Dynamite Entertainment Presents

Garth Ennis John McCrea Darick Robertson

The BOYS

volume five: HEROGASM

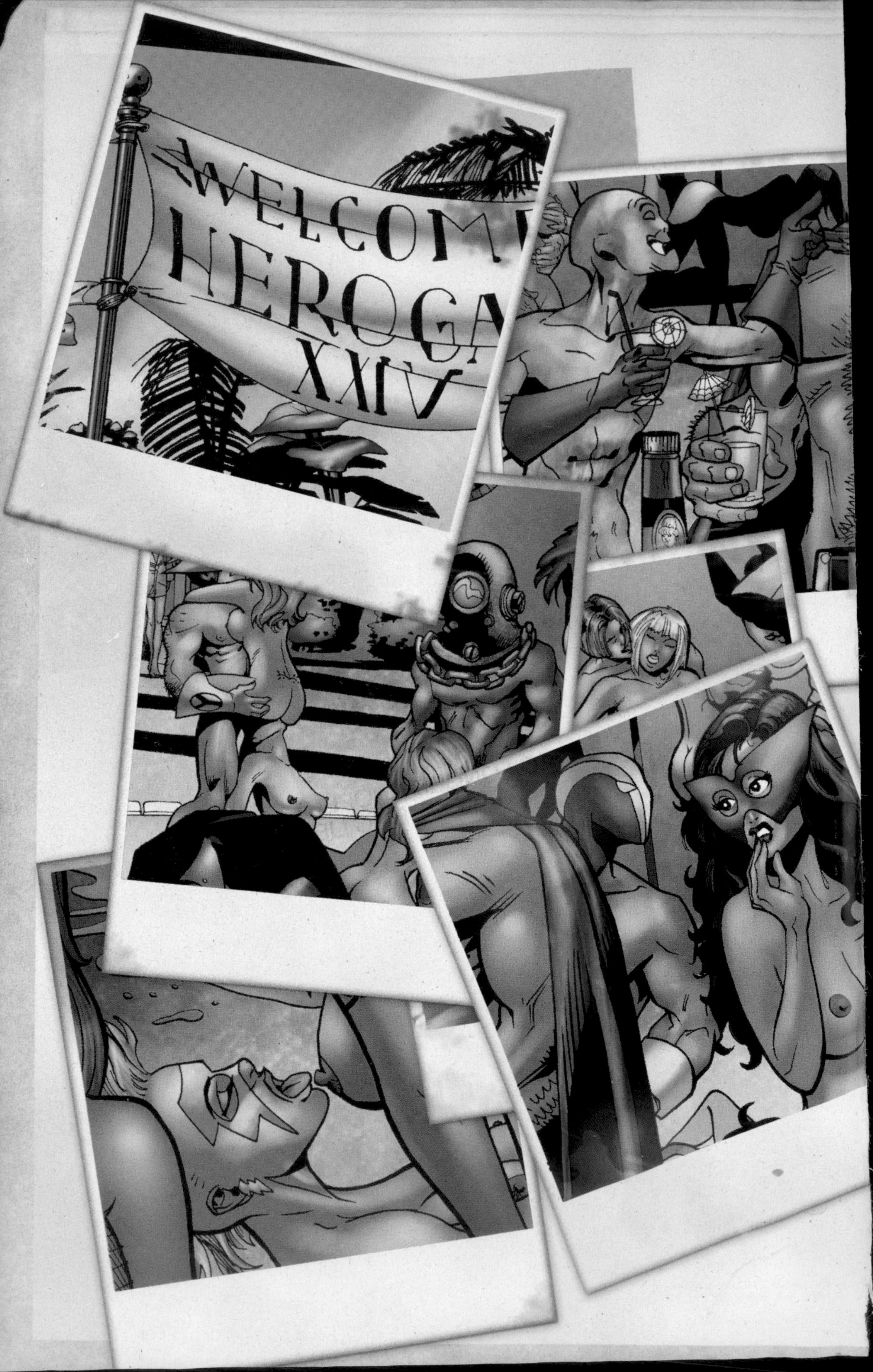
WELCOM
HEROGA
XXIV

The BOYS™

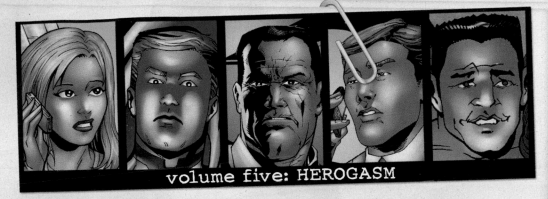

volume five: HEROGASM

Written by:
GARTH ENNIS

Pencils by:
JOHN McCREA
w/ KEITH BURNS

Inks by:
KEITH BURNS
w/ JOHN McCREA

Lettered by:
SIMON BOWLAND

Colored by:
TONY AVIÑA

Covers by:
DARICK ROBERTSON
& TONY AVIÑA

The Boys created by:
GARTH ENNIS & DARICK ROBERTSON

Collects issues one through six of The Boys: Herogasm
by Dynamite Entertainment.

Trade Design By: JASON ULLMEYER

DYNAMITE ENTERTAINMENT

To find a comic shop in your area, call the comic shop locator service at: 1-888-266-4226

DYNAMITE ENTERTAINMENT
NICK BARRUCCI • PRESIDENT
JUAN COLLADO • CHIEF OPERATING OFFICER
JOSEPH RYBANDT • EDITOR
JOSH JOHNSON • CREATIVE DIRECTOR
JASON ULLMEYER • GRAPHIC DESIGNER

First Printing
SC ISBN-10: 1-60690-082-X
SC ISBN-13: 978-1-60690-082-6
10 9 8 7 6 5 4 3 2 1

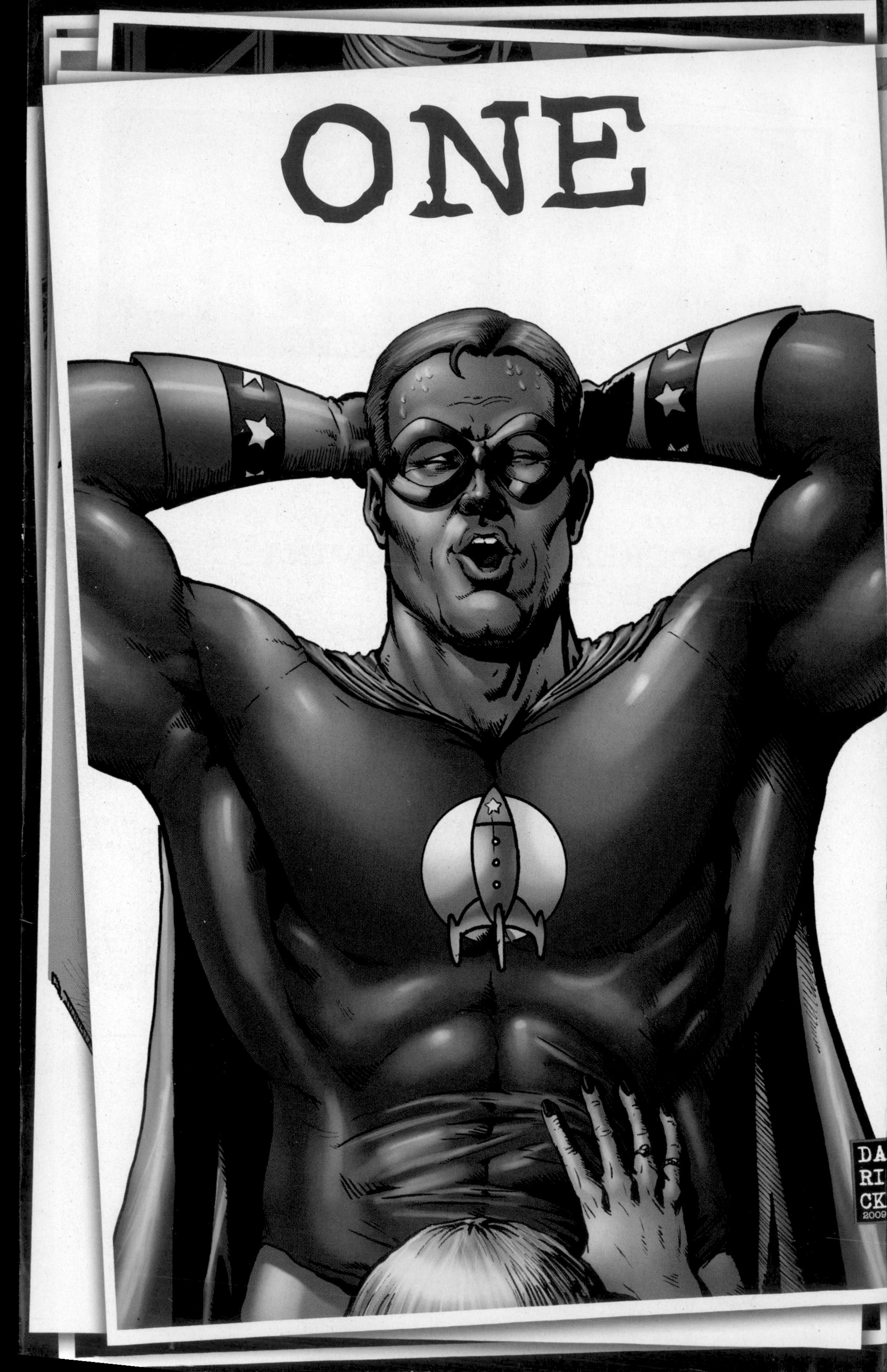
ONE

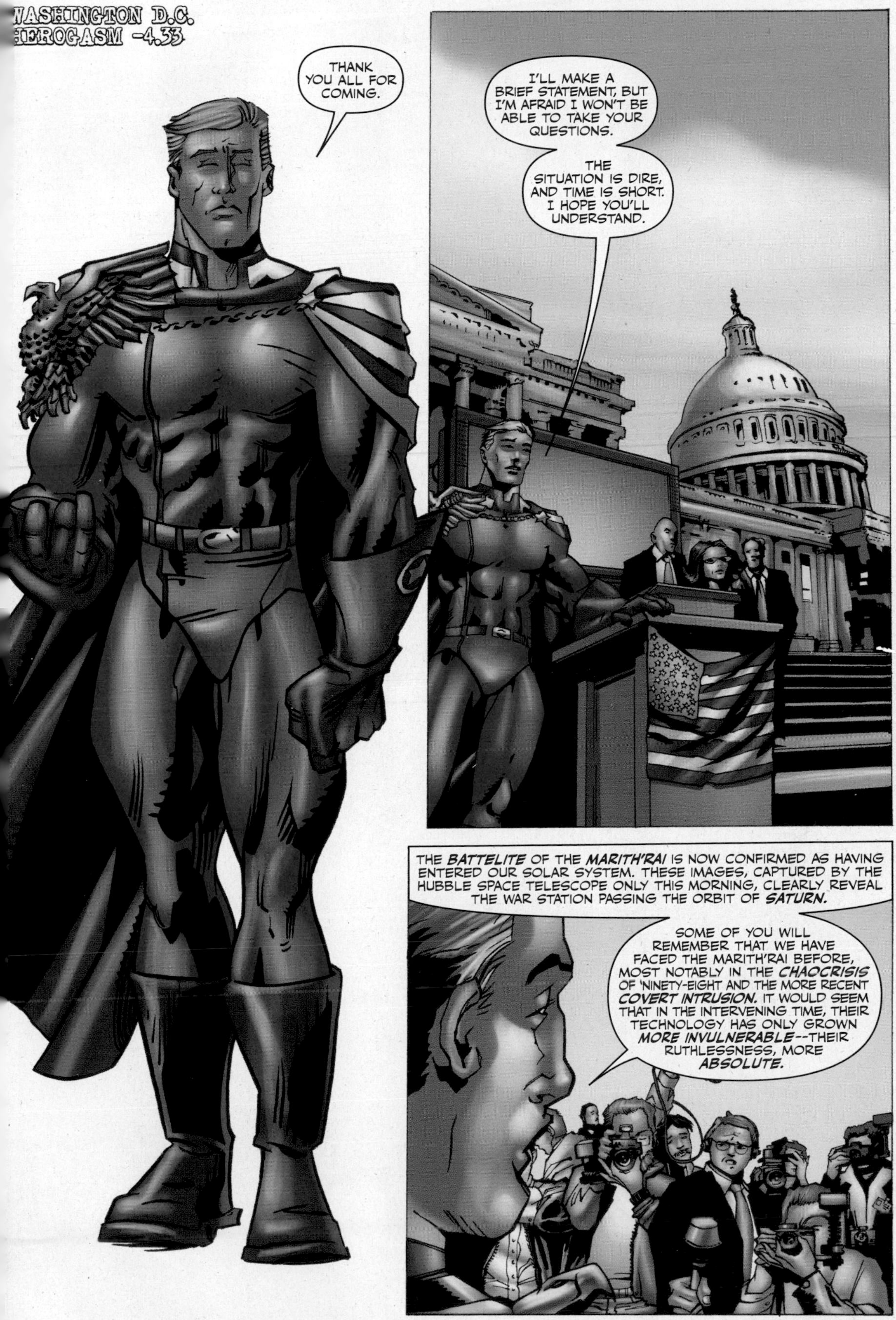
WASHINGTON D.C.
HEROGASM -4.33
THANK YOU ALL FOR COMING.
I'LL MAKE A BRIEF STATEMENT, BUT I'M AFRAID I WON'T BE ABLE TO TAKE YOUR QUESTIONS.
THE SITUATION IS DIRE, AND TIME IS SHORT. I HOPE YOU'LL UNDERSTAND.
THE BATTELITE OF THE MARITH'RAI IS NOW CONFIRMED AS HAVING ENTERED OUR SOLAR SYSTEM. THESE IMAGES, CAPTURED BY THE HUBBLE SPACE TELESCOPE ONLY THIS MORNING, CLEARLY REVEAL THE WAR STATION PASSING THE ORBIT OF SATURN.
SOME OF YOU WILL REMEMBER THAT WE HAVE FACED THE MARITH'RAI BEFORE, MOST NOTABLY IN THE CHAOCRISIS OF 'NINETY-EIGHT AND THE MORE RECENT COVERT INTRUSION. IT WOULD SEEM THAT IN THE INTERVENING TIME, THEIR TECHNOLOGY HAS ONLY GROWN MORE INVULNERABLE--THEIR RUTHLESSNESS, MORE ABSOLUTE.

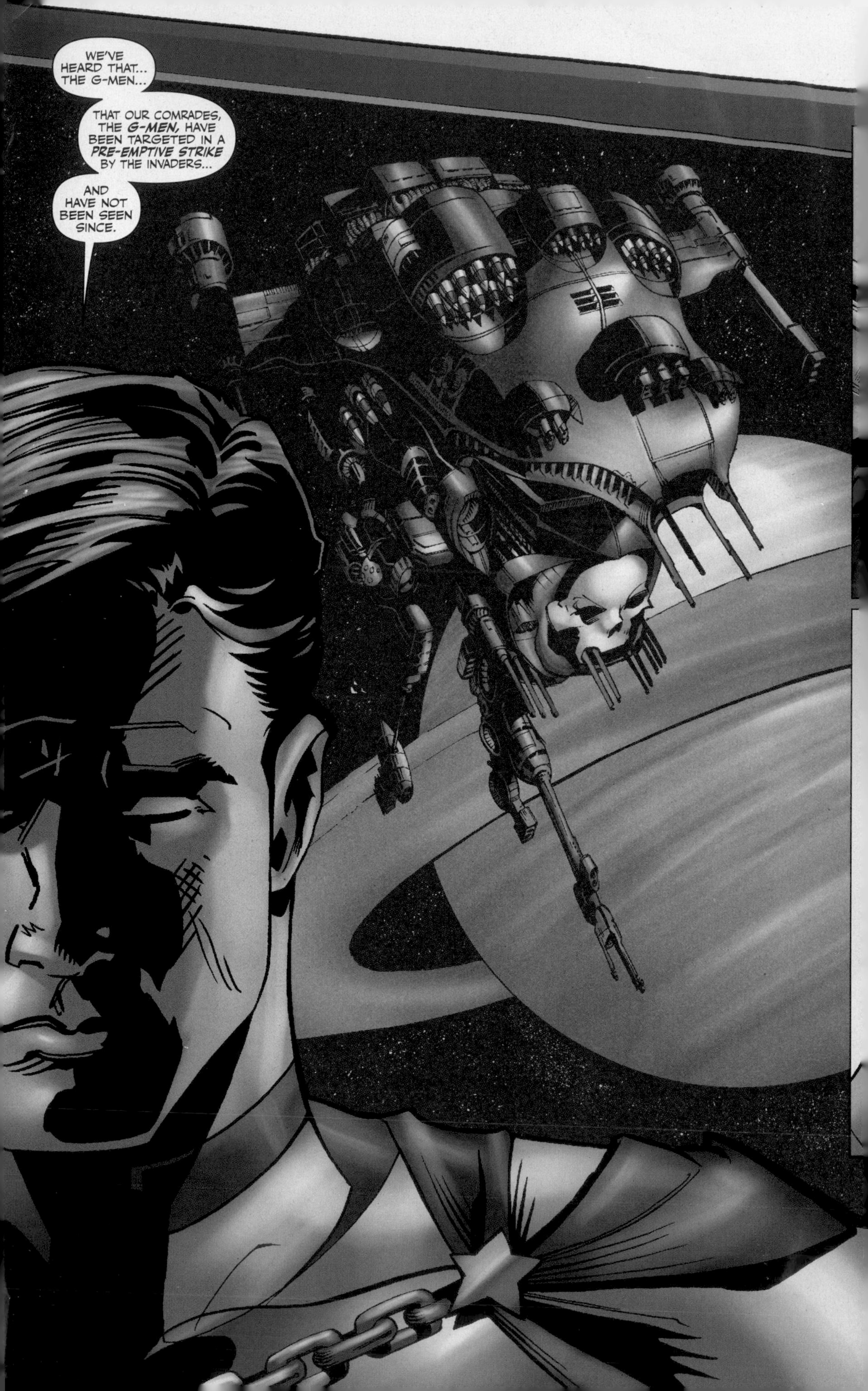
WE'VE HEARD THAT... THE G-MEN...
THAT OUR COMRADES, THE G-MEN, HAVE BEEN TARGETED IN A PRE-EMPTIVE STRIKE BY THE INVADERS...
AND HAVE NOT BEEN SEEN SINCE.

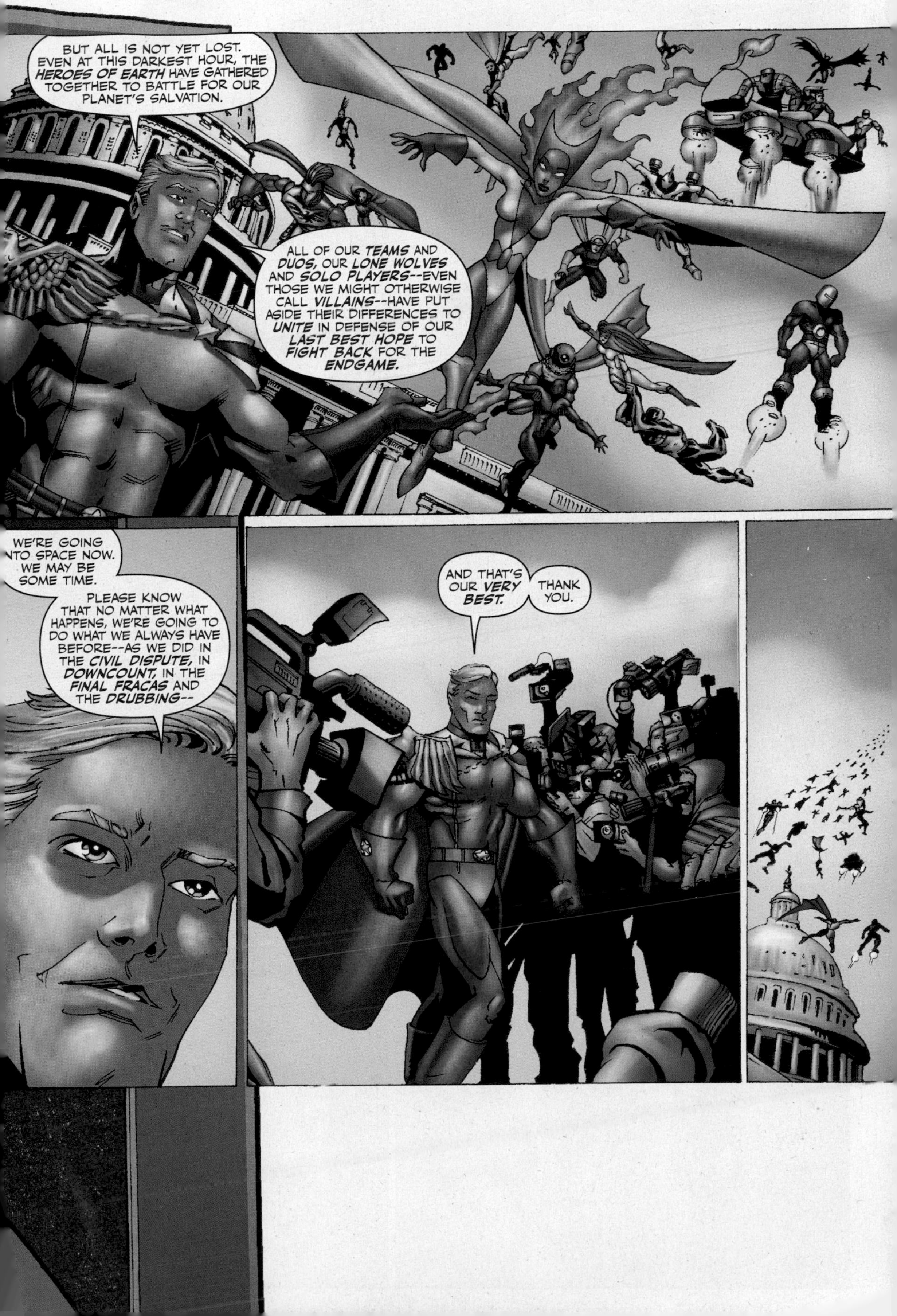
BUT ALL IS NOT YET LOST. EVEN AT THIS DARKEST HOUR, THE HEROES OF EARTH HAVE GATHERED TOGETHER TO BATTLE FOR OUR PLANET'S SALVATION.
ALL OF OUR TEAMS AND DUOS, OUR LONE WOLVES AND SOLO PLAYERS--EVEN THOSE WE MIGHT OTHERWISE CALL VILLAINS--HAVE PUT ASIDE THEIR DIFFERENCES TO UNITE IN DEFENSE OF OUR LAST BEST HOPE TO FIGHT BACK FOR THE ENDGAME.
WE'RE GOING NTO SPACE NOW. WE MAY BE SOME TIME.
PLEASE KNOW THAT NO MATTER WHAT HAPPENS, WE'RE GOING TO DO WHAT WE ALWAYS HAVE BEFORE--AS WE DID IN THE CIVIL DISPUTE, IN DOWNCOUNT, IN THE FINAL FRACAS AND THE DRUBBING--
AND THAT'S OUR VERY BEST.
THANK YOU.

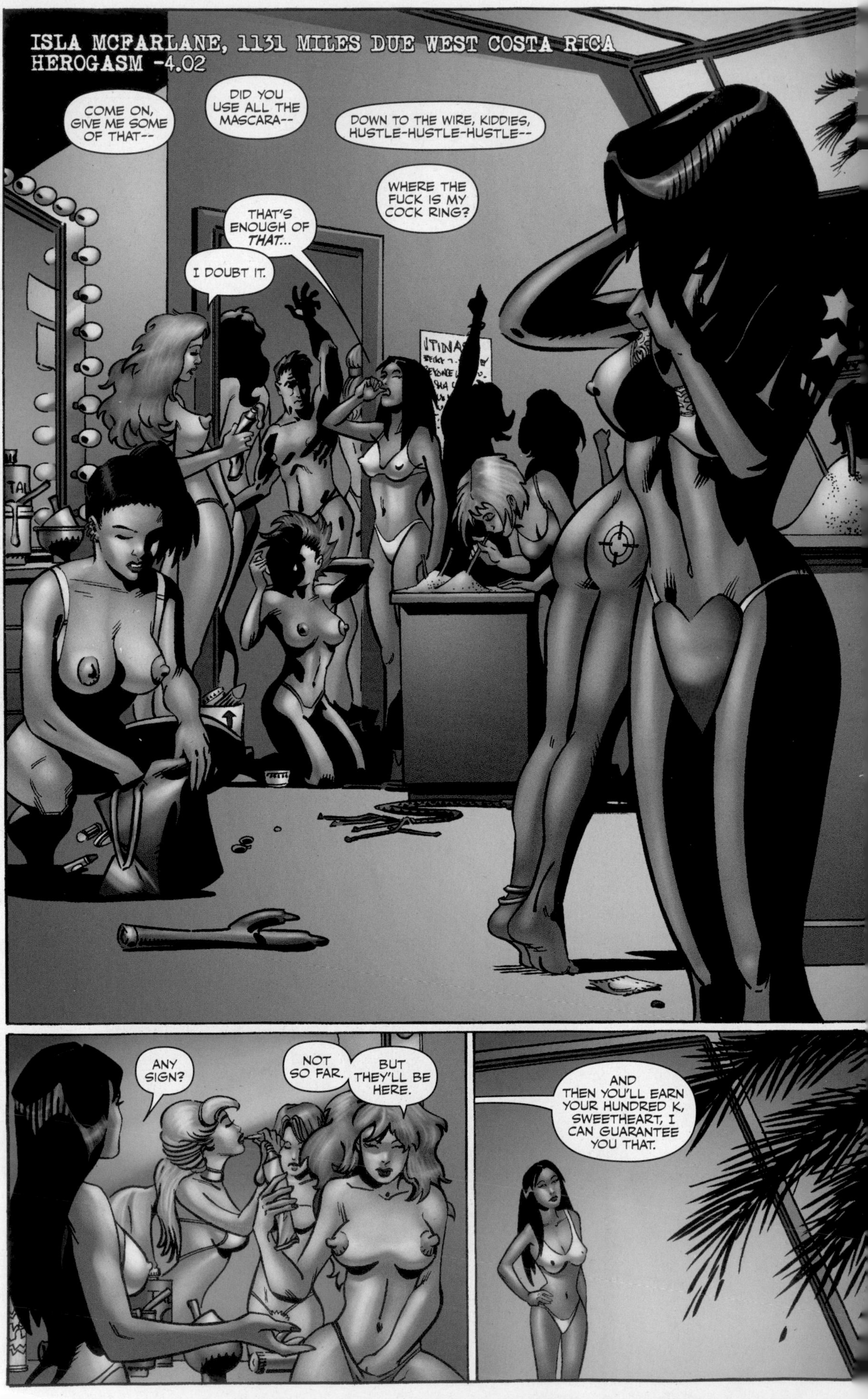
ISLA MCFARLANE, 1131 MILES DUE WEST COSTA RICA
HEROGASM -4.02
COME ON, GIVE ME SOME OF THAT--
DID YOU USE ALL THE MASCARA--
DOWN TO THE WIRE, KIDDIES, HUSTLE-HUSTLE-HUSTLE--
WHERE THE FUCK IS MY COCK RING?
THAT'S ENOUGH OF *THAT*...
I DOUBT IT.
ANY SIGN?
NOT SO FAR.
BUT THEY'LL BE HERE.
AND THEN YOU'LL EARN YOUR HUNDRED K, SWEETHEART, I CAN GUARANTEE YOU THAT.

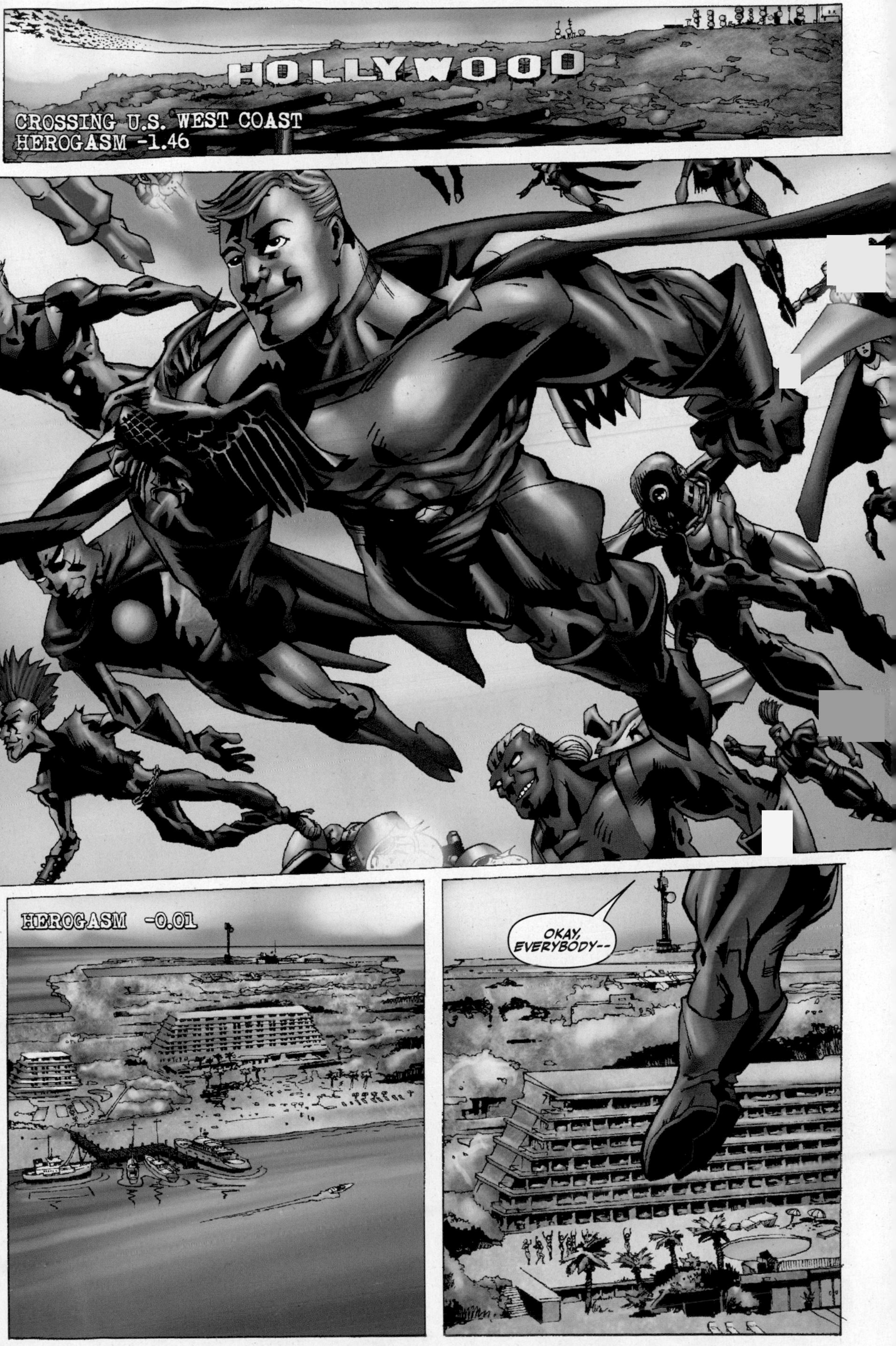
HOLLYWOOD
CROSSING U.S. WEST COAST
HEROGASM -1.46
HEROGASM -0.01
OKAY, EVERYBODY--

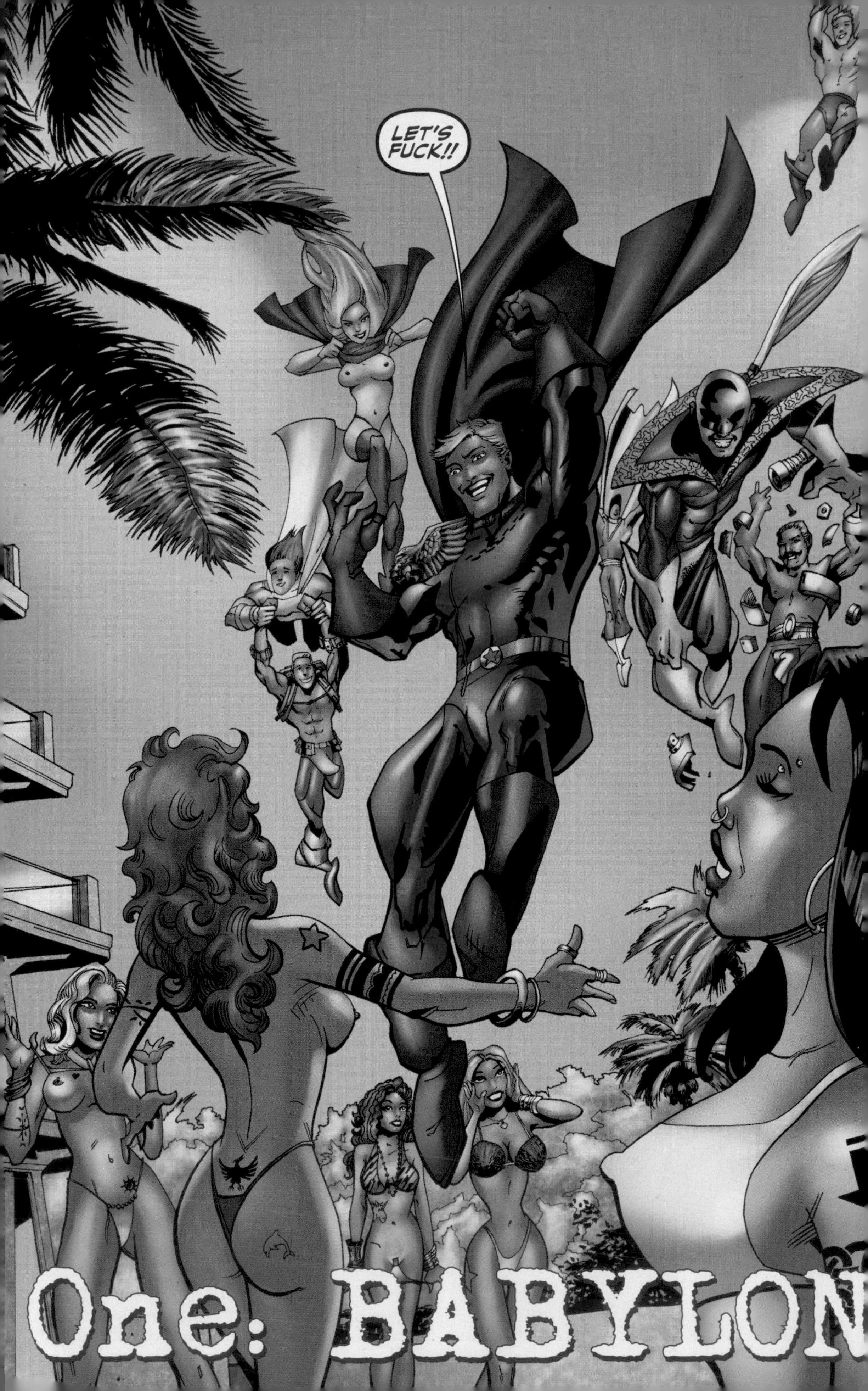
LET'S FUCK!!
One: BABYLON

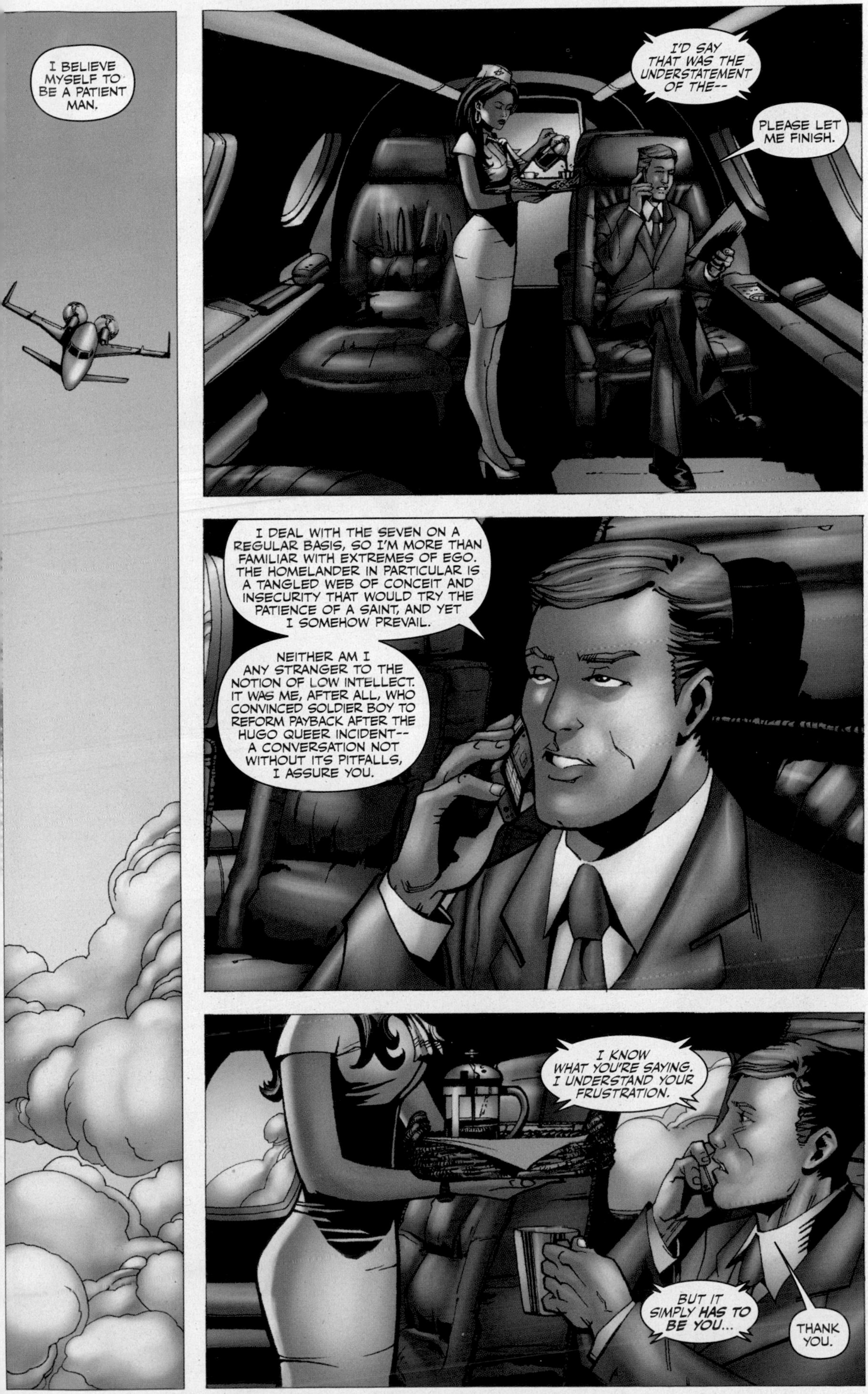
I BELIEVE MYSELF TO BE A PATIENT MAN.
I'D SAY THAT WAS THE UNDERSTATEMENT OF THE--
PLEASE LET ME FINISH.
I DEAL WITH THE SEVEN ON A REGULAR BASIS, SO I'M MORE THAN FAMILIAR WITH EXTREMES OF EGO. THE HOMELANDER IN PARTICULAR IS A TANGLED WEB OF CONCEIT AND INSECURITY THAT WOULD TRY THE PATIENCE OF A SAINT, AND YET I SOMEHOW PREVAIL.
NEITHER AM I ANY STRANGER TO THE NOTION OF LOW INTELLECT. IT WAS ME, AFTER ALL, WHO CONVINCED SOLDIER BOY TO REFORM PAYBACK AFTER THE HUGO QUEER INCIDENT-- A CONVERSATION NOT WITHOUT ITS PITFALLS, I ASSURE YOU.
I KNOW WHAT YOU'RE SAYING. I UNDERSTAND YOUR FRUSTRATION.
BUT IT SIMPLY **HAS TO BE YOU...**
THANK YOU.

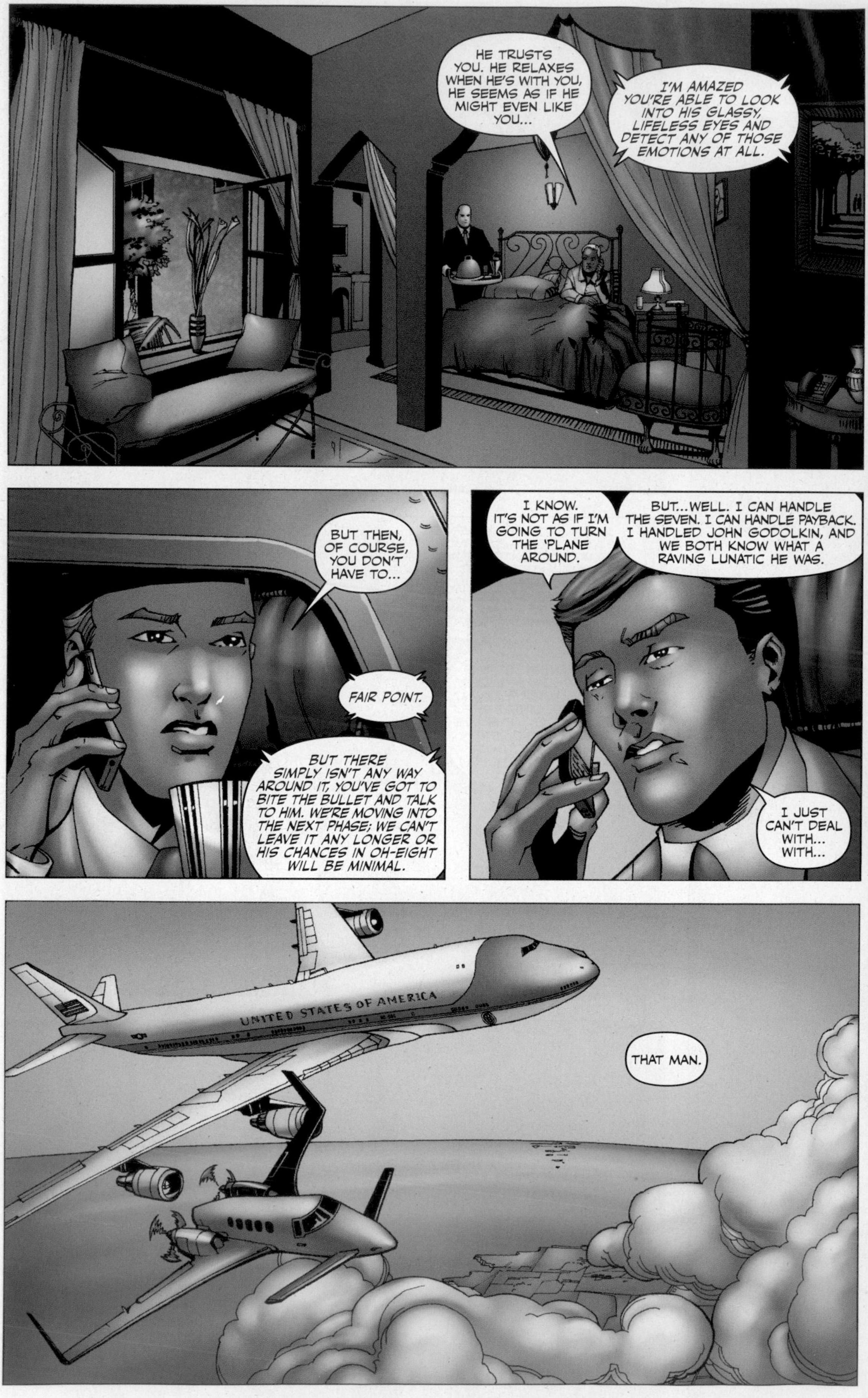

HE TRUSTS YOU. HE RELAXES WHEN HE'S WITH YOU, HE SEEMS AS IF HE MIGHT EVEN LIKE YOU...
I'M AMAZED YOU'RE ABLE TO LOOK INTO HIS GLASSY, LIFELESS EYES AND DETECT ANY OF THOSE EMOTIONS AT ALL.
BUT THEN, OF COURSE, YOU DON'T HAVE TO...
FAIR POINT.
BUT THERE SIMPLY ISN'T ANY WAY AROUND IT, YOU'VE GOT TO BITE THE BULLET AND TALK TO HIM. WE'RE MOVING INTO THE NEXT PHASE; WE CAN'T LEAVE IT ANY LONGER OR HIS CHANCES IN OH-EIGHT WILL BE MINIMAL.
I KNOW. IT'S NOT AS IF I'M GOING TO TURN THE 'PLANE AROUND.
BUT...WELL. I CAN HANDLE THE SEVEN. I CAN HANDLE PAYBACK. I HANDLED JOHN GODOLKIN, AND WE BOTH KNOW WHAT A RAVING LUNATIC HE WAS.
I JUST CAN'T DEAL WITH... WITH...
UNITED STATES OF AMERICA
THAT MAN.

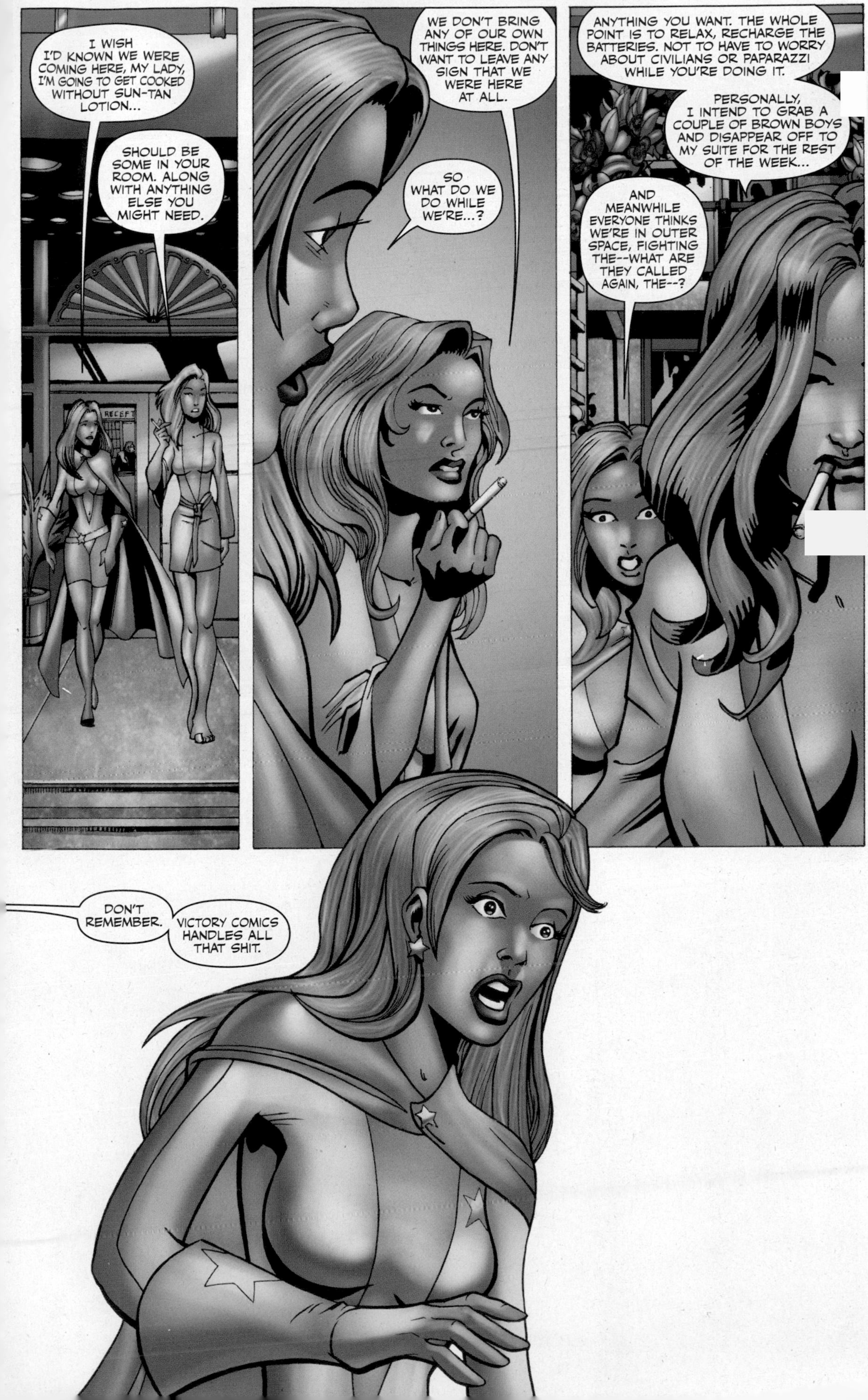
I WISH I'D KNOWN WE WERE COMING HERE, MY LADY, I'M GOING TO GET COOKED WITHOUT SUN-TAN LOTION...
SHOULD BE SOME IN YOUR ROOM. ALONG WITH ANYTHING ELSE YOU MIGHT NEED.
RECEPT
WE DON'T BRING ANY OF OUR OWN THINGS HERE. DON'T WANT TO LEAVE ANY SIGN THAT WE WERE HERE AT ALL.
SO WHAT DO WE DO WHILE WE'RE...?
ANYTHING YOU WANT. THE WHOLE POINT IS TO RELAX, RECHARGE THE BATTERIES. NOT TO HAVE TO WORRY ABOUT CIVILIANS OR PAPARAZZI WHILE YOU'RE DOING IT.
PERSONALLY, I INTEND TO GRAB A COUPLE OF BROWN BOYS AND DISAPPEAR OFF TO MY SUITE FOR THE REST OF THE WEEK...
AND MEANWHILE EVERYONE THINKS WE'RE IN OUTER SPACE, FIGHTING THE--WHAT ARE THEY CALLED AGAIN, THE--?
DON'T REMEMBER.
VICTORY COMICS HANDLES ALL THAT SHIT.

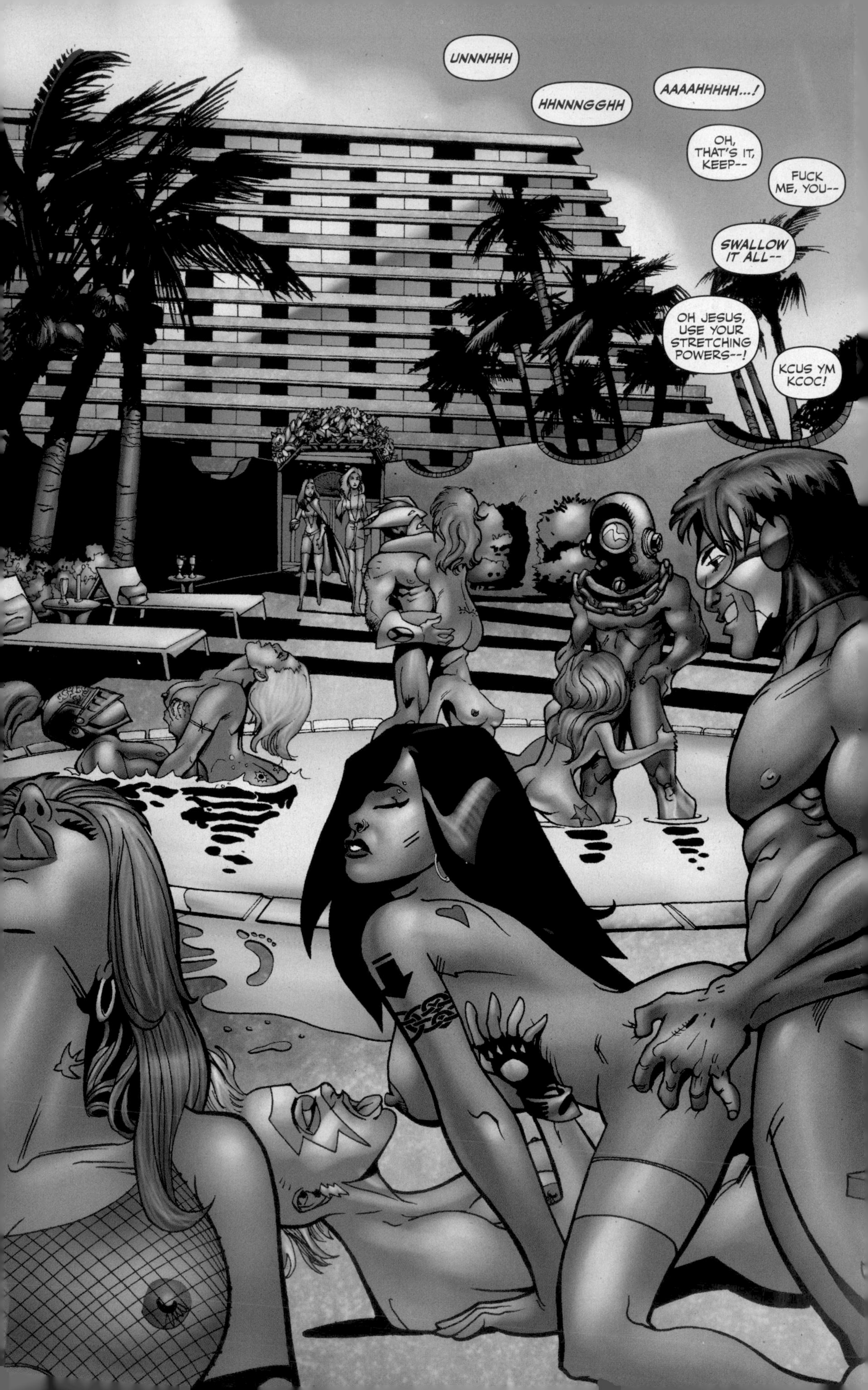
UNNNHHH
HHNNNGGHH
AAAAHHHHH...!
OH, THAT'S IT, KEEP--
FUCK ME, YOU--
SWALLOW IT ALL--
OH JESUS, USE YOUR STRETCHING POWERS--!
KCUS YM KCOC!

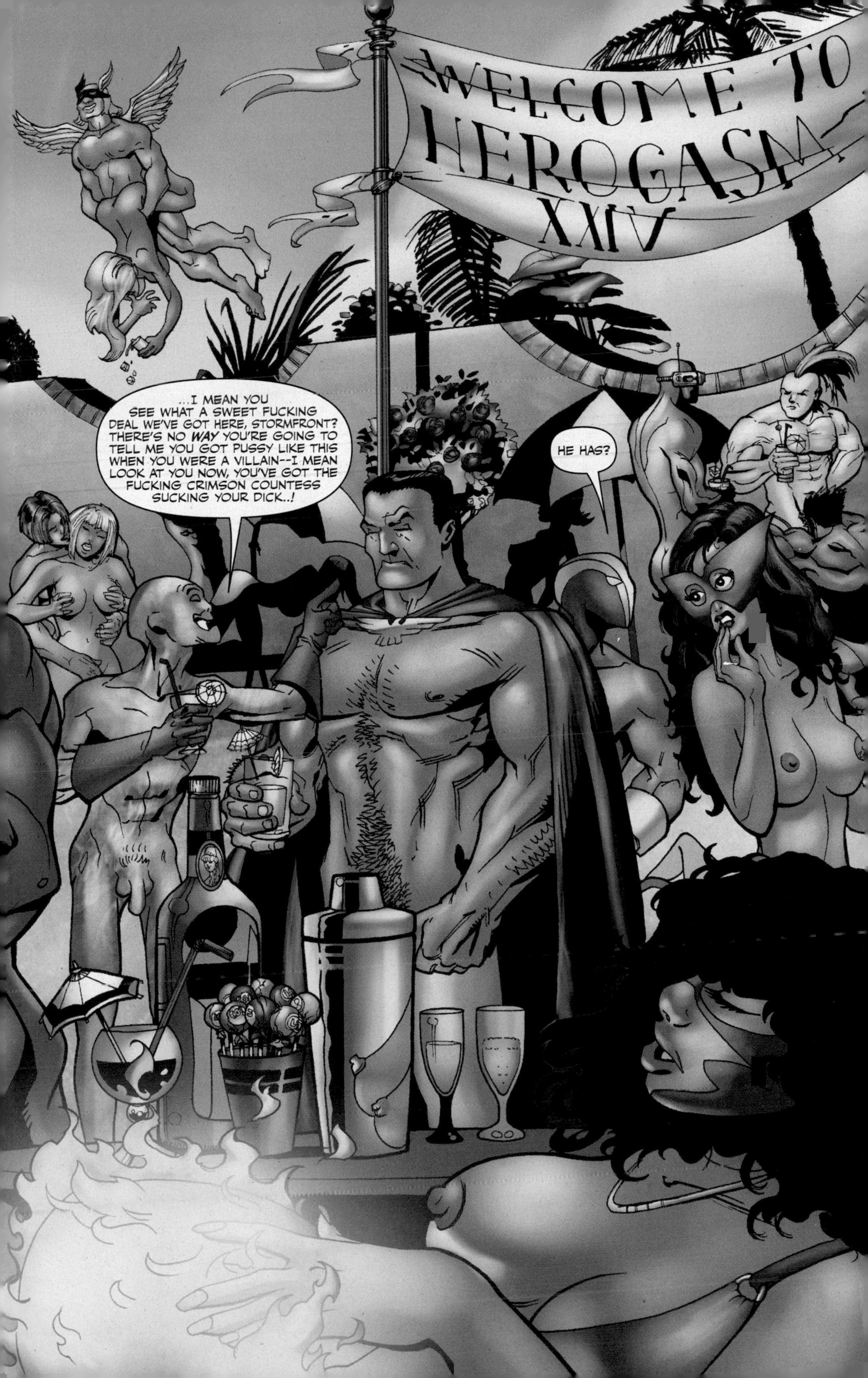
WELCOME TO HEROGASM XXIV
...I MEAN YOU SEE WHAT A SWEET FUCKING DEAL WE'VE GOT HERE, STORMFRONT? THERE'S NO WAY YOU'RE GOING TO TELL ME YOU GOT PUSSY LIKE THIS WHEN YOU WERE A VILLAIN--I MEAN LOOK AT YOU NOW, YOU'VE GOT THE FUCKING CRIMSON COUNTESS SUCKING YOUR DICK..!
HE HAS?

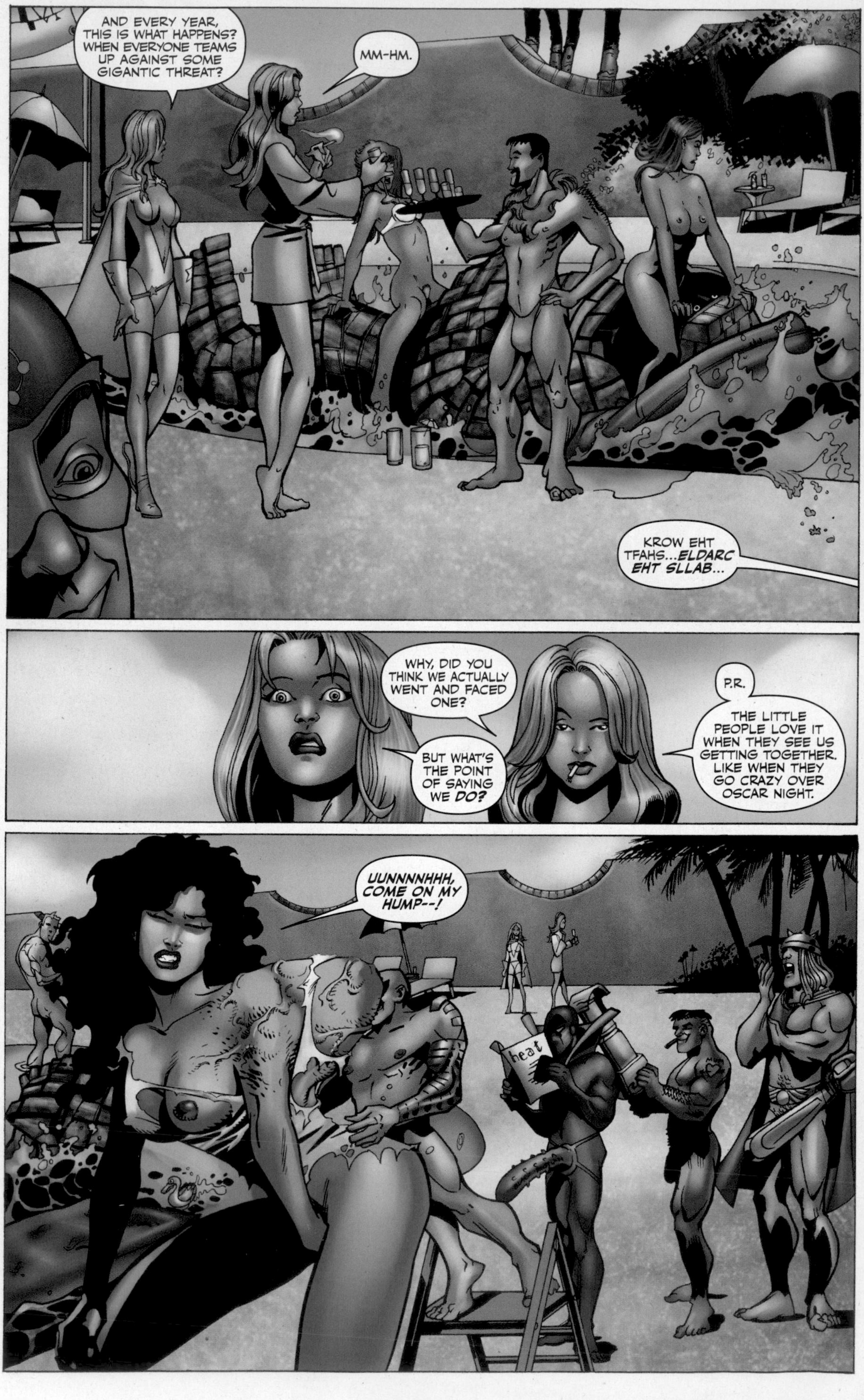
AND EVERY YEAR, THIS IS WHAT HAPPENS? WHEN EVERYONE TEAMS UP AGAINST SOME GIGANTIC THREAT?
MM-HM.
KROW EHT TFAHS...*ELDARC EHT SLLAB*...
WHY, DID YOU THINK WE ACTUALLY WENT AND FACED ONE?
BUT WHAT'S THE POINT OF SAYING WE *DO?*
P.R.
THE LITTLE PEOPLE LOVE IT WHEN THEY SEE US GETTING TOGETHER. LIKE WHEN THEY GO CRAZY OVER OSCAR NIGHT.
UUNNNNHHH, COME ON MY HUMP--!
heat

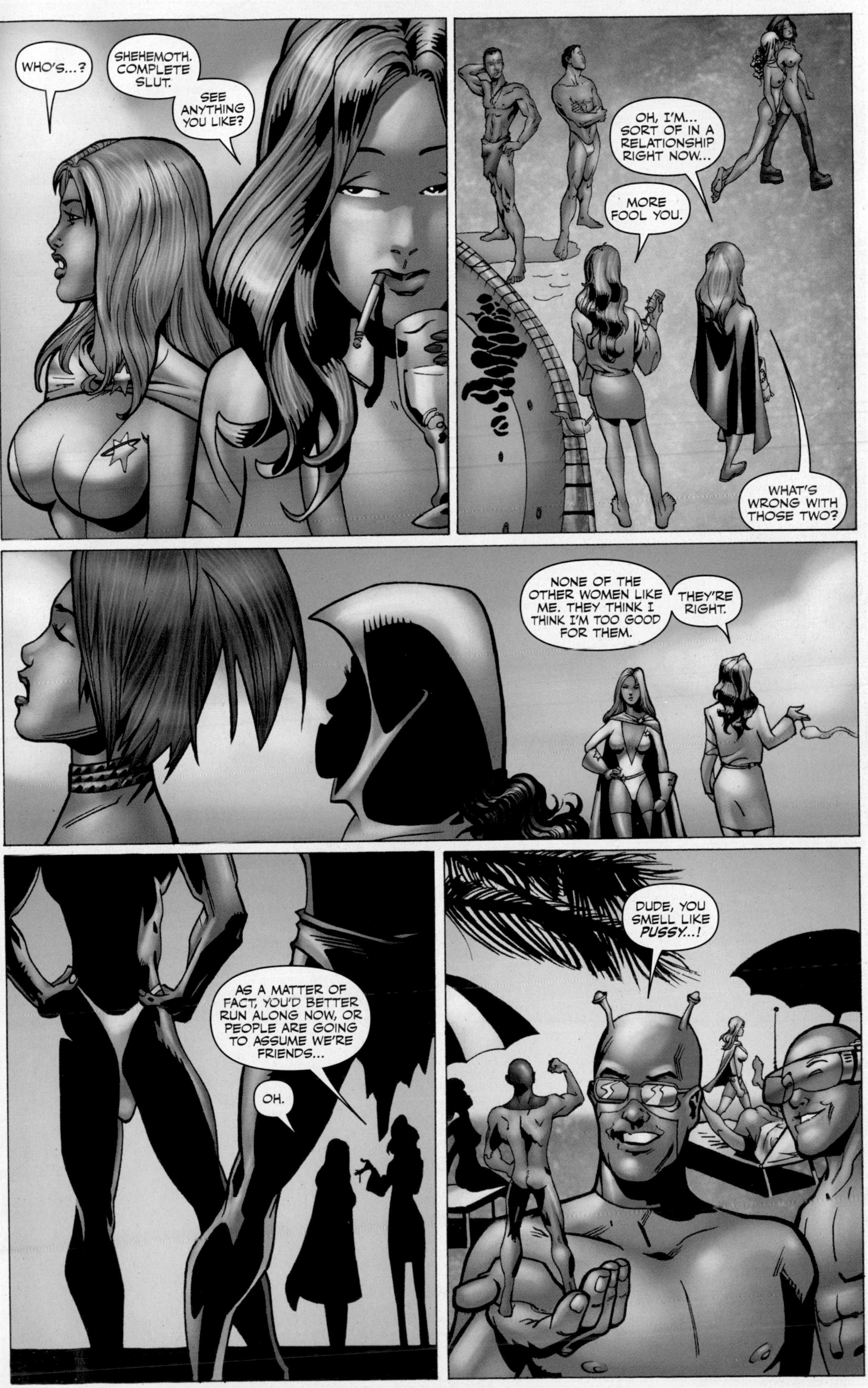
WHO'S...?
SHEHEMOTH. COMPLETE SLUT.
SEE ANYTHING YOU LIKE?
OH, I'M... SORT OF IN A RELATIONSHIP RIGHT NOW...
MORE FOOL YOU.
WHAT'S WRONG WITH THOSE TWO?
NONE OF THE OTHER WOMEN LIKE ME. THEY THINK I THINK I'M TOO GOOD FOR THEM.
THEY'RE RIGHT.
AS A MATTER OF FACT, YOU'D BETTER RUN ALONG NOW, OR PEOPLE ARE GOING TO ASSUME WE'RE FRIENDS...
OH.
DUDE, YOU SMELL LIKE *PUSSY*...!

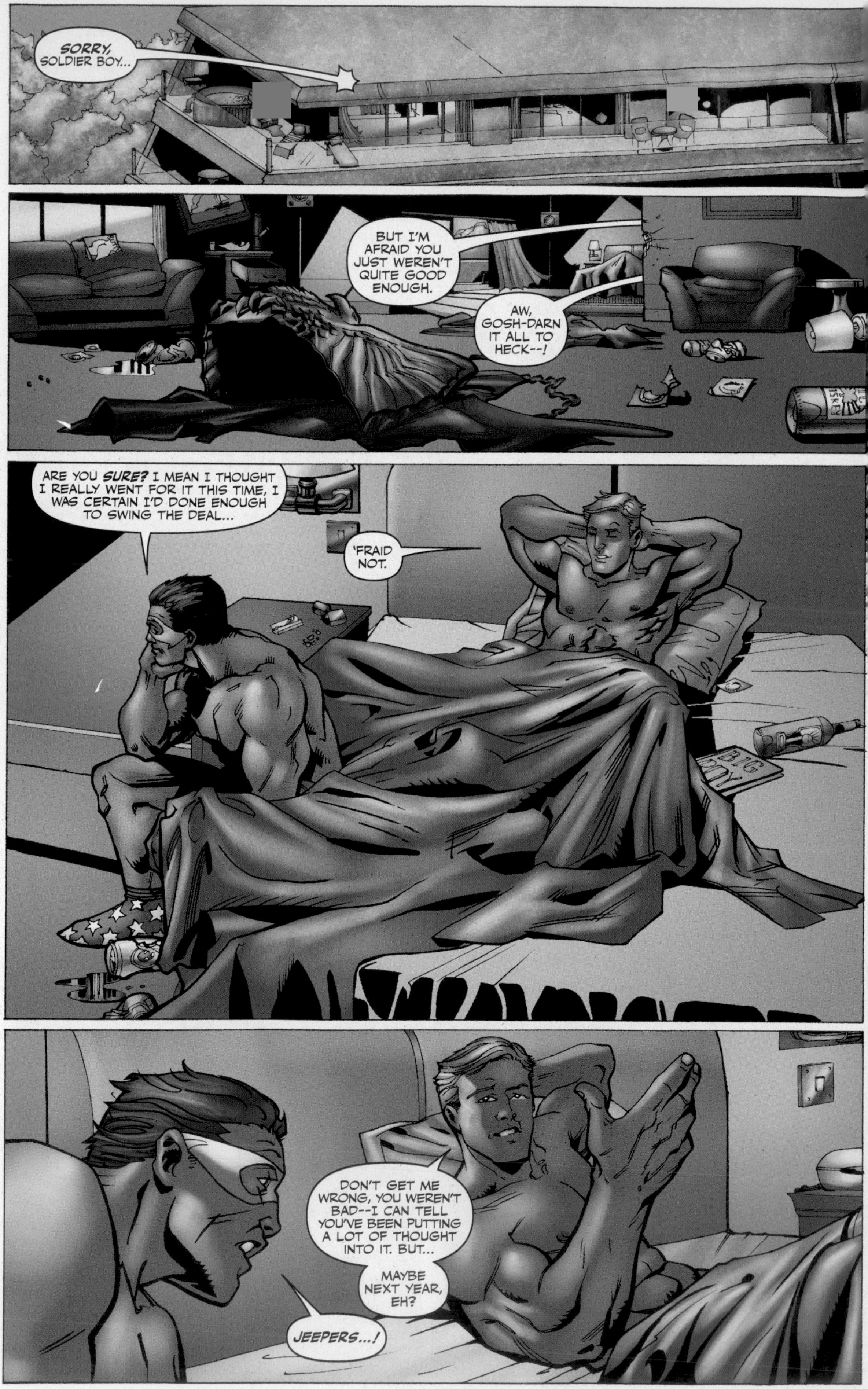

SORRY, SOLDIER BOY...
BUT I'M AFRAID YOU JUST WEREN'T QUITE GOOD ENOUGH.
AW, GOSH-DARN IT ALL TO HECK--!
ARE YOU SURE? I MEAN I THOUGHT I REALLY WENT FOR IT THIS TIME, I WAS CERTAIN I'D DONE ENOUGH TO SWING THE DEAL...
'FRAID NOT.
BIG BOY
DON'T GET ME WRONG, YOU WEREN'T BAD--I CAN TELL YOU'VE BEEN PUTTING A LOT OF THOUGHT INTO IT. BUT...
MAYBE NEXT YEAR, EH?
JEEPERS...!

ANOTHER YEAR IN PAYBACK, I DON'T KNOW IF I CAN STAND IT... TEK-KNIGHT AND EAGLE WERE THE ONLY ONES WHO WERE NICE TO ME, AND EVER SINCE THEY DIED IT'S LIKE THE OTHERS HAVE GOTTEN EVEN MEANER...

SWATTO'S NO USE, HE JUST SITS AROUND MAKING THAT NUTTY BUZZING SOUND. MIND-DROID AND THE CRIMSON COUNTESS FIGHT ALL THE TIME, AND STORMFRONT KEEPS CALLING ME *SCHWEINER AMERIKANER.* IT'S ALL JUST SO LAME, YOU KNOW?

SO... SECOND BEST.

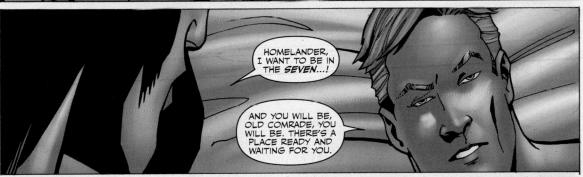

HOMELANDER, I WANT TO BE IN THE *SEVEN...!*

AND YOU WILL BE, OLD COMRADE, YOU WILL BE. THERE'S A PLACE READY AND WAITING FOR YOU.

BUT YOU'VE GOT TO PASS THE ENTRANCE TEST FIRST...

AND I TRY, EVERY YEAR I TRY! BUT IT'S LIKE I'M *NEVER* GOING TO BE GOOD ENOUGH!

AW, HECK.

JUST *HECK.*

I GUESS I'LL SEE YOU LATER, THEN.

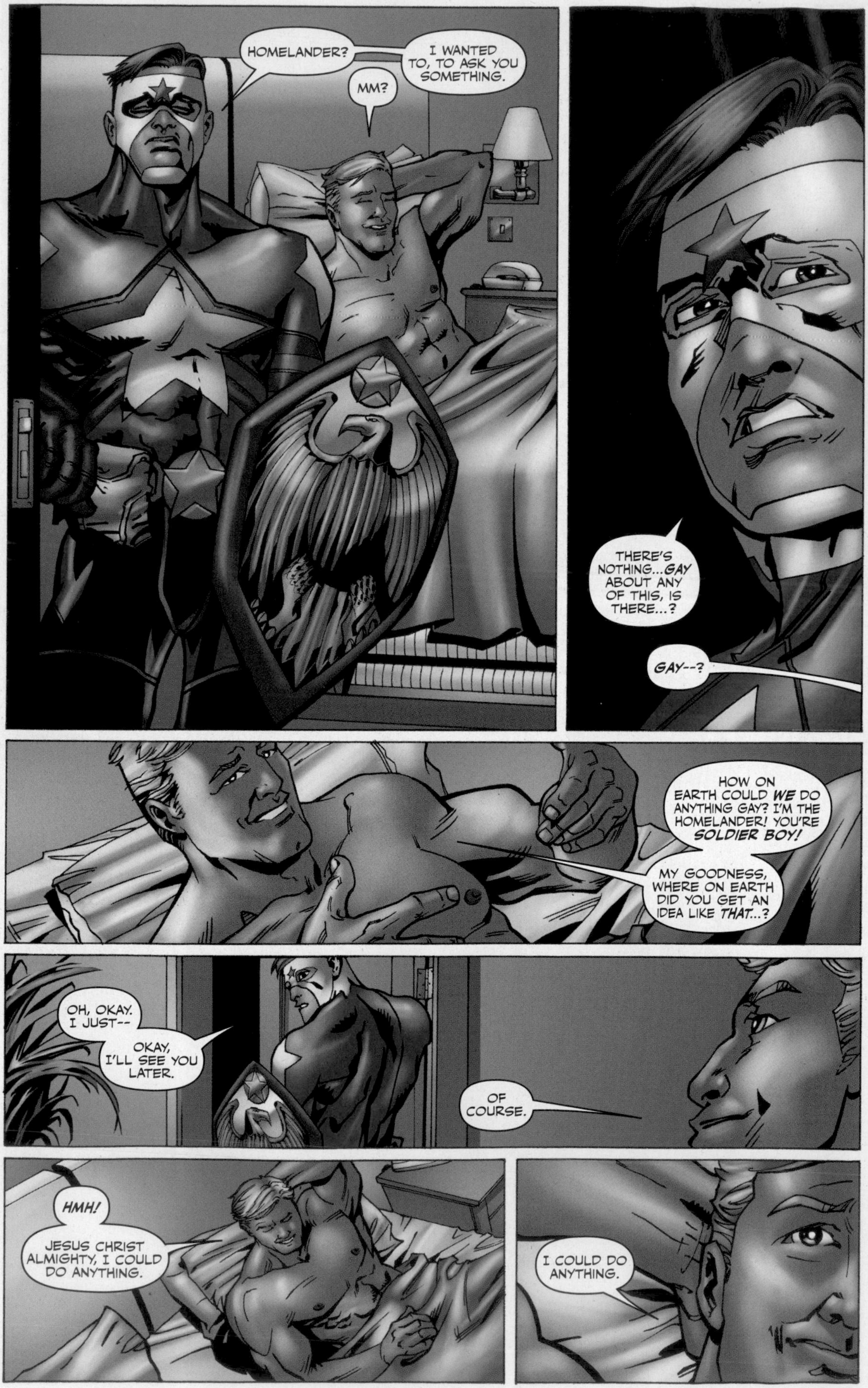
HOMELANDER?
I WANTED TO, TO ASK YOU SOMETHING.
MM?
THERE'S NOTHING...GAY ABOUT ANY OF THIS, IS THERE...?
GAY--?
HOW ON EARTH COULD WE DO ANYTHING GAY? I'M THE HOMELANDER! YOU'RE SOLDIER BOY!
MY GOODNESS, WHERE ON EARTH DID YOU GET AN IDEA LIKE THAT...?
OH, OKAY. I JUST--
OKAY, I'LL SEE YOU LATER.
OF COURSE.
HMH!
JESUS CHRIST ALMIGHTY, I COULD DO ANYTHING.
I COULD DO ANYTHING.

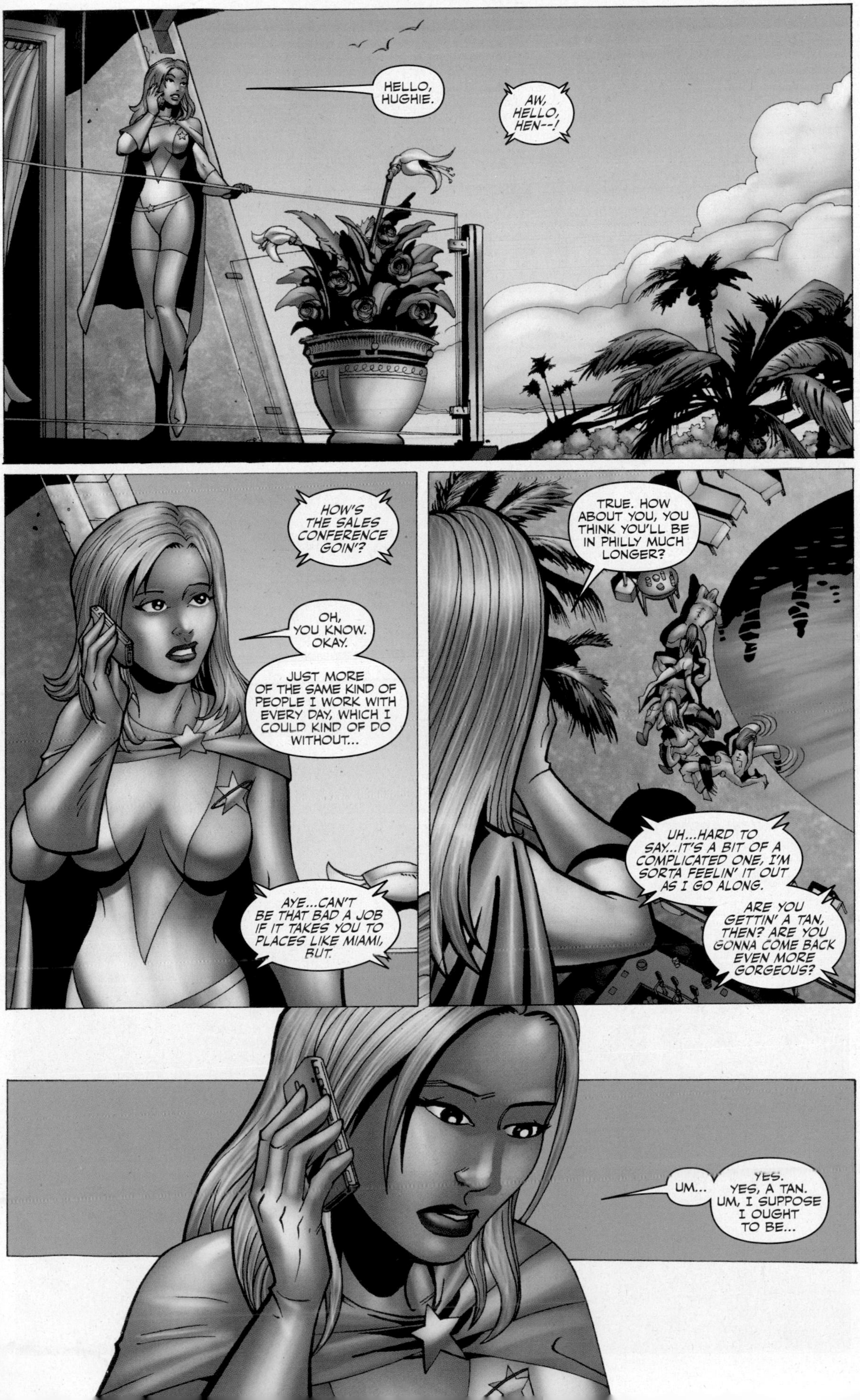

HELLO, HUGHIE.
AW, HELLO, HEN--!
HOW'S THE SALES CONFERENCE GOIN'?
OH, YOU KNOW. OKAY.
JUST MORE OF THE SAME KIND OF PEOPLE I WORK WITH EVERY DAY, WHICH I COULD KIND OF DO WITHOUT...
AYE...CAN'T BE THAT BAD A JOB IF IT TAKES YOU TO PLACES LIKE MIAMI, BUT.
TRUE. HOW ABOUT YOU, YOU THINK YOU'LL BE IN PHILLY MUCH LONGER?
UH...HARD TO SAY...IT'S A BIT OF A COMPLICATED ONE, I'M SORTA FEELIN' IT OUT AS I GO ALONG.
ARE YOU GETTIN' A TAN, THEN? ARE YOU GONNA COME BACK EVEN MORE GORGEOUS?
UM...
YES. YES, A TAN. UM, I SUPPOSE I OUGHT TO BE...

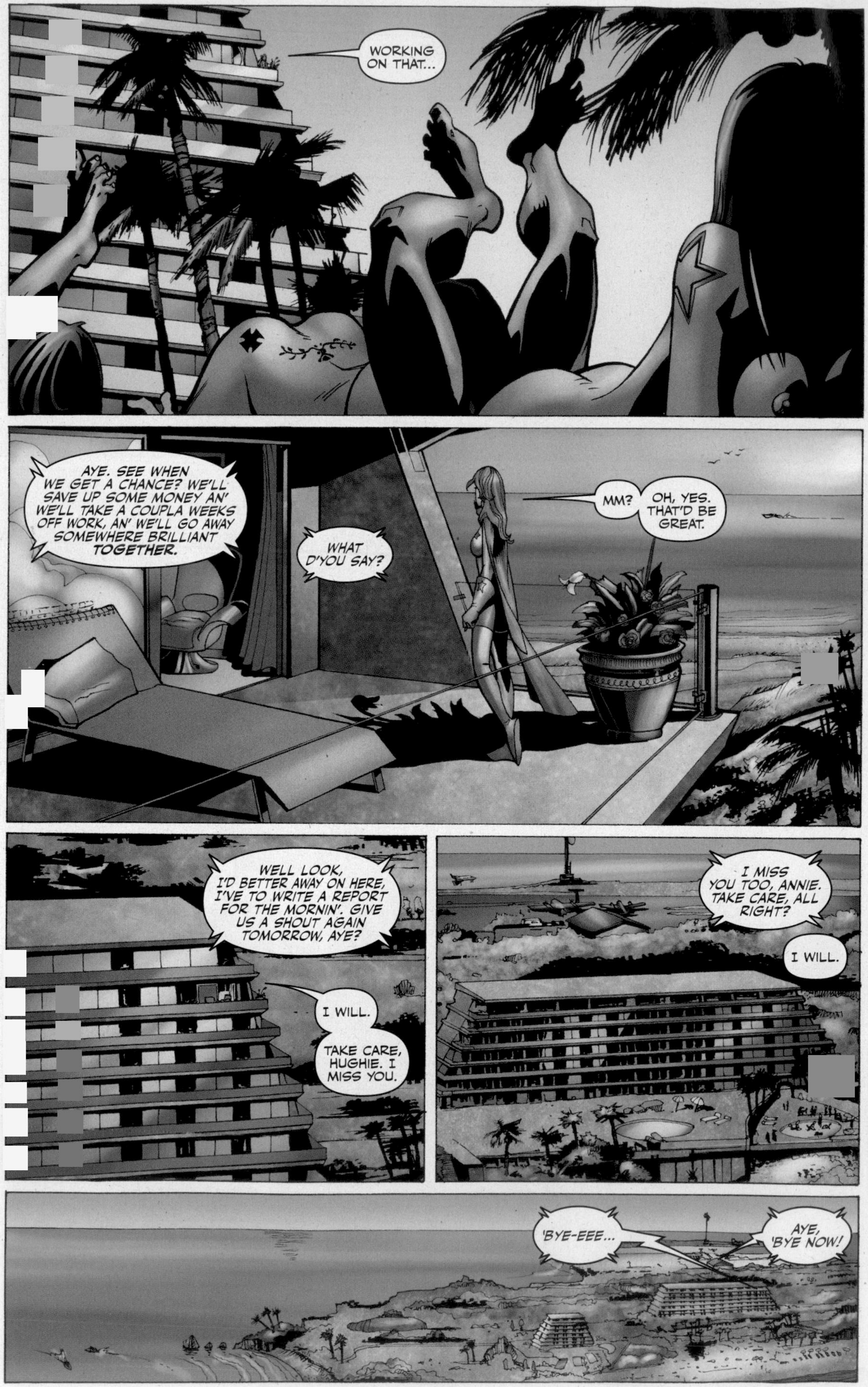
WORKING ON THAT...
AYE. SEE WHEN WE GET A CHANCE? WE'LL SAVE UP SOME MONEY AN' WE'LL TAKE A COUPLA WEEKS OFF WORK, AN' WE'LL GO AWAY SOMEWHERE BRILLIANT TOGETHER.
WHAT D'YOU SAY?
MM?
OH, YES. THAT'D BE GREAT.
WELL LOOK, I'D BETTER AWAY ON HERE, I'VE TO WRITE A REPORT FOR THE MORNIN'. GIVE US A SHOUT AGAIN TOMORROW, AYE?
I WILL.
TAKE CARE, HUGHIE. I MISS YOU.
I MISS YOU TOO, ANNIE. TAKE CARE, ALL RIGHT?
I WILL.
'BYE-EEE...
AYE, 'BYE NOW!

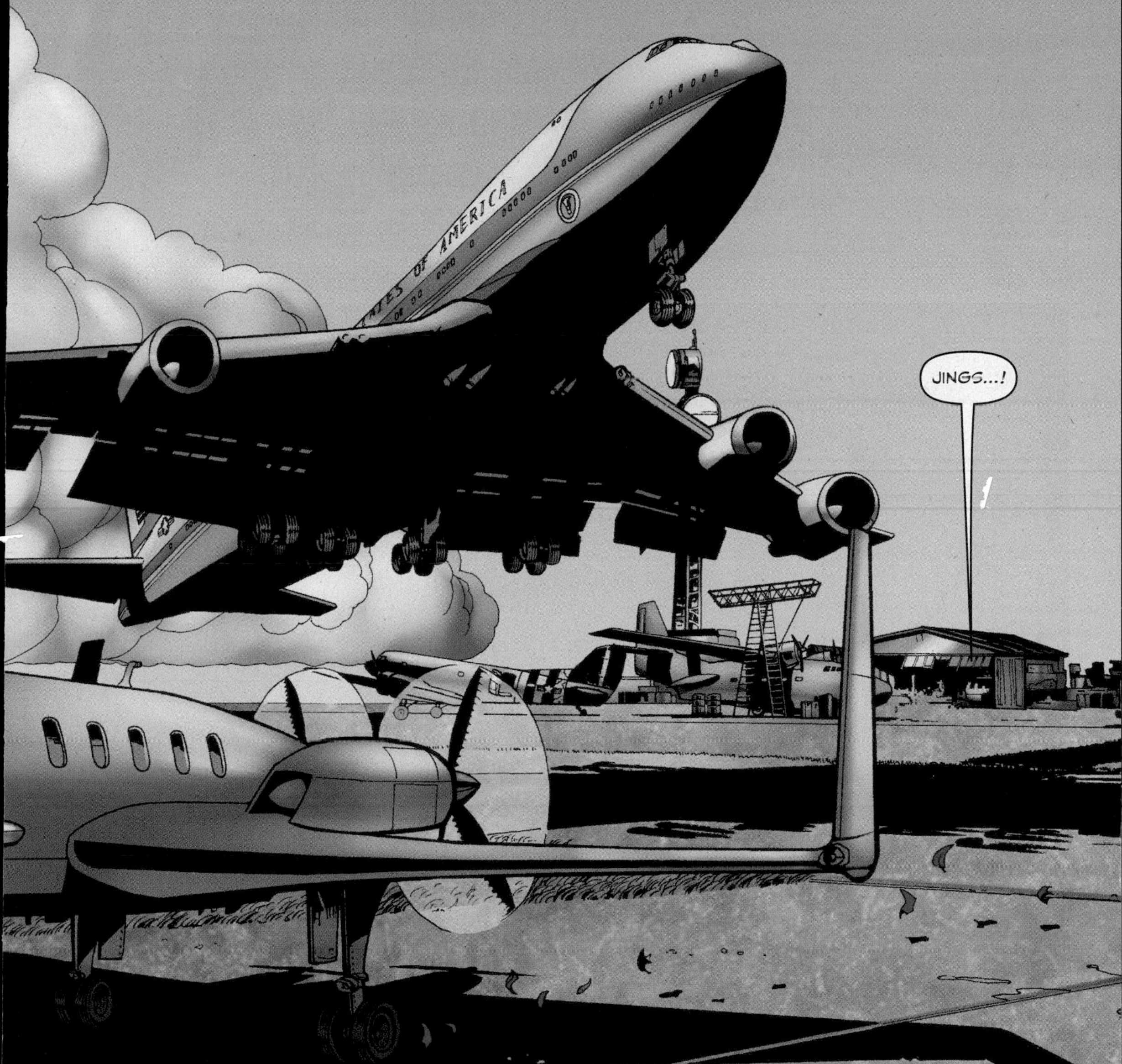
JINGS...!

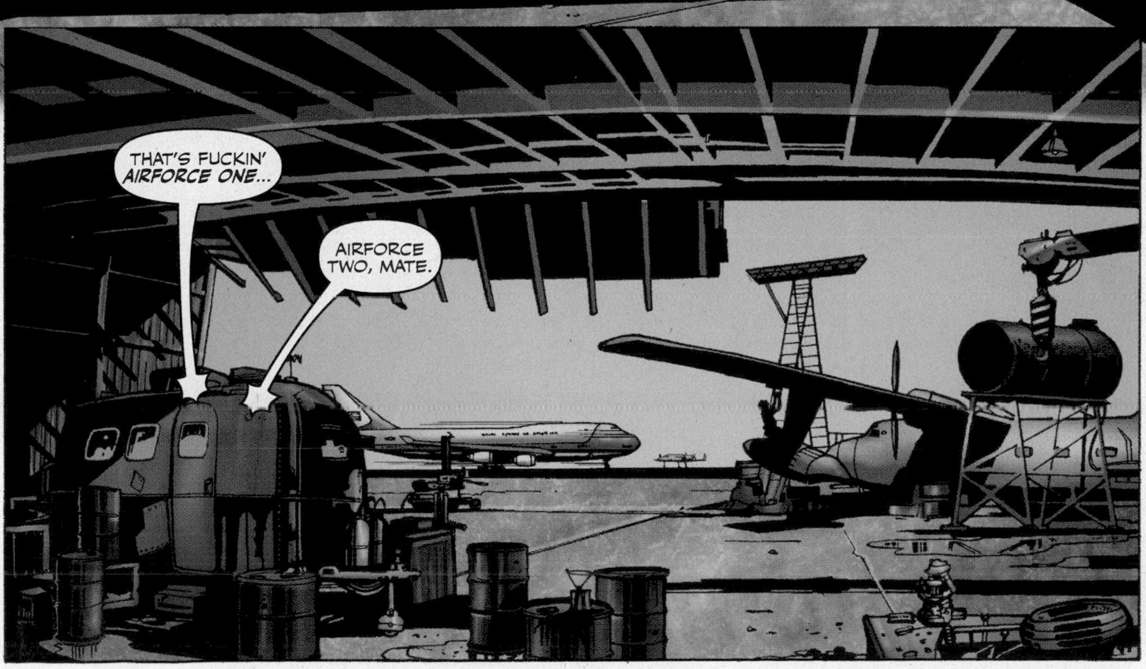
THAT'S FUCKIN' *AIRFORCE ONE*...
AIRFORCE TWO, MATE.

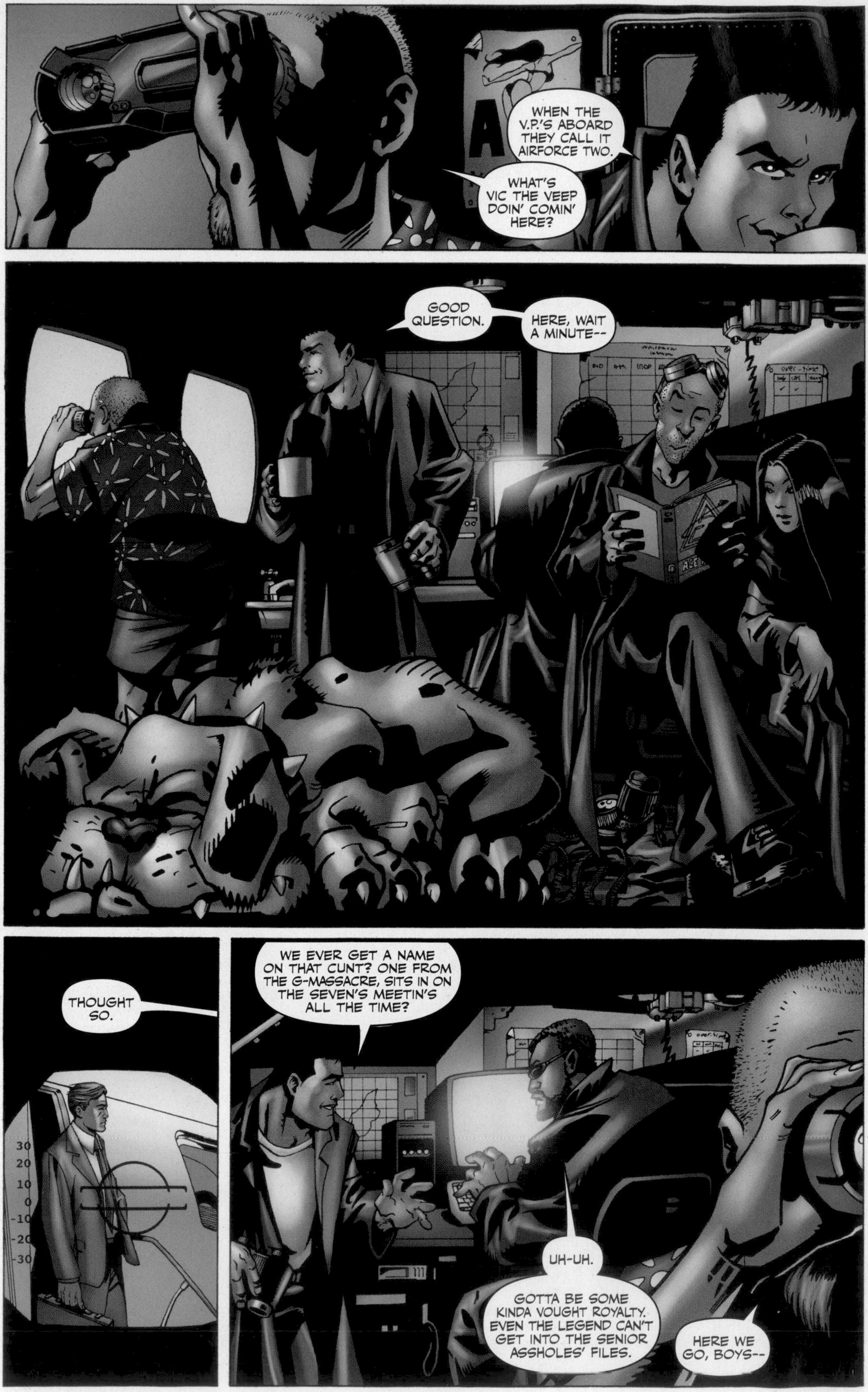
WHEN THE V.P.'S ABOARD THEY CALL IT AIRFORCE TWO.
WHAT'S VIC THE VEEP DOIN' COMIN' HERE?
GOOD QUESTION.
HERE, WAIT A MINUTE--
THOUGHT SO.
30
20
10
0
-10
-20
-30
WE EVER GET A NAME ON THAT CUNT? ONE FROM THE G-MASSACRE, SITS IN ON THE SEVEN'S MEETIN'S ALL THE TIME?
UH-UH.
GOTTA BE SOME KINDA VOUGHT ROYALTY. EVEN THE LEGEND CAN'T GET INTO THE SENIOR ASSHOLES' FILES.
HERE WE GO, BOYS--

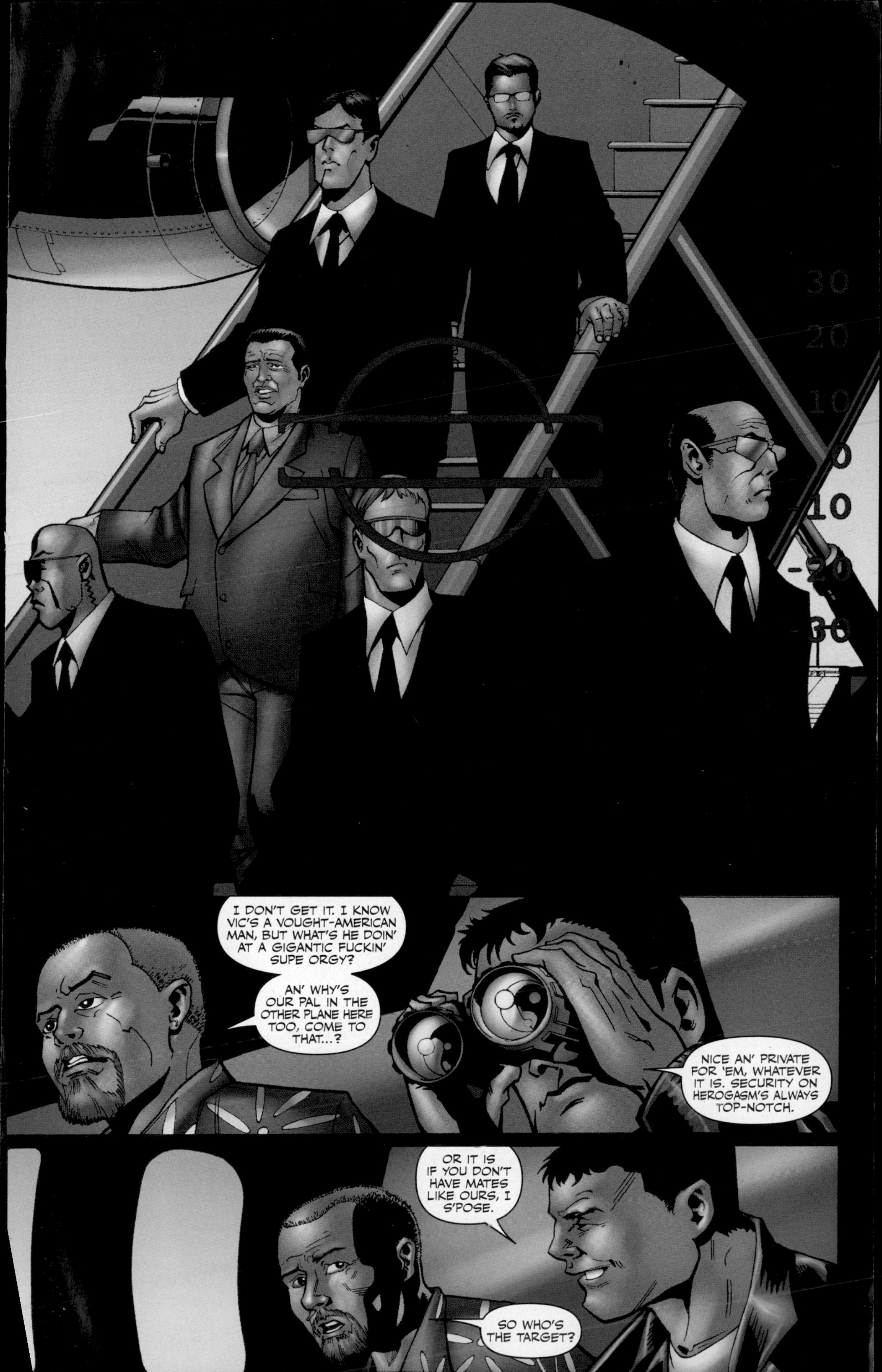
30
20
10
0
10
-20
30
I DON'T GET IT. I KNOW VIC'S A VOUGHT-AMERICAN MAN, BUT WHAT'S HE DOIN' AT A GIGANTIC FUCKIN' SUPE ORGY?
AN' WHY'S OUR PAL IN THE OTHER PLANE HERE TOO, COME TO THAT...?
NICE AN' PRIVATE FOR 'EM, WHATEVER IT IS. SECURITY ON HEROGASM'S ALWAYS TOP-NOTCH.
OR IT IS IF YOU DON'T HAVE MATES LIKE OURS, I S'POSE.
SO WHO'S THE TARGET?

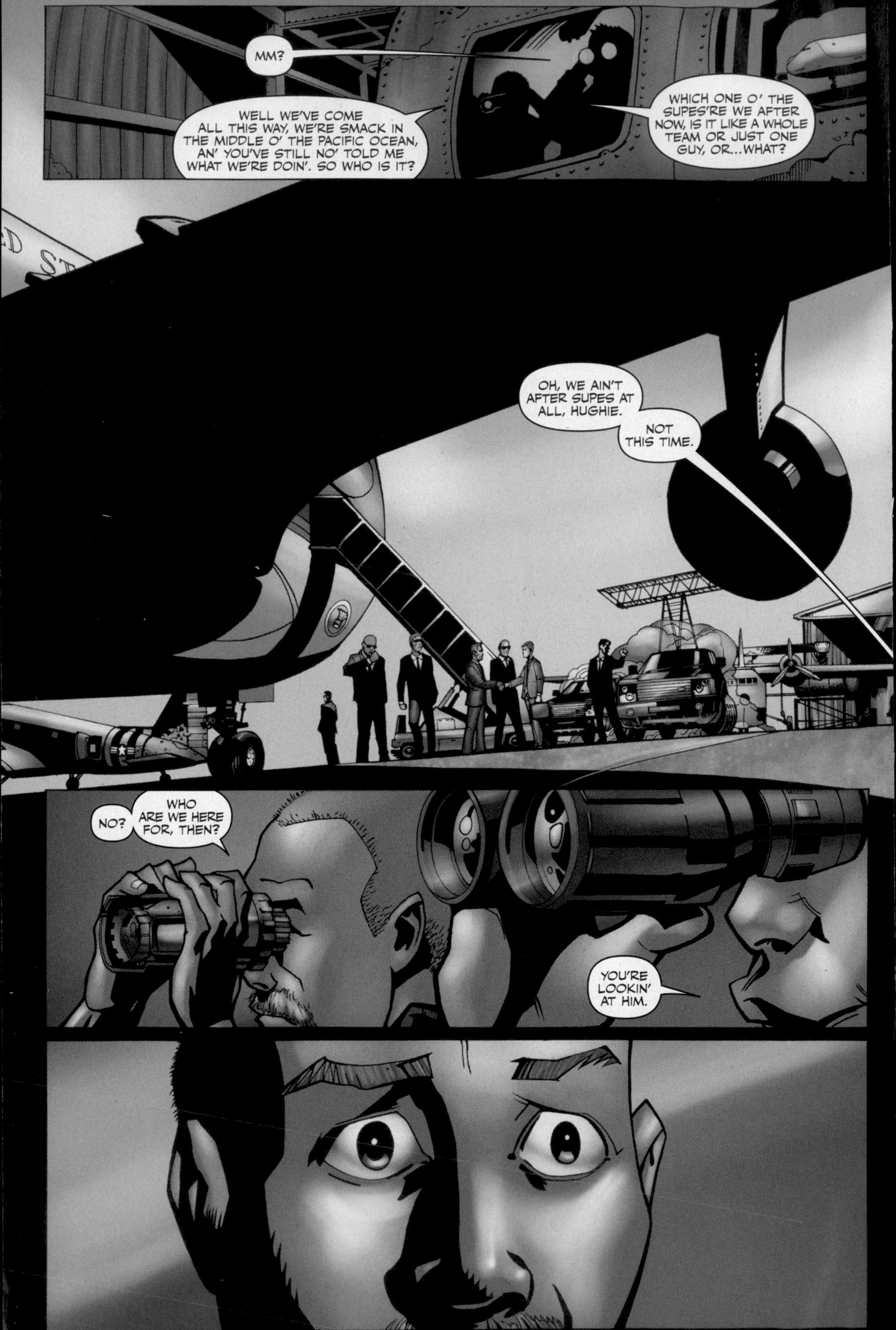
MM?
WELL WE'VE COME ALL THIS WAY, WE'RE SMACK IN THE MIDDLE O' THE PACIFIC OCEAN, AN' YOU'VE STILL NO' TOLD ME WHAT WE'RE DOIN'. SO WHO IS IT?
WHICH ONE O' THE SUPES'RE WE AFTER NOW, IS IT LIKE A WHOLE TEAM OR JUST ONE GUY, OR...WHAT?
OH, WE AIN'T AFTER SUPES AT ALL, HUGHIE.
NOT THIS TIME.
NO?
WHO ARE WE HERE FOR, THEN?
YOU'RE LOOKIN' AT HIM.

TWO

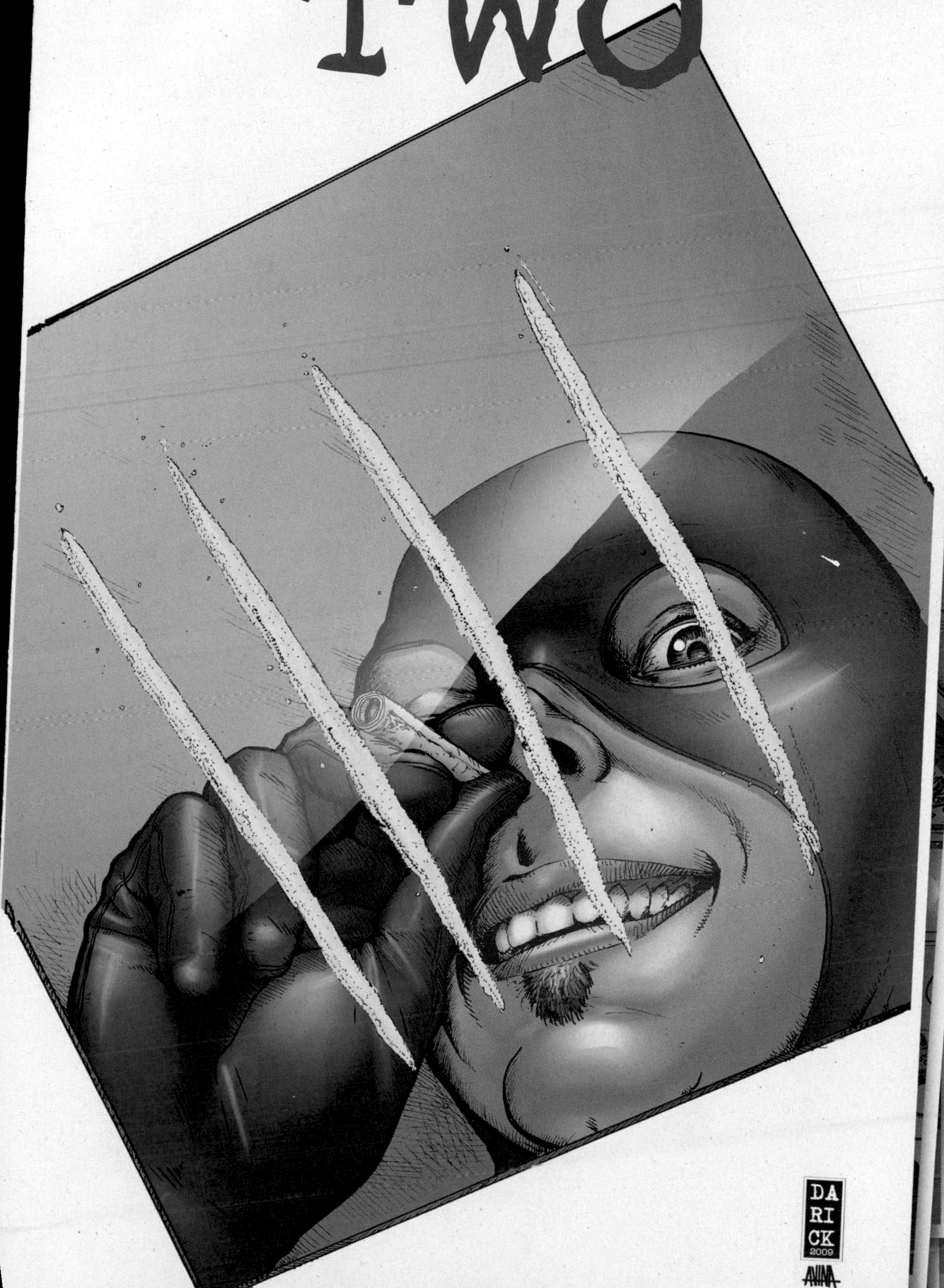
DA
RI
CK
2009
AVINA

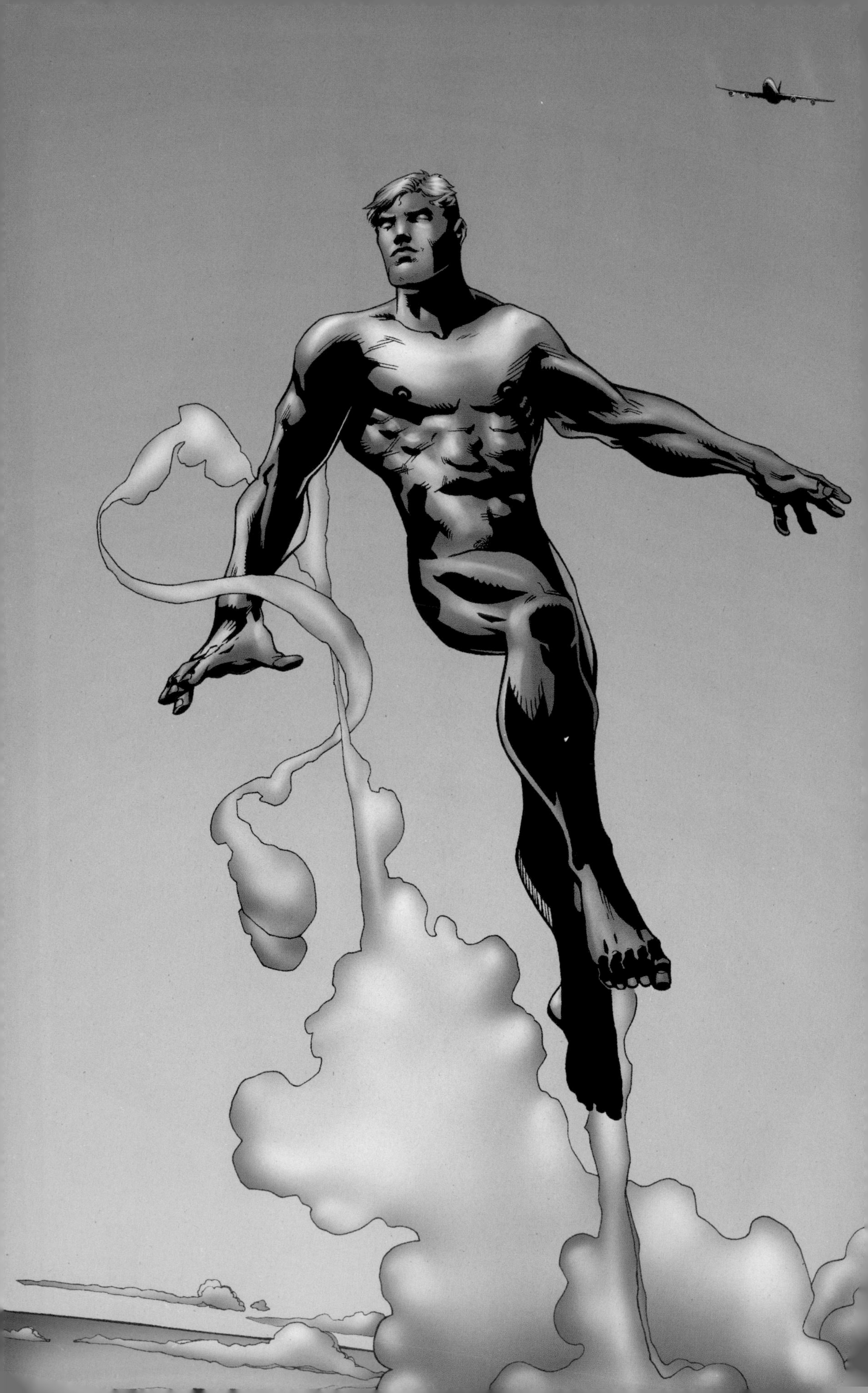

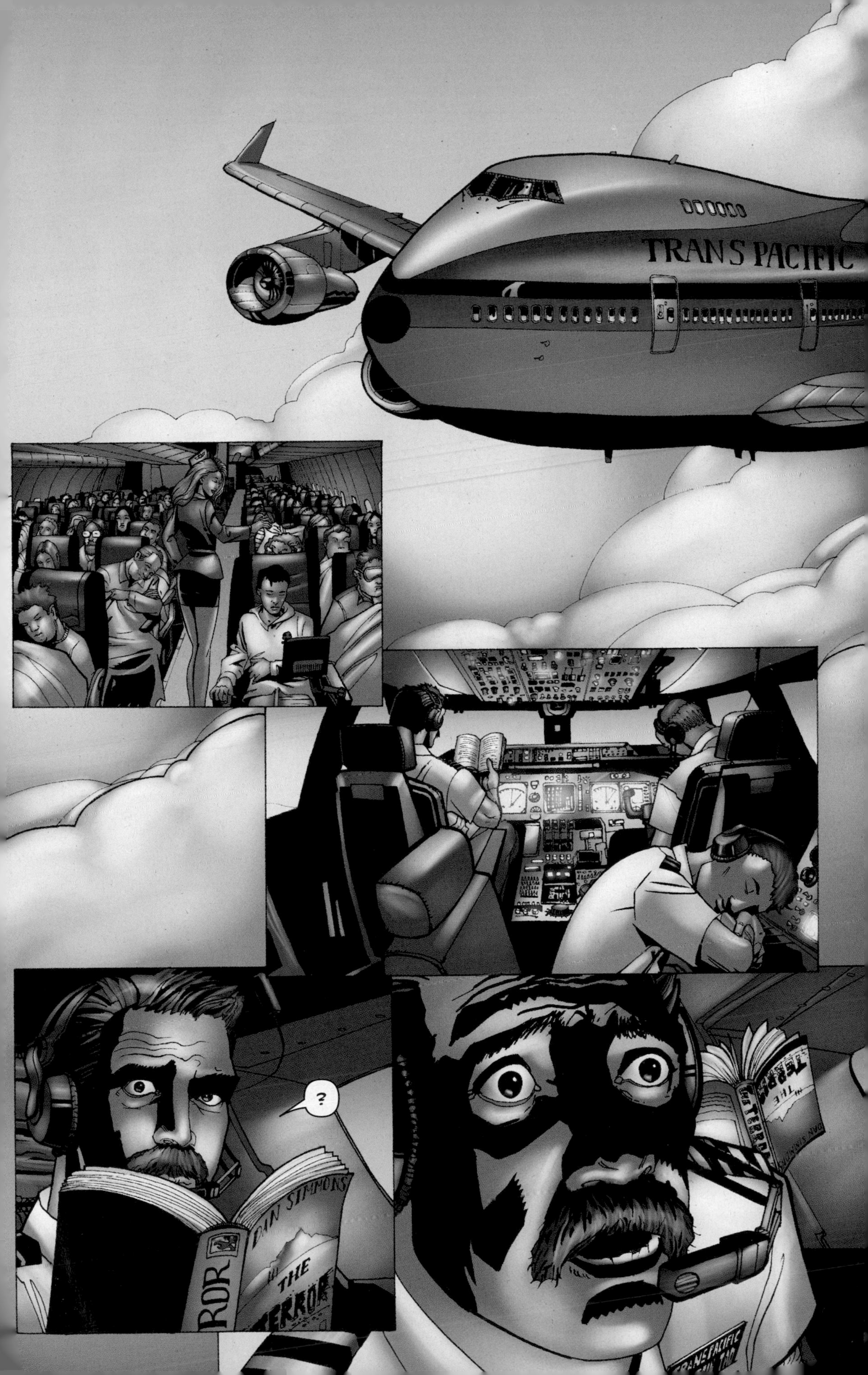

TRANS PACIFIC
?
DAN SIMMONS
THE TERROR

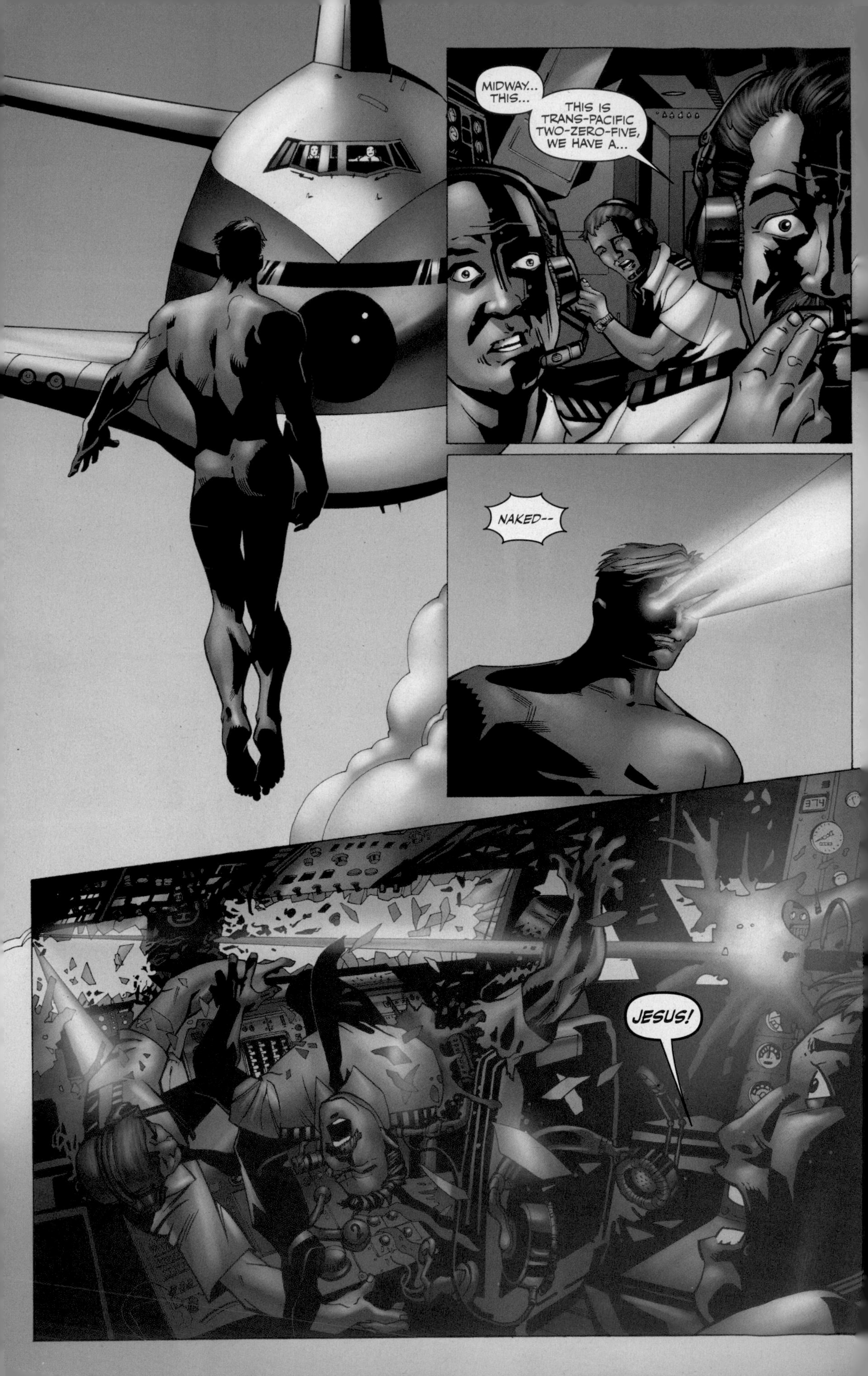
MIDWAY... THIS...
THIS IS TRANS-PACIFIC TWO-ZERO-FIVE, WE HAVE A...
NAKED--
JESUS!

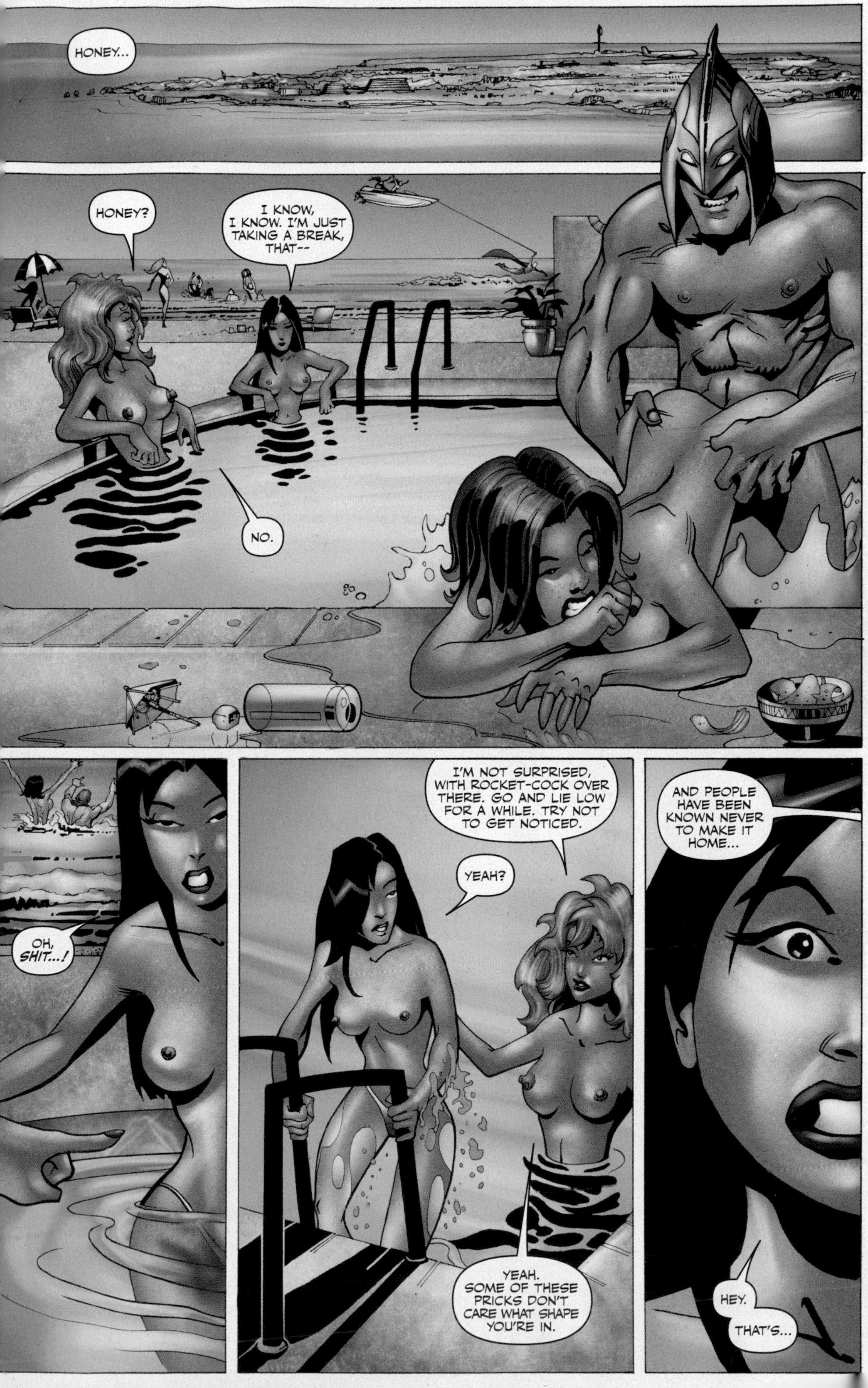
HONEY...
HONEY?
I KNOW, I KNOW. I'M JUST TAKING A BREAK, THAT--
NO.
OH, SHIT...!
I'M NOT SURPRISED, WITH ROCKET-COCK OVER THERE. GO AND LIE LOW FOR A WHILE. TRY NOT TO GET NOTICED.
YEAH?
YEAH. SOME OF THESE PRICKS DON'T CARE WHAT SHAPE YOU'RE IN.
AND PEOPLE HAVE BEEN KNOWN NEVER TO MAKE IT HOME...
HEY.
THAT'S...

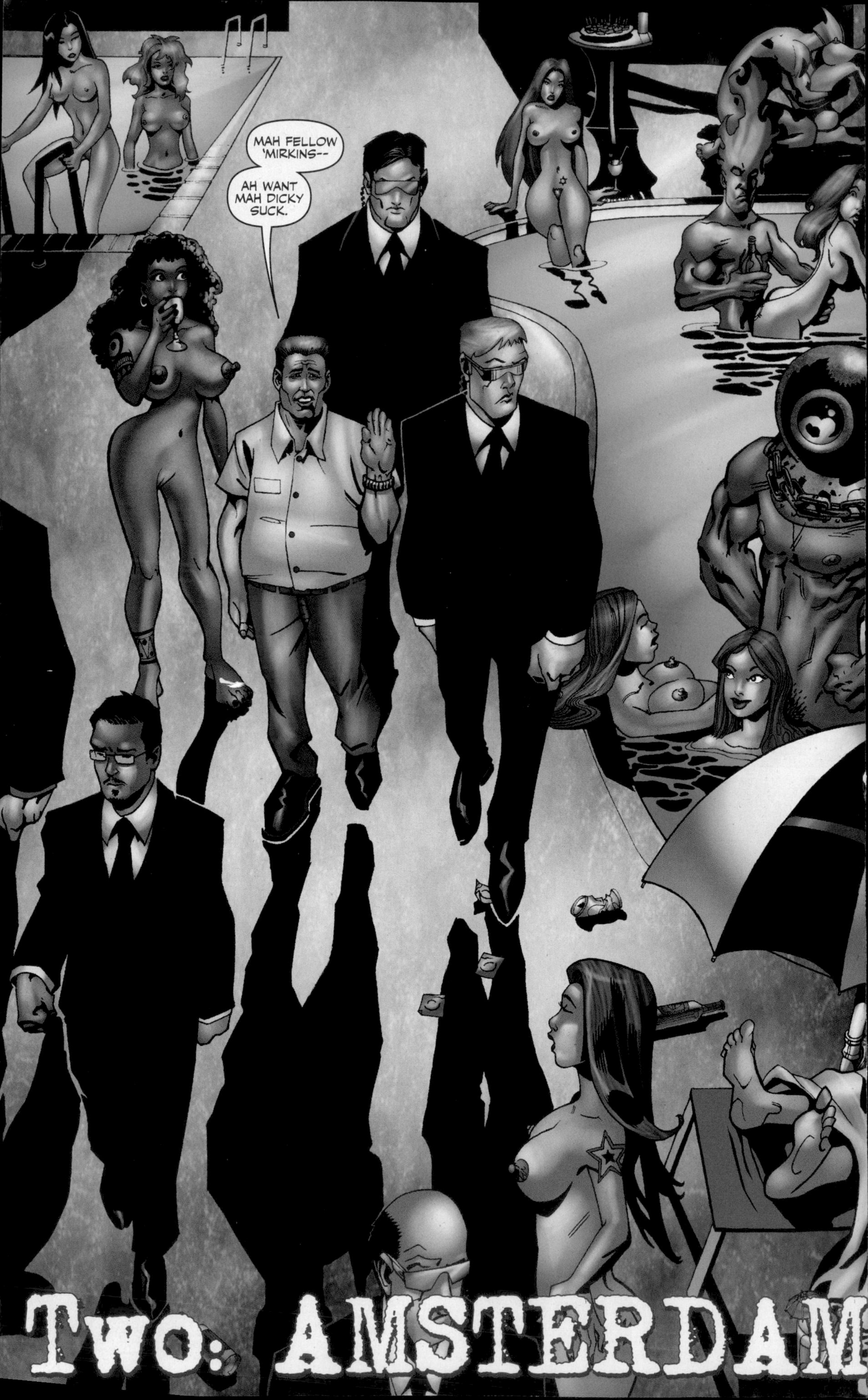
MAH FELLOW 'MIRKINS--
AH WANT MAH DICKY SUCK.
Two: AMSTERDAM

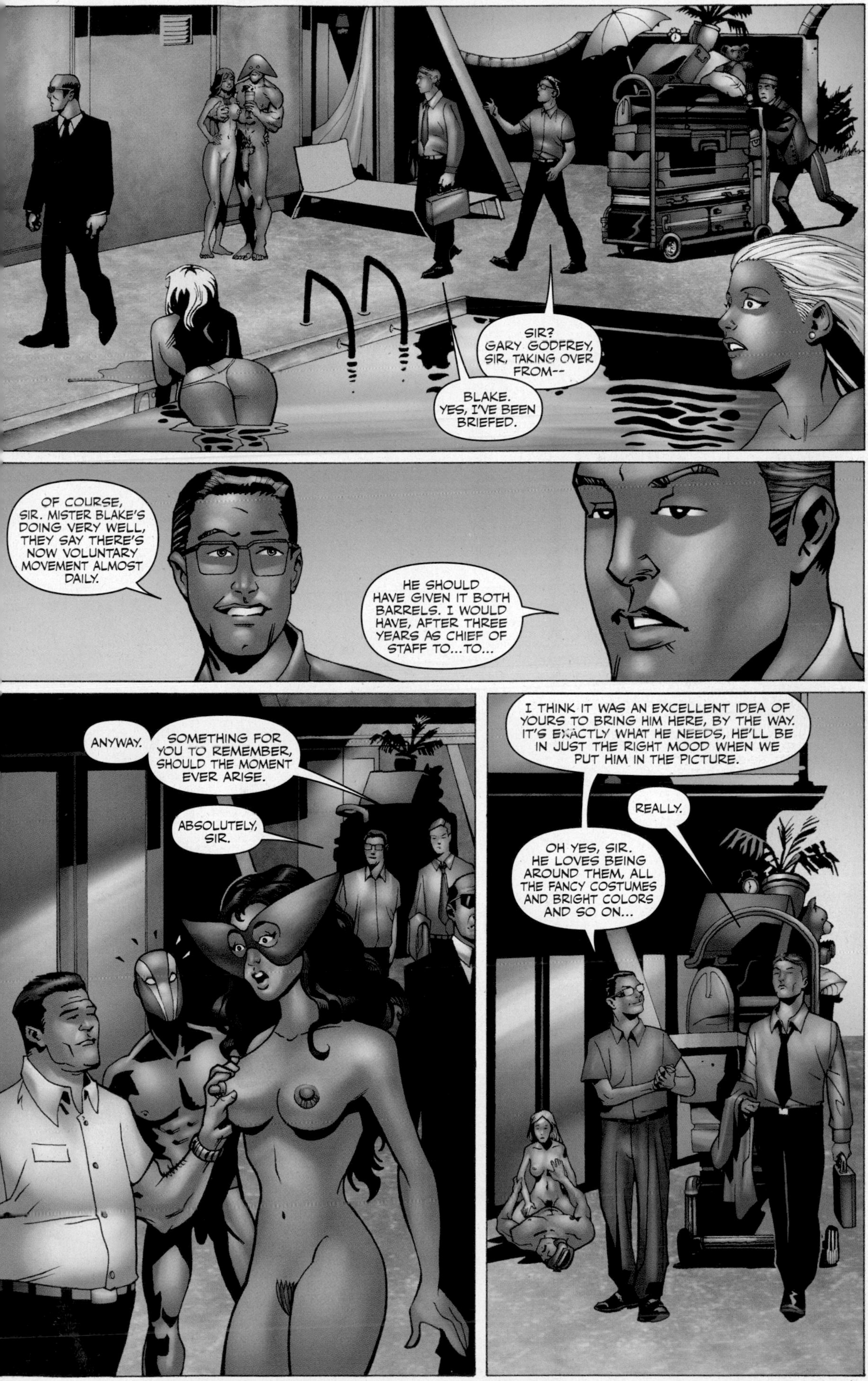
SIR? GARY GODFREY, SIR, TAKING OVER FROM--
BLAKE. YES, I'VE BEEN BRIEFED.
OF COURSE, SIR. MISTER BLAKE'S DOING VERY WELL, THEY SAY THERE'S NOW VOLUNTARY MOVEMENT ALMOST DAILY.
HE SHOULD HAVE GIVEN IT BOTH BARRELS. I WOULD HAVE, AFTER THREE YEARS AS CHIEF OF STAFF TO...TO...
ANYWAY.
SOMETHING FOR YOU TO REMEMBER, SHOULD THE MOMENT EVER ARISE.
ABSOLUTELY, SIR.
I THINK IT WAS AN EXCELLENT IDEA OF YOURS TO BRING HIM HERE, BY THE WAY. IT'S EXACTLY WHAT HE NEEDS, HE'LL BE IN JUST THE RIGHT MOOD WHEN WE PUT HIM IN THE PICTURE.
REALLY.
OH YES, SIR. HE LOVES BEING AROUND THEM, ALL THE FANCY COSTUMES AND BRIGHT COLORS AND SO ON...

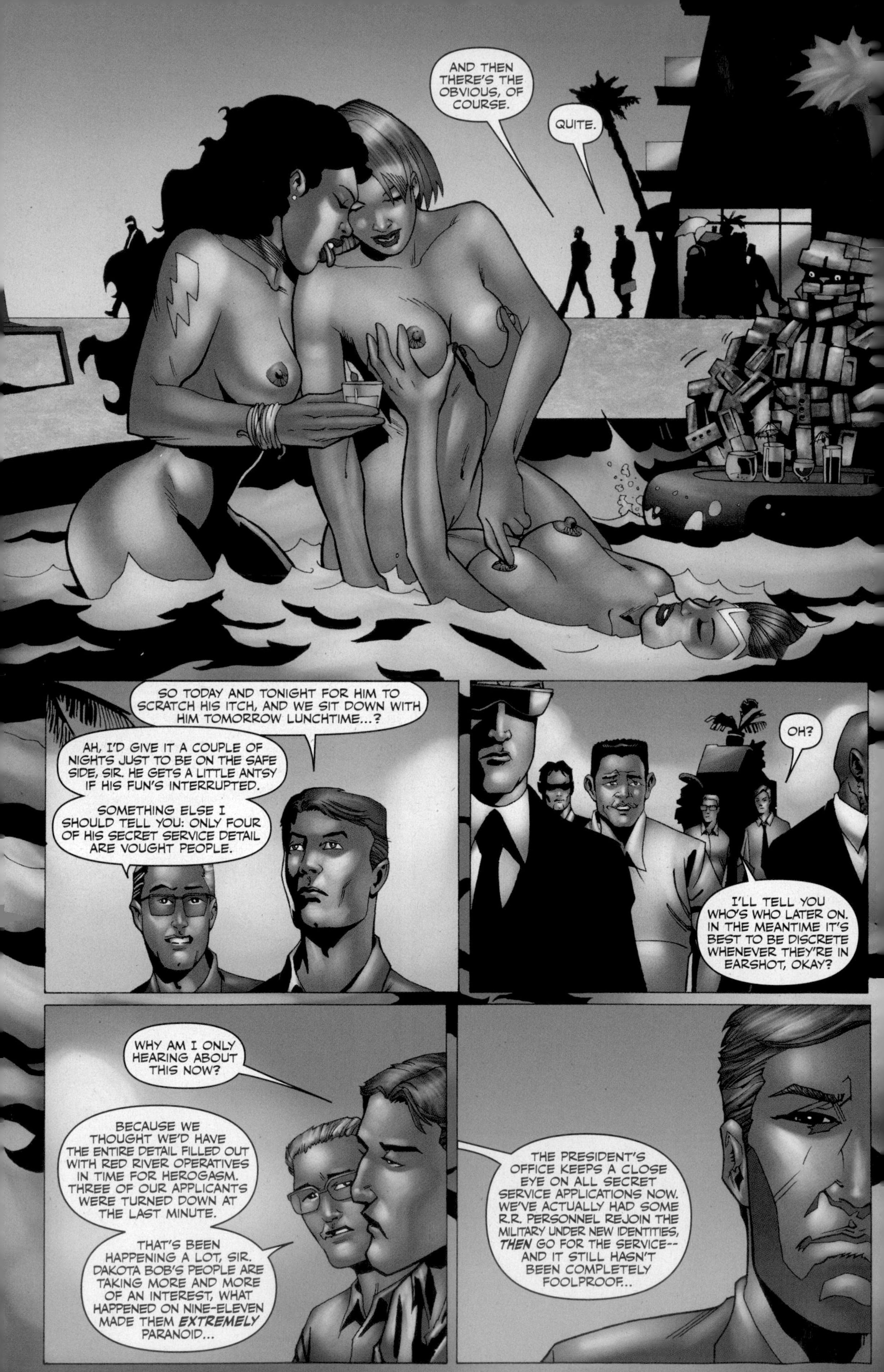
AND THEN THERE'S THE OBVIOUS, OF COURSE.
QUITE.
SO TODAY AND TONIGHT FOR HIM TO SCRATCH HIS ITCH, AND WE SIT DOWN WITH HIM TOMORROW LUNCHTIME...?
AH, I'D GIVE IT A COUPLE OF NIGHTS JUST TO BE ON THE SAFE SIDE, SIR. HE GETS A LITTLE ANTSY IF HIS FUN'S INTERRUPTED.
SOMETHING ELSE I SHOULD TELL YOU: ONLY FOUR OF HIS SECRET SERVICE DETAIL ARE VOUGHT PEOPLE.
OH?
I'LL TELL YOU WHO'S WHO LATER ON. IN THE MEANTIME IT'S BEST TO BE DISCRETE WHENEVER THEY'RE IN EARSHOT, OKAY?
WHY AM I ONLY HEARING ABOUT THIS NOW?
BECAUSE WE THOUGHT WE'D HAVE THE ENTIRE DETAIL FILLED OUT WITH RED RIVER OPERATIVES IN TIME FOR HEROGASM. THREE OF OUR APPLICANTS WERE TURNED DOWN AT THE LAST MINUTE.
THAT'S BEEN HAPPENING A LOT, SIR. DAKOTA BOB'S PEOPLE ARE TAKING MORE AND MORE OF AN INTEREST, WHAT HAPPENED ON NINE-ELEVEN MADE THEM EXTREMELY PARANOID...
THE PRESIDENT'S OFFICE KEEPS A CLOSE EYE ON ALL SECRET SERVICE APPLICATIONS NOW. WE'VE ACTUALLY HAD SOME R.R. PERSONNEL REJOIN THE MILITARY UNDER NEW IDENTITIES, THEN GO FOR THE SERVICE-- AND IT STILL HASN'T BEEN COMPLETELY FOOLPROOF...

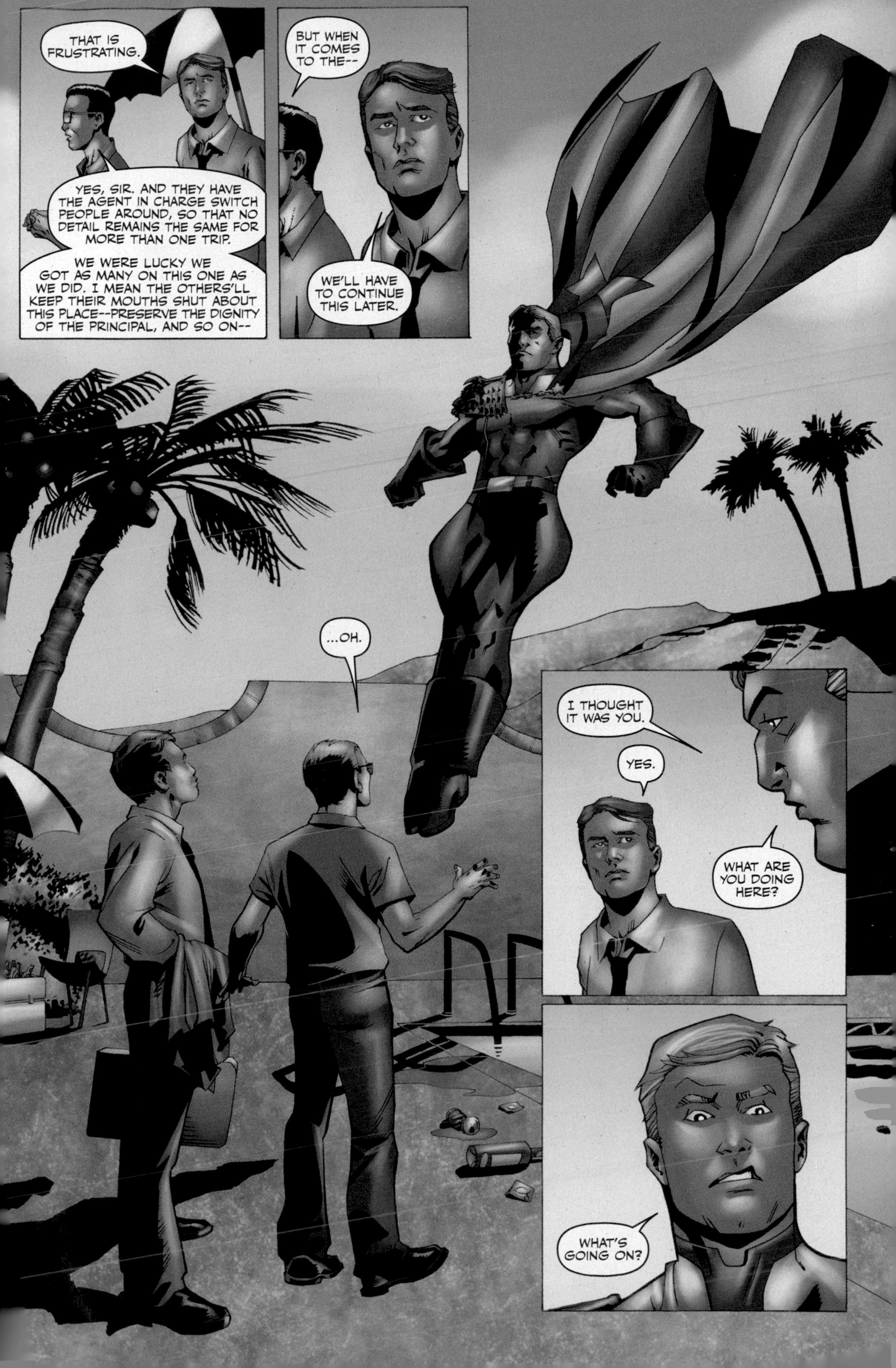
THAT IS FRUSTRATING.
YES, SIR. AND THEY HAVE THE AGENT IN CHARGE SWITCH PEOPLE AROUND, SO THAT NO DETAIL REMAINS THE SAME FOR MORE THAN ONE TRIP.
WE WERE LUCKY WE GOT AS MANY ON THIS ONE AS WE DID. I MEAN THE OTHERS'LL KEEP THEIR MOUTHS SHUT ABOUT THIS PLACE--PRESERVE THE DIGNITY OF THE PRINCIPAL, AND SO ON--
BUT WHEN IT COMES TO THE--
WE'LL HAVE TO CONTINUE THIS LATER.
...OH.
I THOUGHT IT WAS YOU.
YES.
WHAT ARE YOU DOING HERE?
WHAT'S GOING ON?

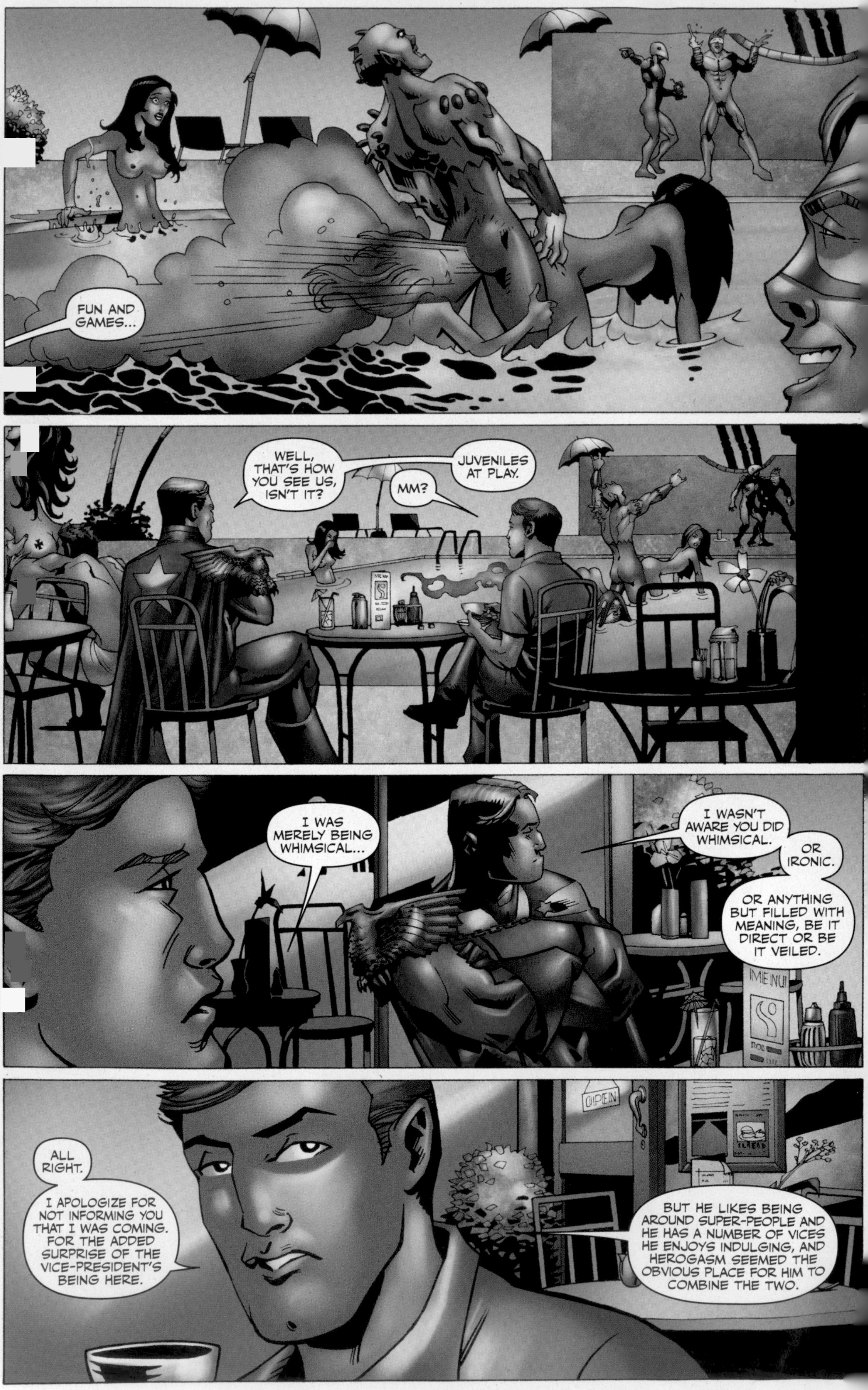
FUN AND GAMES...
WELL, THAT'S HOW YOU SEE US, ISN'T IT?
MM?
JUVENILES AT PLAY.
I WAS MERELY BEING WHIMSICAL...
I WASN'T AWARE YOU DID WHIMSICAL.
OR IRONIC.
OR ANYTHING BUT FILLED WITH MEANING, BE IT DIRECT OR BE IT VEILED.
MENU
ALL RIGHT.
I APOLOGIZE FOR NOT INFORMING YOU THAT I WAS COMING. FOR THE ADDED SURPRISE OF THE VICE-PRESIDENT'S BEING HERE.
OPEN
BUT HE LIKES BEING AROUND SUPER-PEOPLE AND HE HAS A NUMBER OF VICES HE ENJOYS INDULGING, AND HEROGASM SEEMED THE OBVIOUS PLACE FOR HIM TO COMBINE THE TWO.

AND WHAT HAS HE DONE TO DESERVE THIS, EXACTLY?

ABSOLUTELY NOTHING. BUT WE'RE MOVING AHEAD WITH OUR PLANS, AND WE WANT HIM IN THE RIGHT FRAME OF MIND WHEN WE EXPLAIN HIS ROLE.

HE'S HAD THE JOB FOR SEVEN YEARS AND YOU HAVEN'T TOLD HIM WHY YET?

HE HASN'T NEEDED TO KNOW UNTIL NOW.

I THINK I MIGHT KNOW HOW HE FEELS...

YOU DON'T KNOW HOW HE FEELS, BECAUSE YOU HAVE A SIZABLE I.Q. AND HIS IS BARELY IN DOUBLE FIGURES.

WHICH IS WHAT I'M GOING TO BE UP AGAINST WHEN I TELL HIM HE'LL BE PRESIDENT WITHIN THE YEAR.

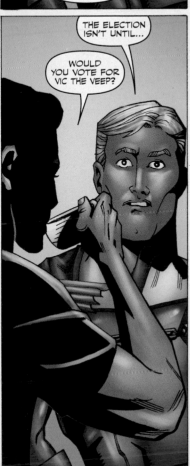

THE ELECTION ISN'T UNTIL...

WOULD YOU VOTE FOR VIC THE VEEP?

JESUS.

BUT THAT'S ABOUT THE BEST NEWS HE COULD POSSIBLY GET, WHY DO YOU HAVE TO GET HIM LAID TO TELL HIM THAT?

BECAUSE THE DETAILS ARE COMPLEX, AND HIS BRAIN IS SMALL.

YOU'VE COMPLAINED BEFORE ABOUT NOT BEING CONSULTED. NOW THAT I'VE TAKEN YOU INTO MY CONFIDENCE--ON WHAT I THINK YOU'LL AGREE IS AN EXTREMELY DELICATE MATTER--CAN I TAKE IT THAT THE V.P. AND HIS PARTY WILL BE WELCOME AT HEROGASM?

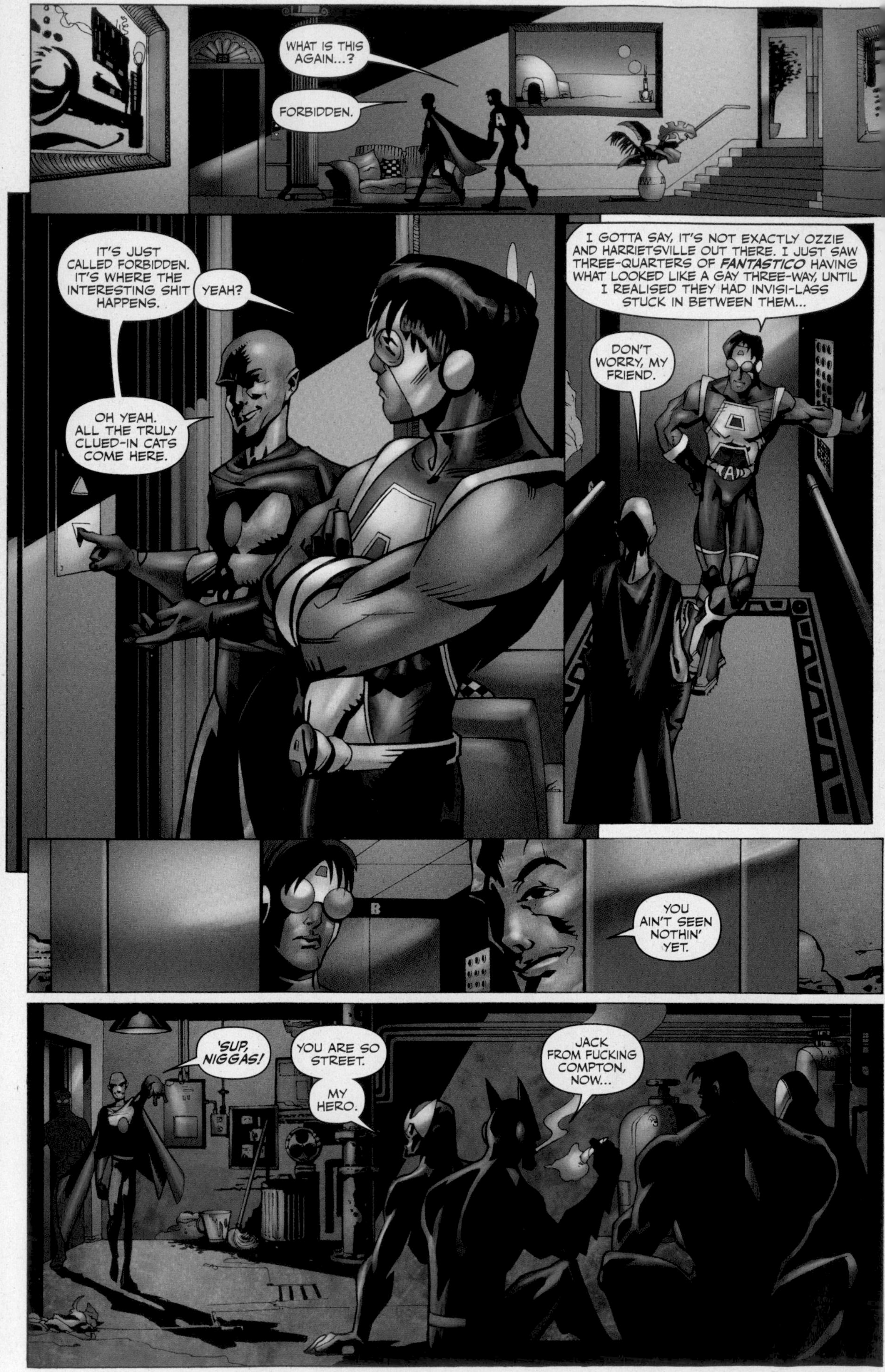
WHAT IS THIS AGAIN...?
FORBIDDEN.
IT'S JUST CALLED FORBIDDEN. IT'S WHERE THE INTERESTING SHIT HAPPENS.
YEAH?
OH YEAH. ALL THE TRULY CLUED-IN CATS COME HERE.
I GOTTA SAY, IT'S NOT EXACTLY OZZIE AND HARRIETSVILLE OUT THERE. I JUST SAW THREE-QUARTERS OF *FANTASTICO* HAVING WHAT LOOKED LIKE A GAY THREE-WAY, UNTIL I REALISED THEY HAD INVISI-LASS STUCK IN BETWEEN THEM...
DON'T WORRY, MY FRIEND.
B
YOU AIN'T SEEN NOTHIN' YET.
'SUP, NIGGAS!
YOU ARE SO STREET.
MY HERO.
JACK FROM FUCKING COMPTON, NOW...

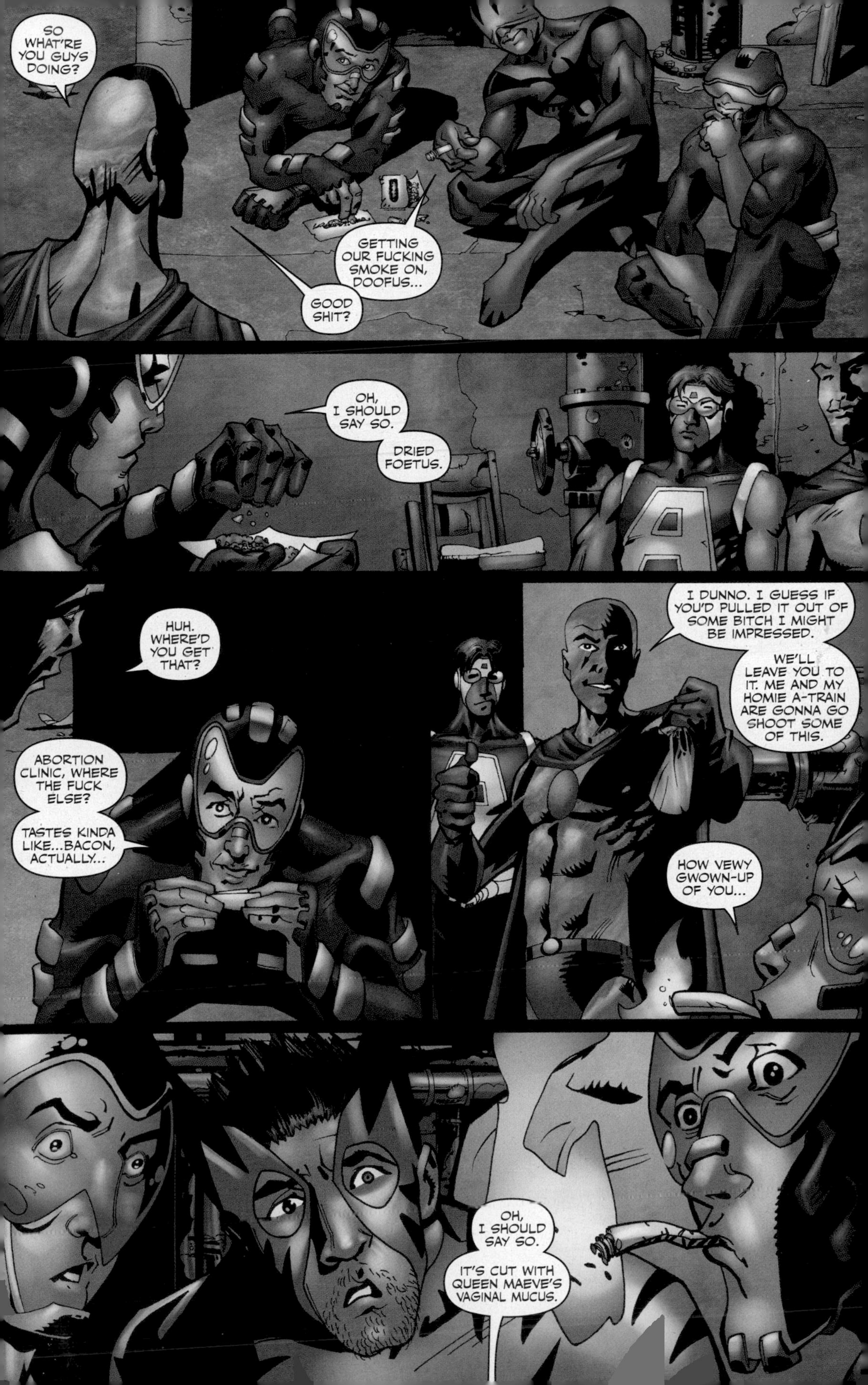
SO WHAT'RE YOU GUYS DOING?
GETTING OUR FUCKING SMOKE ON, DOOFUS...
GOOD SHIT?
OH, I SHOULD SAY SO.
DRIED FOETUS.
HUH. WHERE'D YOU GET THAT?
ABORTION CLINIC, WHERE THE FUCK ELSE?
TASTES KINDA LIKE...BACON, ACTUALLY...
I DUNNO. I GUESS IF YOU'D PULLED IT OUT OF SOME BITCH I MIGHT BE IMPRESSED.
WE'LL LEAVE YOU TO IT. ME AND MY HOMIE A-TRAIN ARE GONNA GO SHOOT SOME OF THIS.
HOW VEWY GWOWN-UP OF YOU...
OH, I SHOULD SAY SO.
IT'S CUT WITH QUEEN MAEVE'S VAGINAL MUCUS.

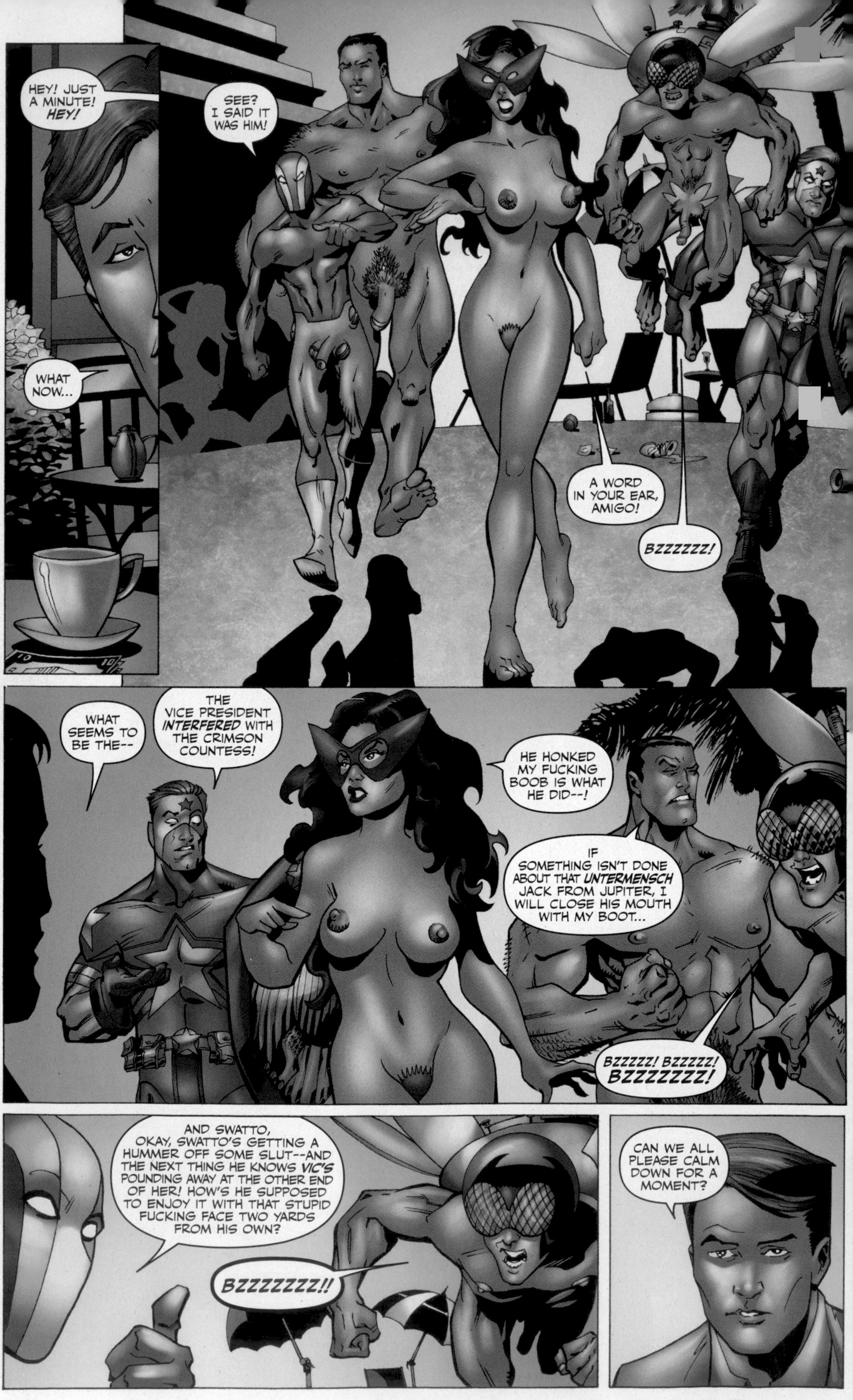

HEY! JUST A MINUTE! *HEY!*
SEE? I SAID IT WAS HIM!
WHAT NOW...
A WORD IN YOUR EAR, AMIGO!
BZZZZZZ!
WHAT SEEMS TO BE THE--
THE VICE PRESIDENT *INTERFERED* WITH THE CRIMSON COUNTESS!
HE HONKED MY FUCKING BOOB IS WHAT HE DID--!
IF SOMETHING ISN'T DONE ABOUT THAT *UNTERMENSCH* JACK FROM JUPITER, I WILL CLOSE HIS MOUTH WITH MY BOOT...
BZZZZZ! BZZZZZ! BZZZZZZZ!
AND SWATTO, OKAY, SWATTO'S GETTING A HUMMER OFF SOME SLUT--AND THE NEXT THING HE KNOWS *VIC'S* POUNDING AWAY AT THE OTHER END OF HER! HOW'S HE SUPPOSED TO ENJOY IT WITH THAT STUPID FUCKING FACE TWO YARDS FROM HIS OWN?
BZZZZZZZ!!
CAN WE ALL PLEASE CALM DOWN FOR A MOMENT?

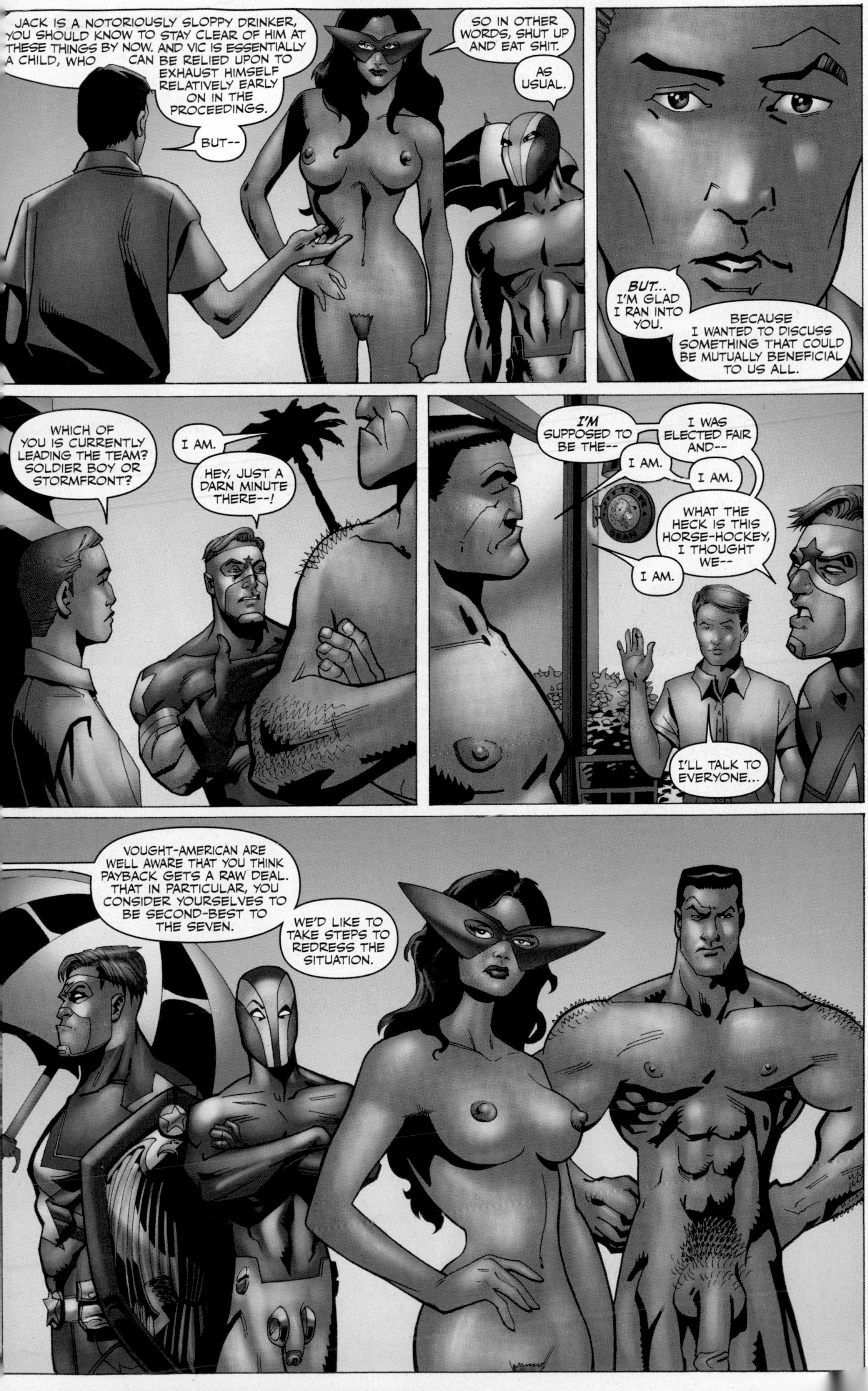
JACK IS A NOTORIOUSLY SLOPPY DRINKER, YOU SHOULD KNOW TO STAY CLEAR OF HIM AT THESE THINGS BY NOW. AND VIC IS ESSENTIALLY A CHILD, WHO CAN BE RELIED UPON TO EXHAUST HIMSELF RELATIVELY EARLY ON IN THE PROCEEDINGS.
BUT--
SO IN OTHER WORDS, SHUT UP AND EAT SHIT.
AS USUAL.
BUT... I'M GLAD I RAN INTO YOU.
BECAUSE I WANTED TO DISCUSS SOMETHING THAT COULD BE MUTUALLY BENEFICIAL TO US ALL.
WHICH OF YOU IS CURRENTLY LEADING THE TEAM? SOLDIER BOY OR STORMFRONT?
I AM.
HEY, JUST A DARN MINUTE THERE--!
I'M SUPPOSED TO BE THE--
I WAS ELECTED FAIR AND--
I AM.
I AM.
WHAT THE HECK IS THIS HORSE-HOCKEY, I THOUGHT WE--
I AM.
I'LL TALK TO EVERYONE...
VOUGHT-AMERICAN ARE WELL AWARE THAT YOU THINK PAYBACK GETS A RAW DEAL. THAT IN PARTICULAR, YOU CONSIDER YOURSELVES TO BE SECOND-BEST TO THE SEVEN.
WE'D LIKE TO TAKE STEPS TO REDRESS THE SITUATION.

I WOULDN'T SAY SECOND-BEST, EXACTLY...

YEAH, NOT TO THAT BUNCH OF STUCK-UP ASSHOLES...

WELL, YOU DO KEEP TRYING TO JOIN THEM. EACH OF YOU HAS MADE SEVERAL ATTEMPTS.

TEK-KNIGHT WAS CALLING THEM THE SAME WEEK HE WAS KILLED...

HOW DID YOU--

YOU TRIED TO LEAVE WITHOUT ME--?

LOOK, LET'S JUST LISTEN TO THE MAN!

BZZZZZ! BZZZZZ!

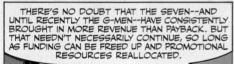

THERE'S NO DOUBT THAT THE SEVEN--AND UNTIL RECENTLY THE G-MEN--HAVE CONSISTENTLY BROUGHT IN MORE REVENUE THAN PAYBACK. BUT THAT NEEDN'T NECESSARILY CONTINUE, SO LONG AS FUNDING CAN BE FREED UP AND PROMOTIONAL RESOURCES REALLOCATED.

WHAT WE NEED IS SOME ASSISTANCE WITH A PROBLEM BACK IN NEW YORK, A SMALL GROUP WHO'VE BEEN CAUSING US QUITE A LOT OF TROUBLE...

YEAH? JESUS, JUST TELL US THEIR NAMES, WE'LL OBLITERATE THE PRICKS...

WHAT ARE WE TALKING ABOUT, SOME ROGUE TEAM OR OTHER?

NO.

NOT A SUPER-TEAM AT ALL, AS A MATTER OF FACT.

WHY DON'T WE SIT DOWN, AND I'LL TELL YOU MORE ABOUT THEM OVER COFFEE?

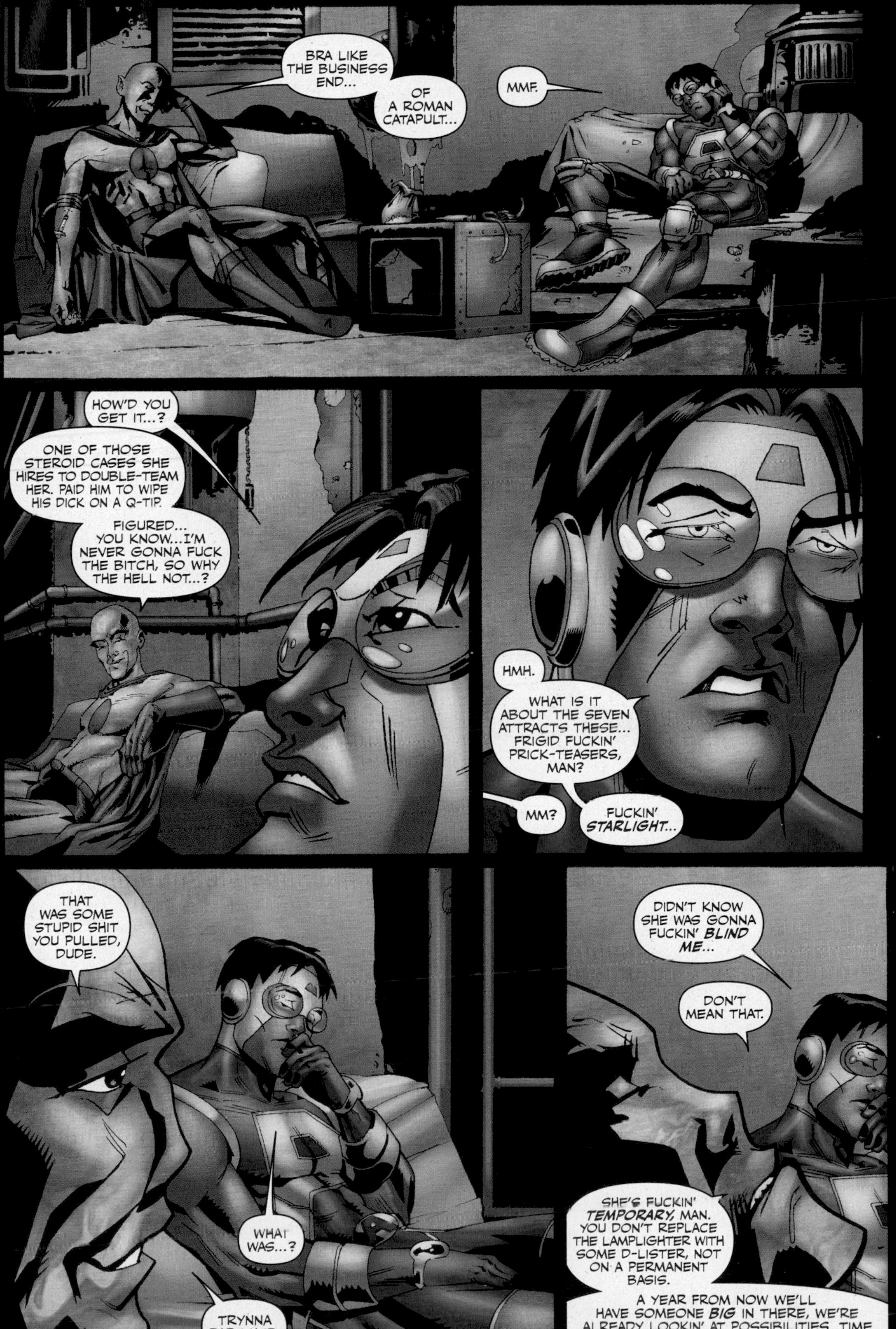
BRA LIKE THE BUSINESS END...
OF A ROMAN CATAPULT...
MMF.
HOW'D YOU GET IT...?
ONE OF THOSE STEROID CASES SHE HIRES TO DOUBLE-TEAM HER. PAID HIM TO WIPE HIS DICK ON A Q-TIP.
FIGURED... YOU KNOW...I'M NEVER GONNA FUCK THE BITCH, SO WHY THE HELL NOT...?
HMH.
WHAT IS IT ABOUT THE SEVEN ATTRACTS THESE... FRIGID FUCKIN' PRICK-TEASERS, MAN?
MM?
FUCKIN' STARLIGHT...
THAT WAS SOME STUPID SHIT YOU PULLED, DUDE.
WHAT WAS...?
TRYNNA RAPE HER.
DIDN'T KNOW SHE WAS GONNA FUCKIN' BLIND ME...
DON'T MEAN THAT.
SHE'S FUCKIN' TEMPORARY, MAN. YOU DON'T REPLACE THE LAMPLIGHTER WITH SOME D-LISTER, NOT ON A PERMANENT BASIS.
A YEAR FROM NOW WE'LL HAVE SOMEONE BIG IN THERE, WE'RE ALREADY LOOKIN' AT POSSIBILITIES. TIME COMES AN' SHE'S ALL YOURS, AN NO ONE'S GONNA FUCKIN' SAY DICK ABOUT IT...

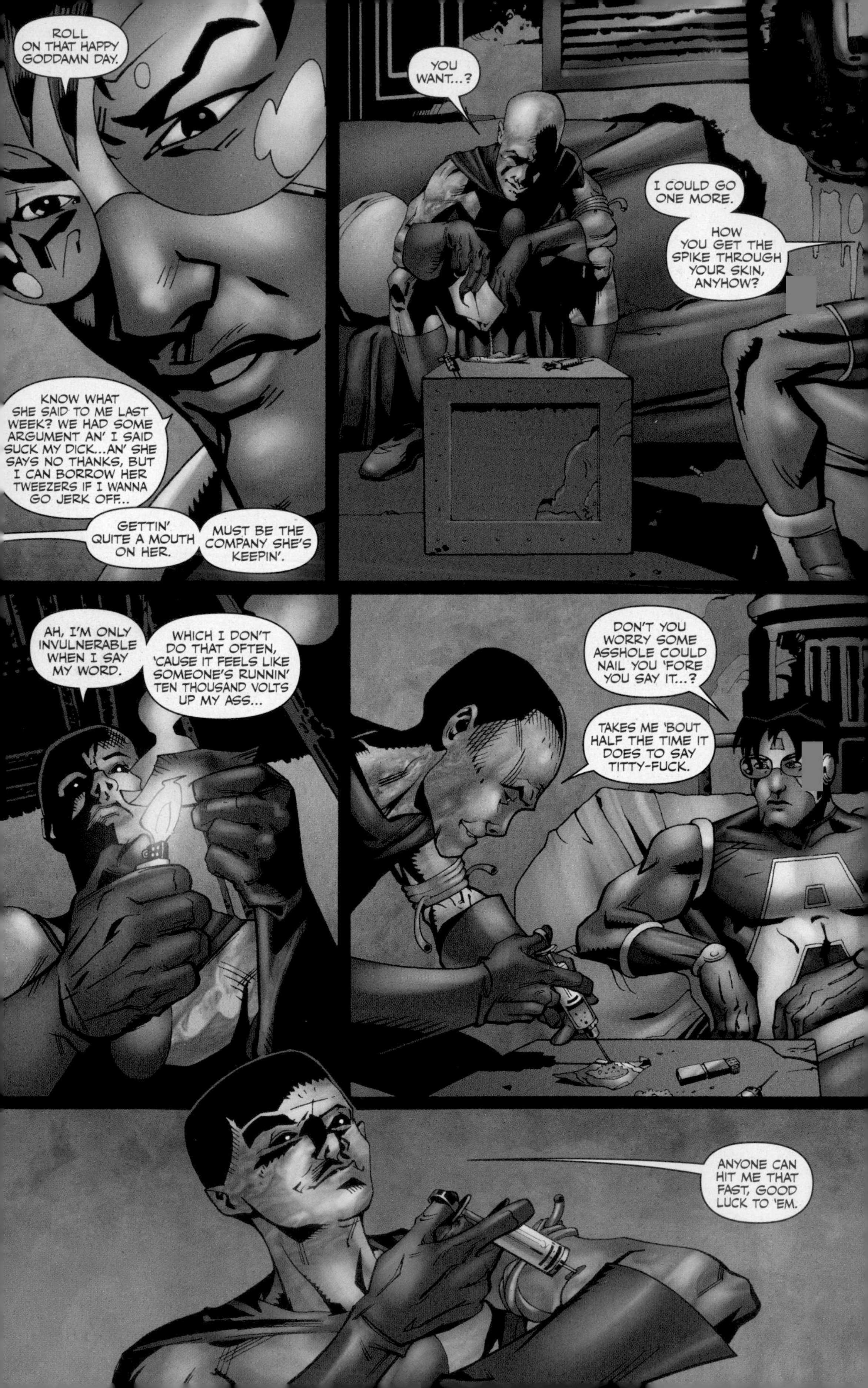
ROLL ON THAT HAPPY GODDAMN DAY.
KNOW WHAT SHE SAID TO ME LAST WEEK? WE HAD SOME ARGUMENT AN' I SAID SUCK MY DICK...AN' SHE SAYS NO THANKS, BUT I CAN BORROW HER TWEEZERS IF I WANNA GO JERK OFF...
GETTIN' QUITE A MOUTH ON HER.
MUST BE THE COMPANY SHE'S KEEPIN'.
YOU WANT...?
I COULD GO ONE MORE.
HOW YOU GET THE SPIKE THROUGH YOUR SKIN, ANYHOW?
AH, I'M ONLY INVULNERABLE WHEN I SAY MY WORD.
WHICH I DON'T DO THAT OFTEN, 'CAUSE IT FEELS LIKE SOMEONE'S RUNNIN' TEN THOUSAND VOLTS UP MY ASS...
DON'T YOU WORRY SOME ASSHOLE COULD NAIL YOU 'FORE YOU SAY IT...?
TAKES ME 'BOUT HALF THE TIME IT DOES TO SAY TITTY-FUCK.
ANYONE CAN HIT ME THAT FAST, GOOD LUCK TO 'EM.

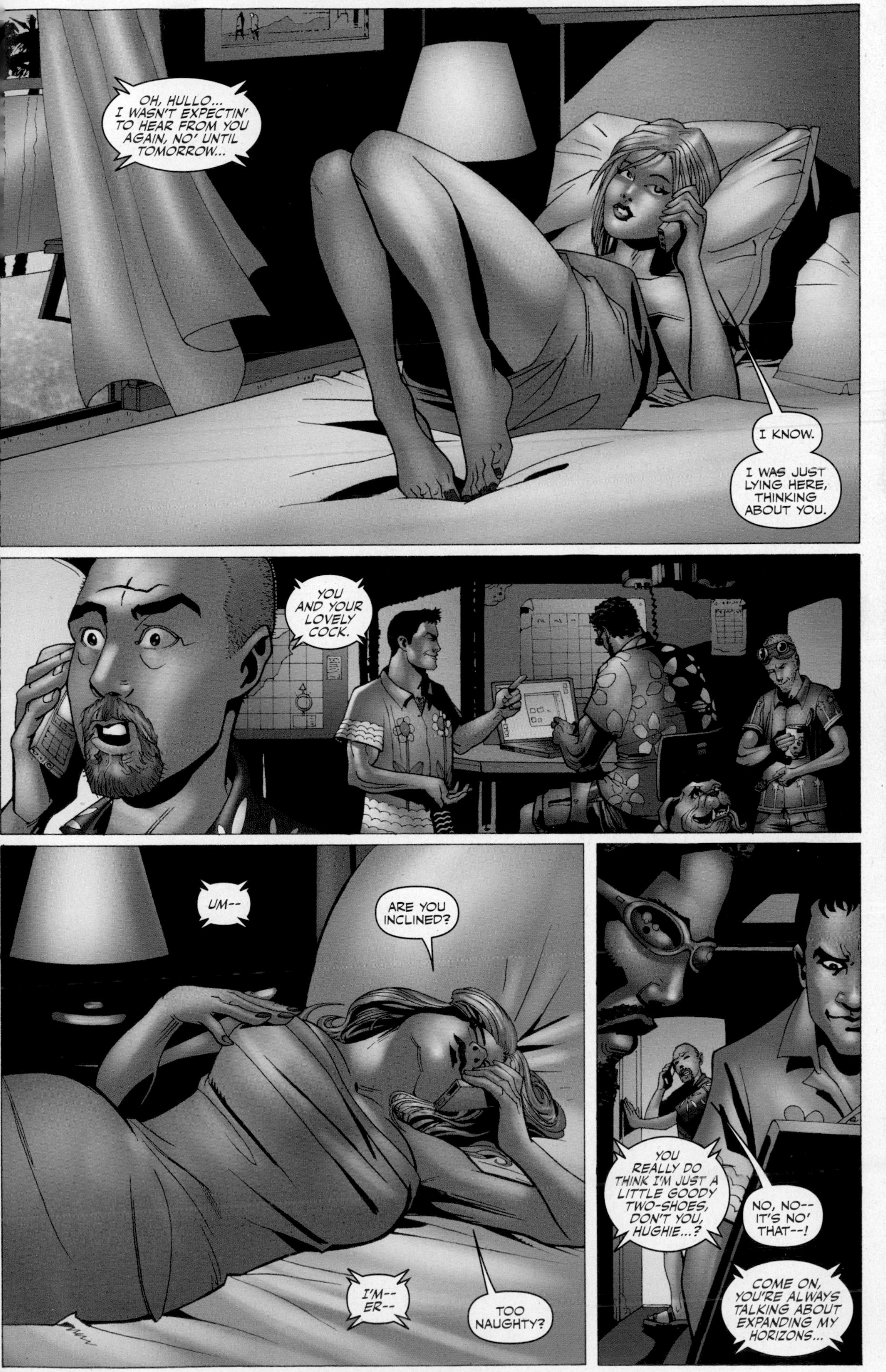
OH, HULLO... I WASN'T EXPECTIN' TO HEAR FROM YOU AGAIN, NO' UNTIL TOMORROW...
I KNOW.
I WAS JUST LYING HERE, THINKING ABOUT YOU.
YOU AND YOUR LOVELY COCK.
UM--
ARE YOU INCLINED?
I'M-- ER--
TOO NAUGHTY?
YOU REALLY DO THINK I'M JUST A LITTLE GOODY TWO-SHOES, DON'T YOU, HUGHIE...?
NO, NO-- IT'S NO' THAT--!
COME ON, YOU'RE ALWAYS TALKING ABOUT EXPANDING MY HORIZONS...

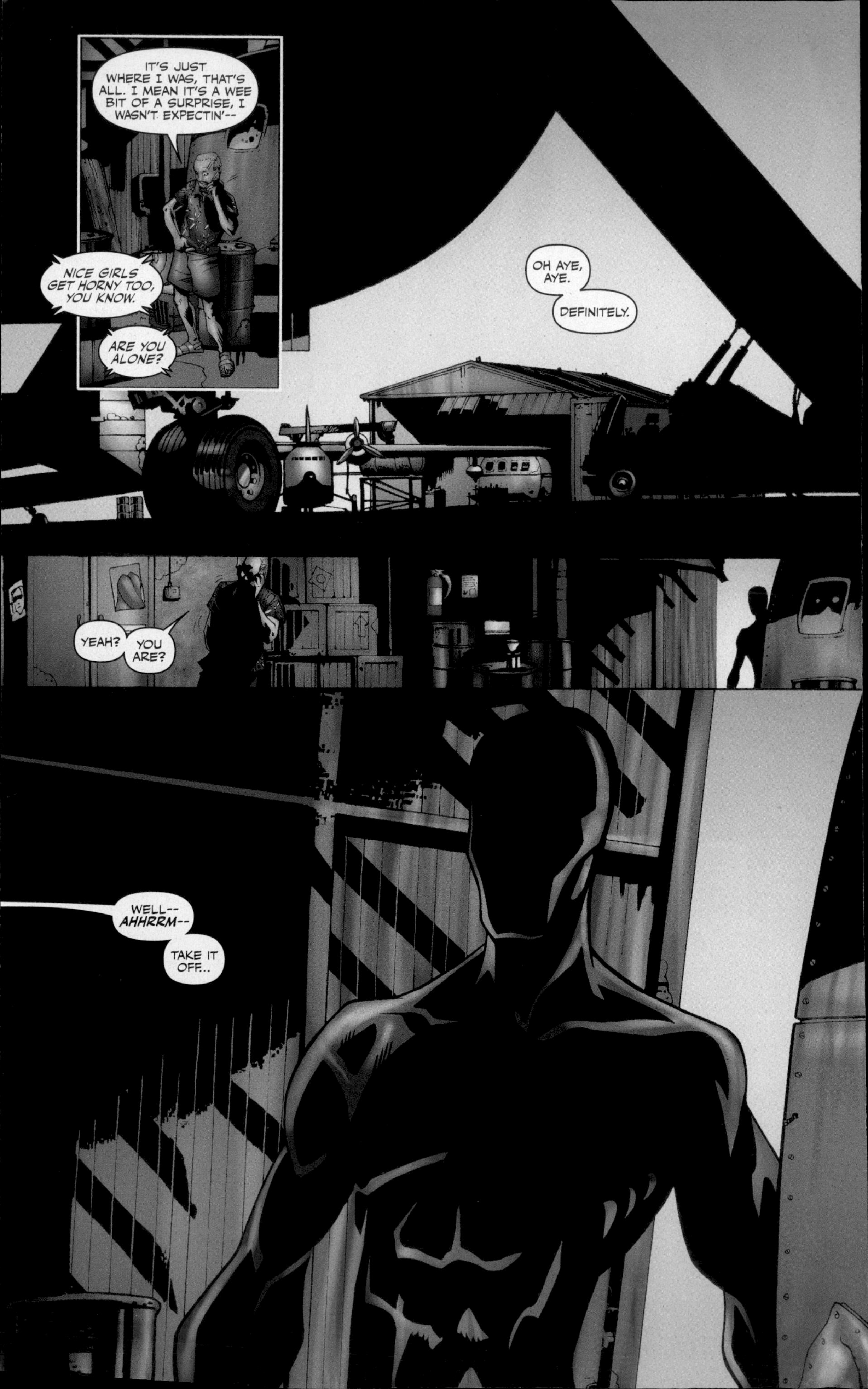
IT'S JUST WHERE I WAS, THAT'S ALL. I MEAN IT'S A WEE BIT OF A SURPRISE, I WASN'T EXPECTIN'--
NICE GIRLS GET HORNY TOO, YOU KNOW.
ARE YOU ALONE?
OH AYE, AYE.
DEFINITELY.
YEAH?
YOU ARE?
WELL-- AHHRRM--
TAKE IT OFF...

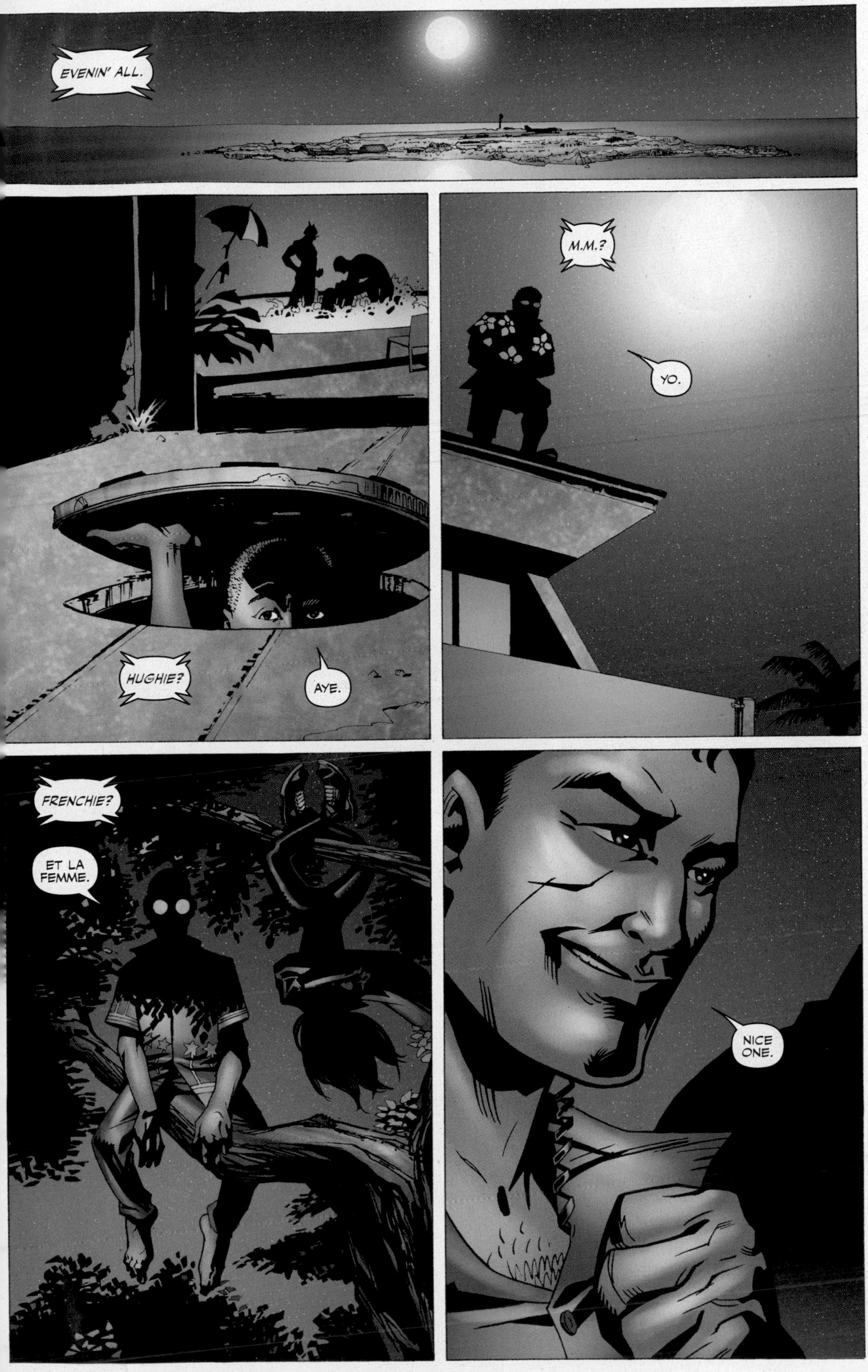
EVENIN' ALL.
HUGHIE?
AYE.
M.M.?
YO.
FRENCHIE?
ET LA FEMME.
NICE ONE.

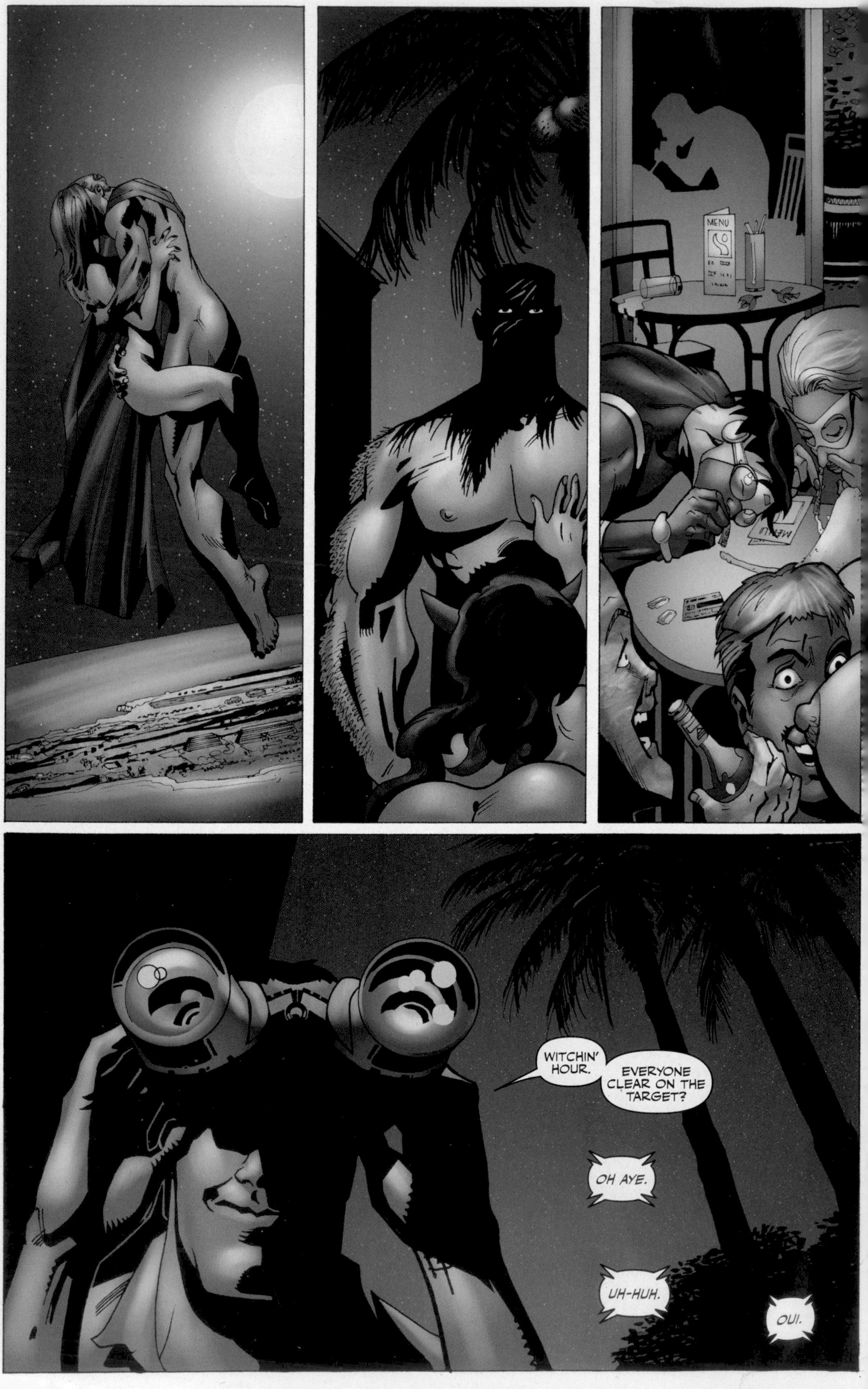
MENU
WITCHIN' HOUR.
EVERYONE CLEAR ON THE TARGET?
OH AYE.
UH-HUH.
OUI.

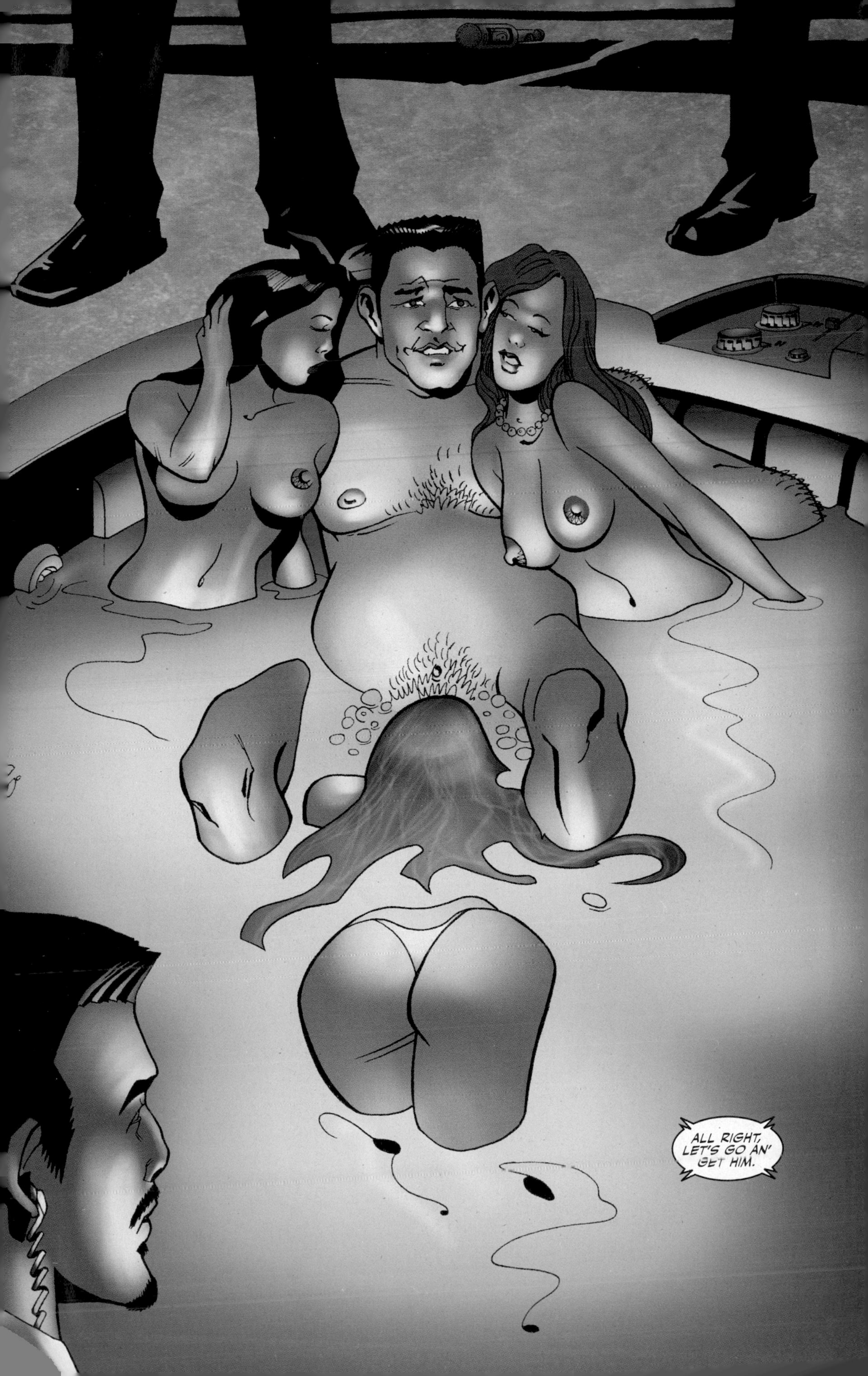
ALL RIGHT, LET'S GO AN' GET HIM.

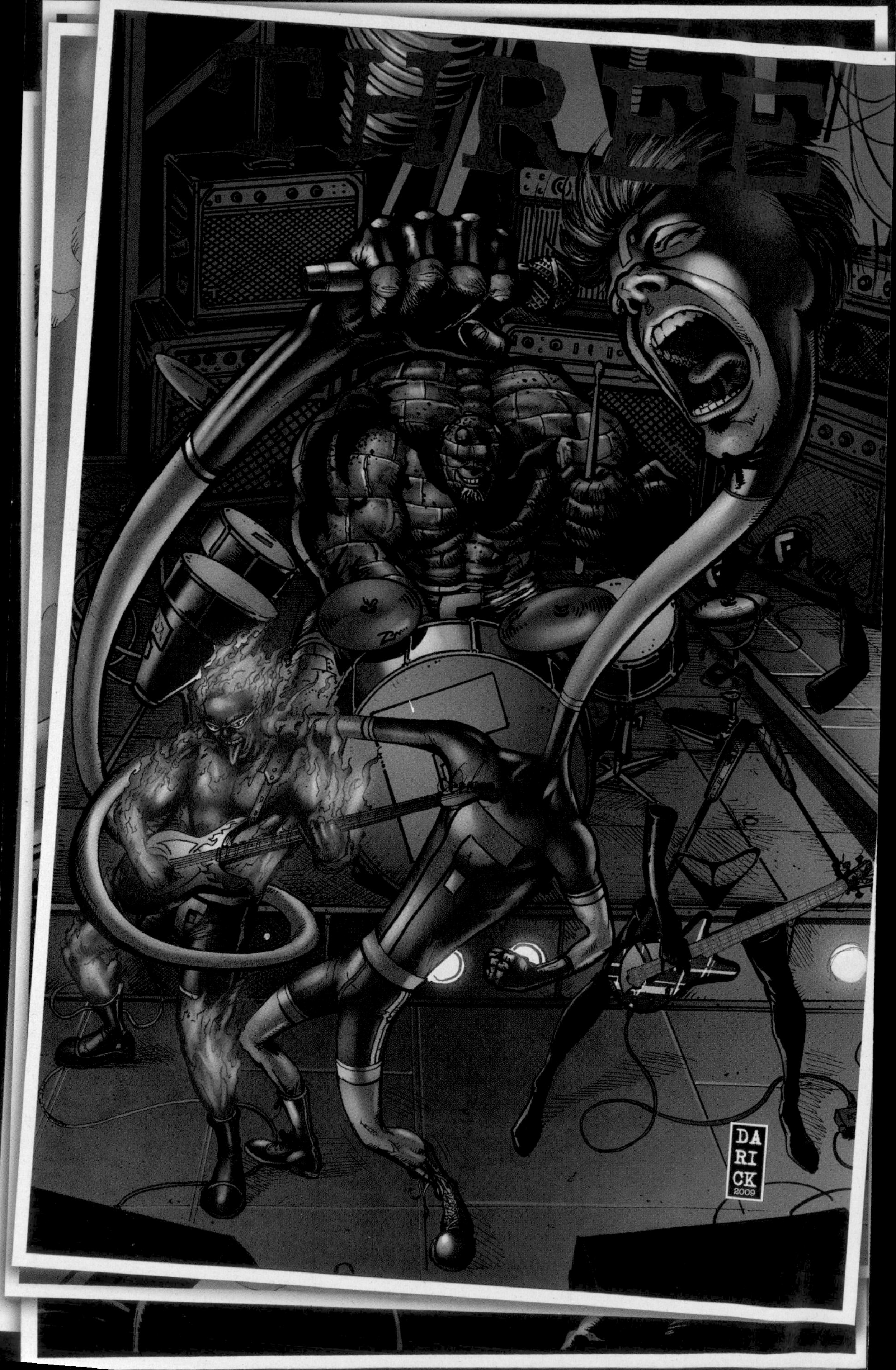
THREE
DA
RI
CK
2009

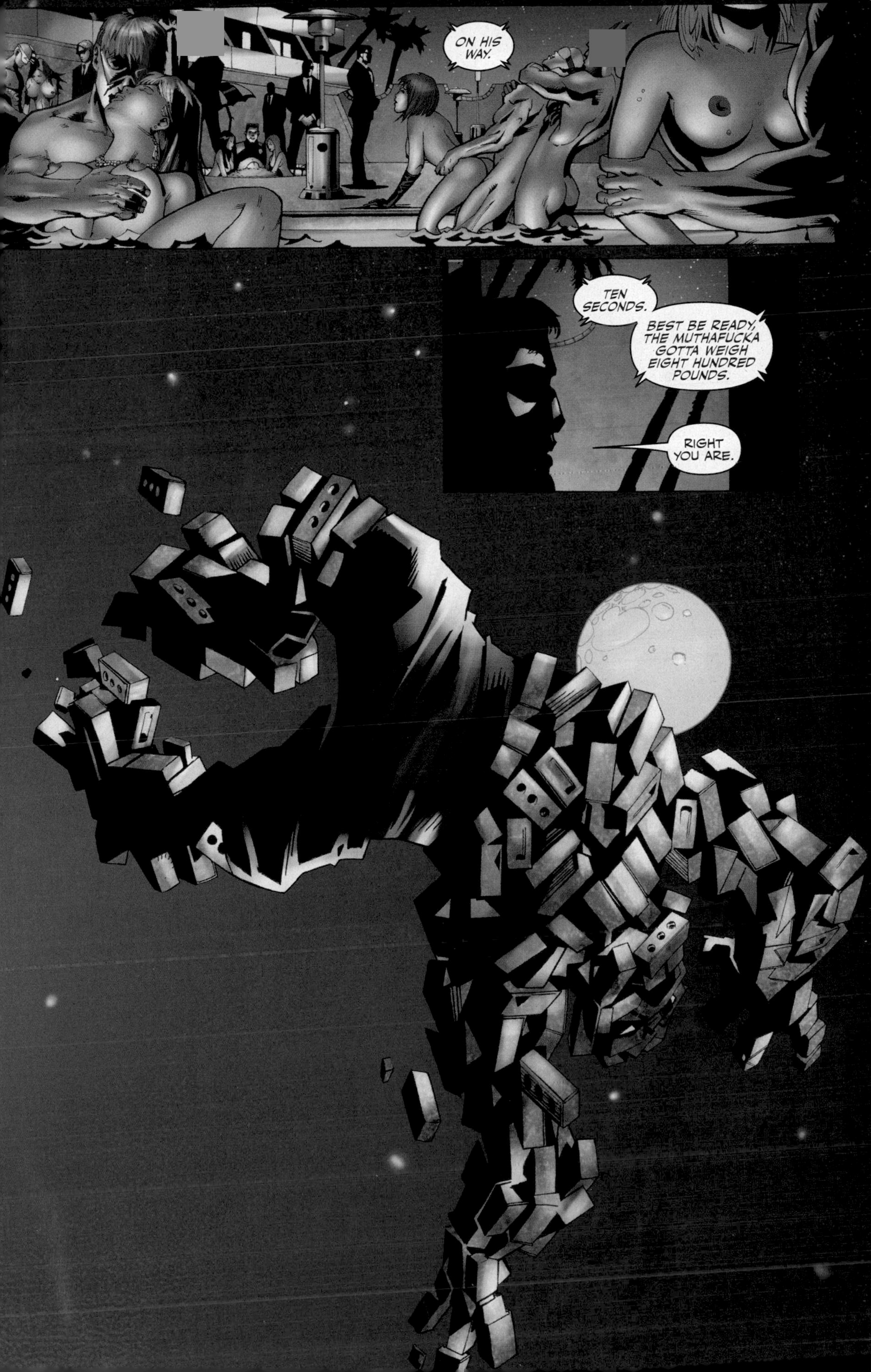
ON HIS WAY.
TEN SECONDS.
BEST BE READY, THE MUTHAFUCKA GOTTA WEIGH EIGHT HUNDRED POUNDS.
RIGHT YOU ARE.

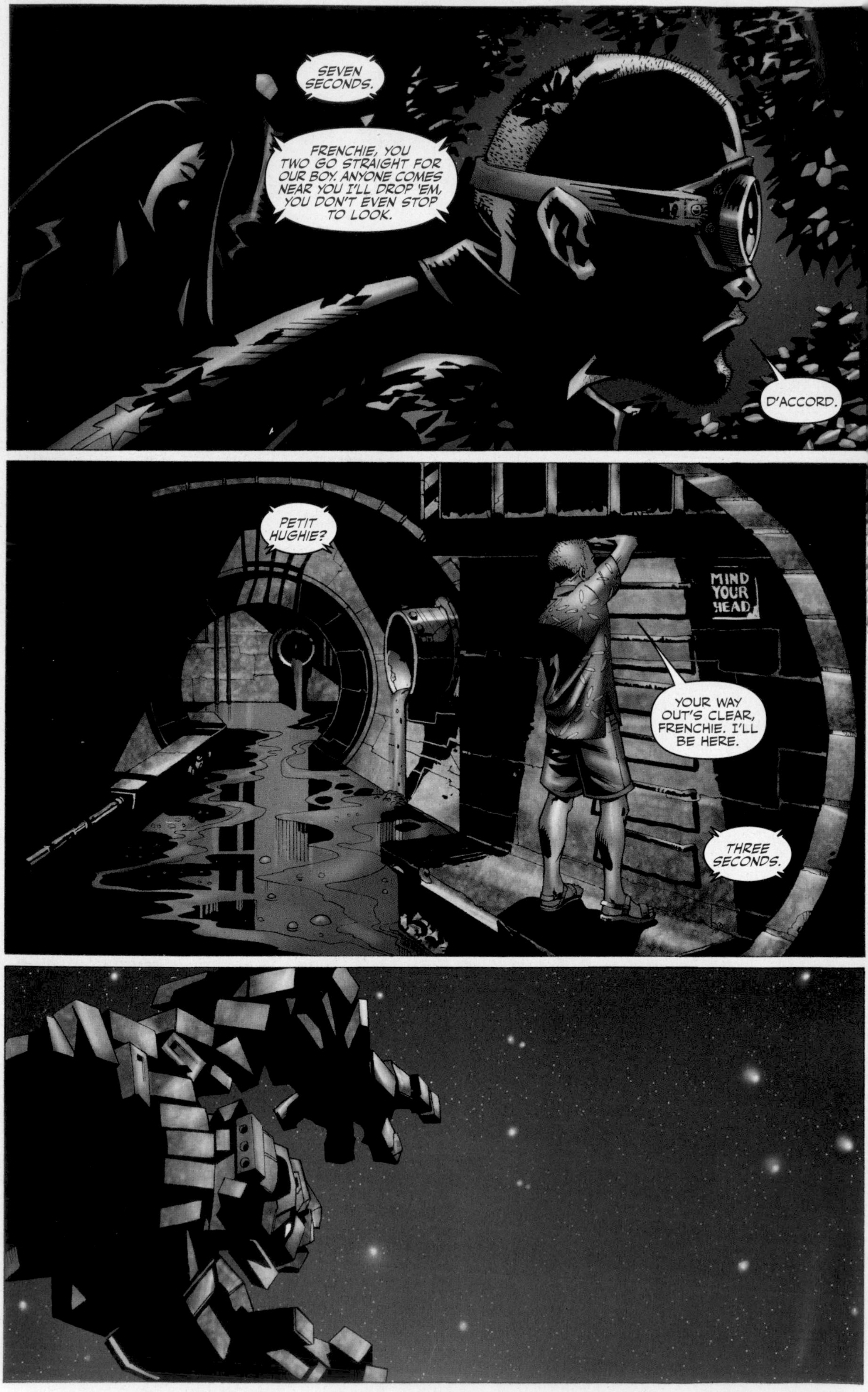
SEVEN SECONDS.
FRENCHIE, YOU TWO GO STRAIGHT FOR OUR BOY. ANYONE COMES NEAR YOU I'LL DROP 'EM, YOU DON'T EVEN STOP TO LOOK.
D'ACCORD.
PETIT HUGHIE?
MIND YOUR HEAD
YOUR WAY OUT'S CLEAR, FRENCHIE. I'LL BE HERE.
THREE SECONDS.

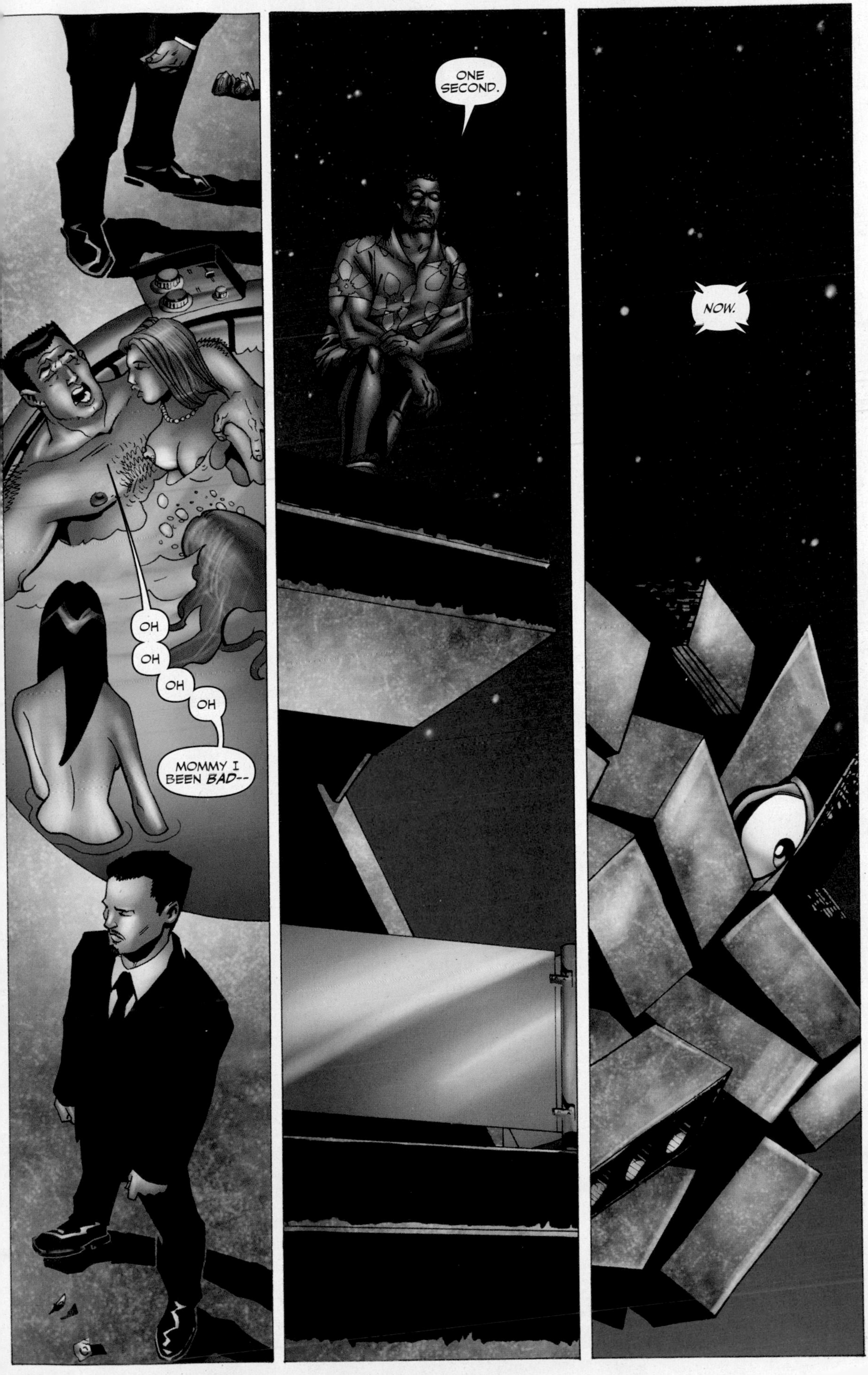
OH
OH
OH
OH
MOMMY I BEEN *BAD*--
ONE SECOND.
NOW.

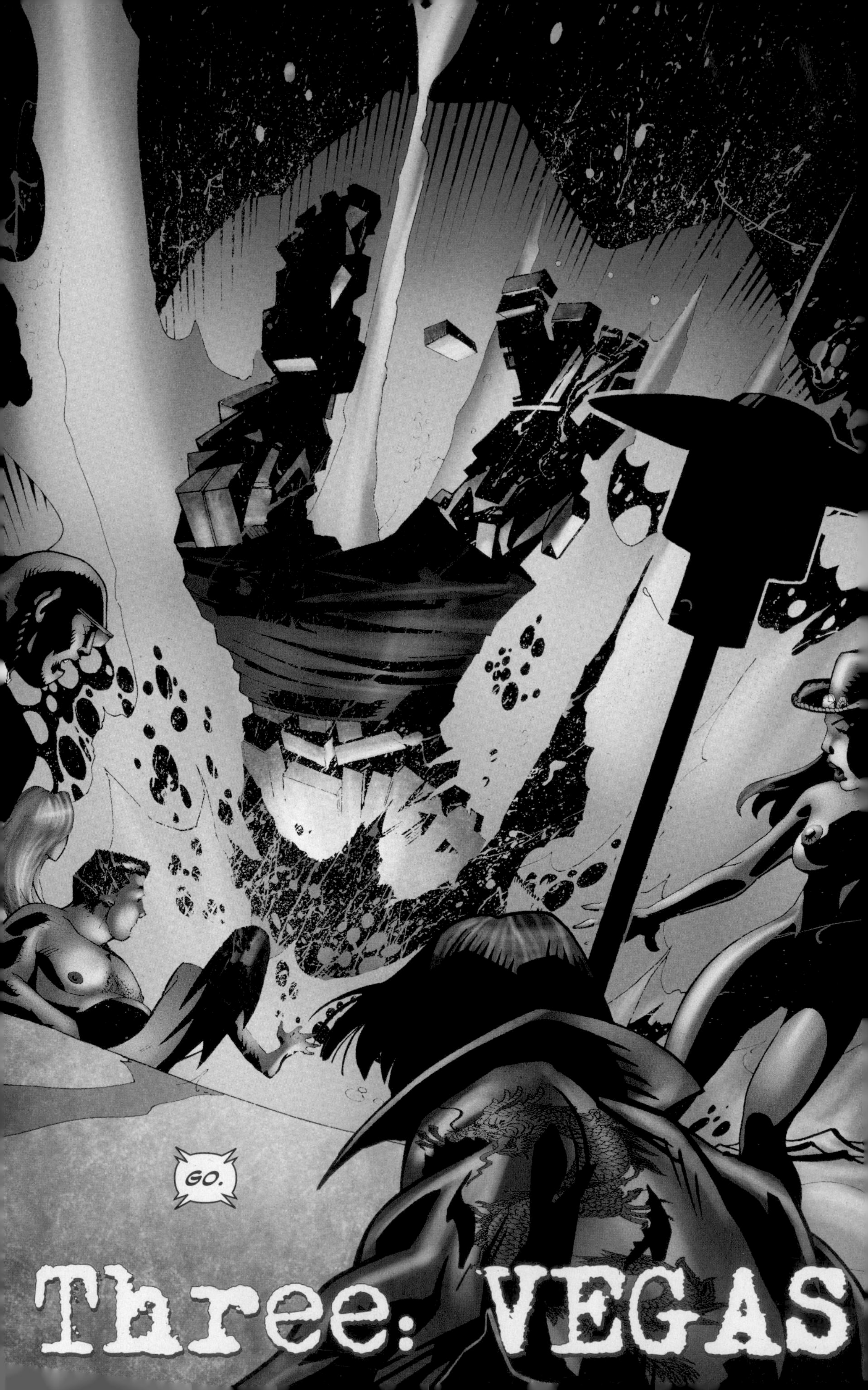
GO.
Three: VEGAS

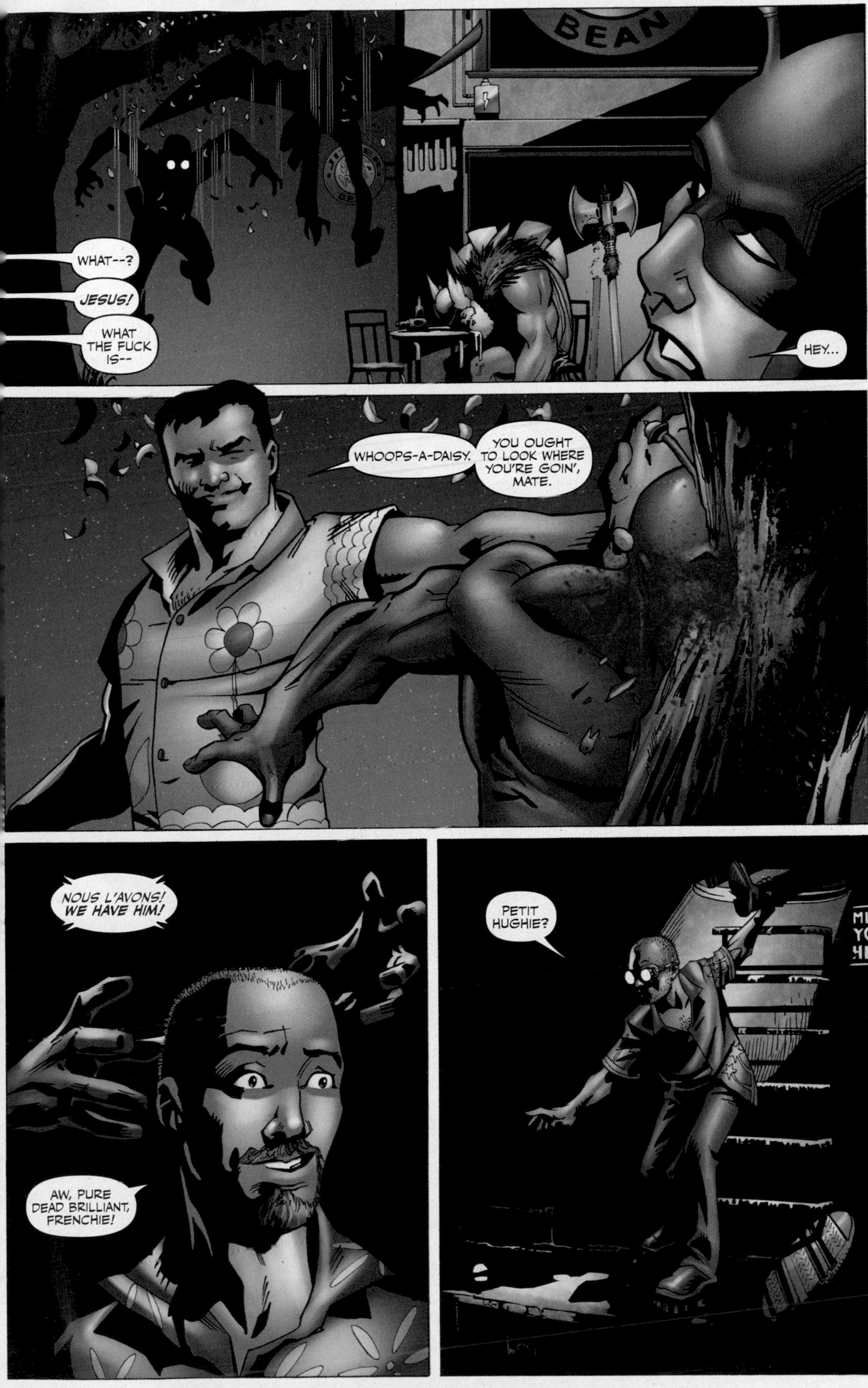

BEAN
WHAT--?
JESUS!
WHAT THE FUCK IS--
HEY...
WHOOPS-A-DAISY.
YOU OUGHT TO LOOK WHERE YOU'RE GOIN', MATE.
NOUS L'AVONS! WE HAVE HIM!
AW, PURE DEAD BRILLIANT, FRENCHIE!
PETIT HUGHIE?

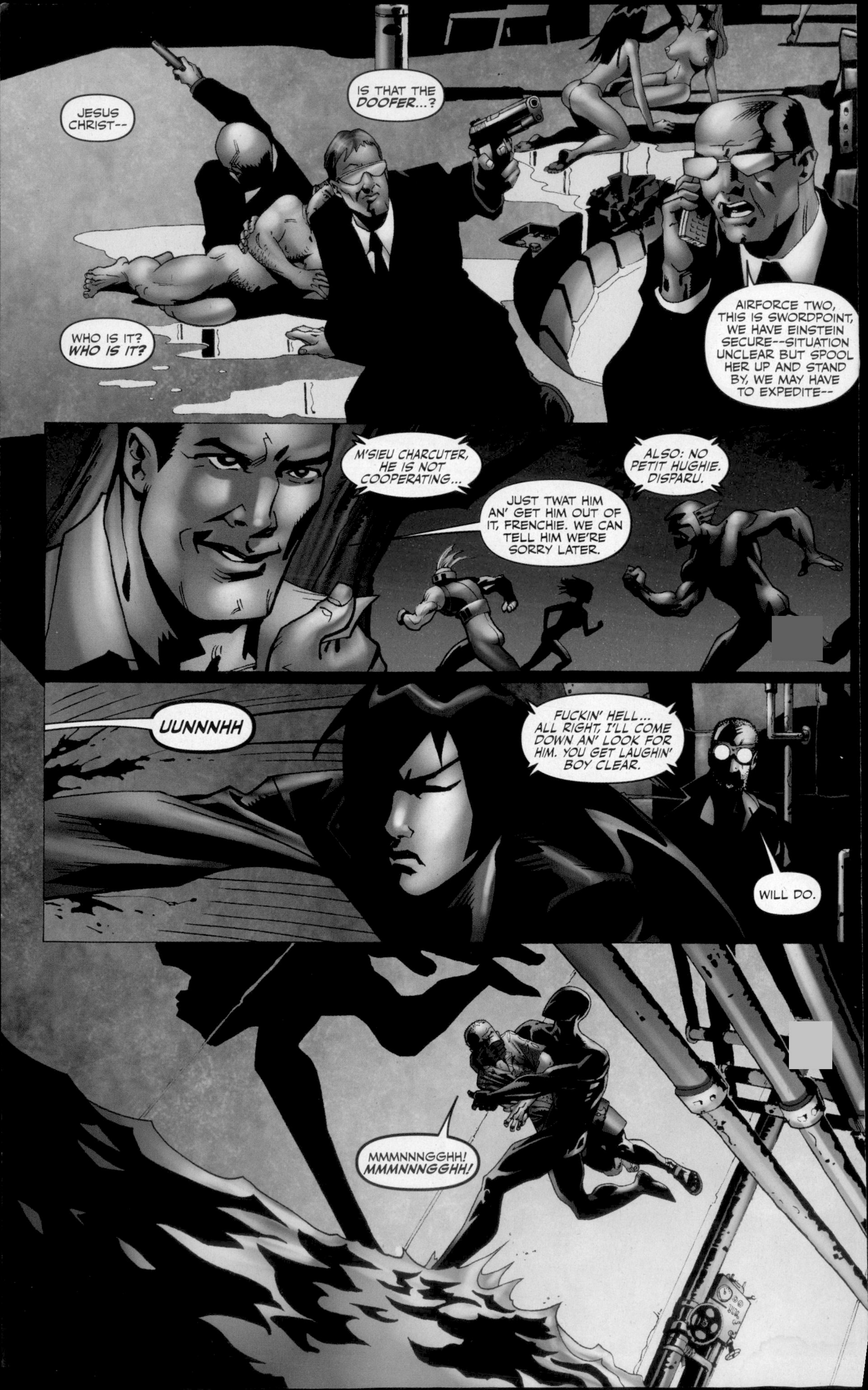

JESUS CHRIST--
IS THAT THE DOOFER...?
WHO IS IT? WHO IS IT?
AIRFORCE TWO, THIS IS SWORDPOINT, WE HAVE EINSTEIN SECURE--SITUATION UNCLEAR BUT SPOOL HER UP AND STAND BY, WE MAY HAVE TO EXPEDITE--
M'SIEU CHARCUTER, HE IS NOT COOPERATING...
ALSO: NO PETIT HUGHIE. DISPARU.
JUST TWAT HIM AN' GET HIM OUT OF IT, FRENCHIE. WE CAN TELL HIM WE'RE SORRY LATER.
UUNNNHH
FUCKIN' HELL... ALL RIGHT, I'LL COME DOWN AN' LOOK FOR HIM. YOU GET LAUGHIN' BOY CLEAR.
WILL DO.
MMMNNNGGHH! MMMNNNGGHH!

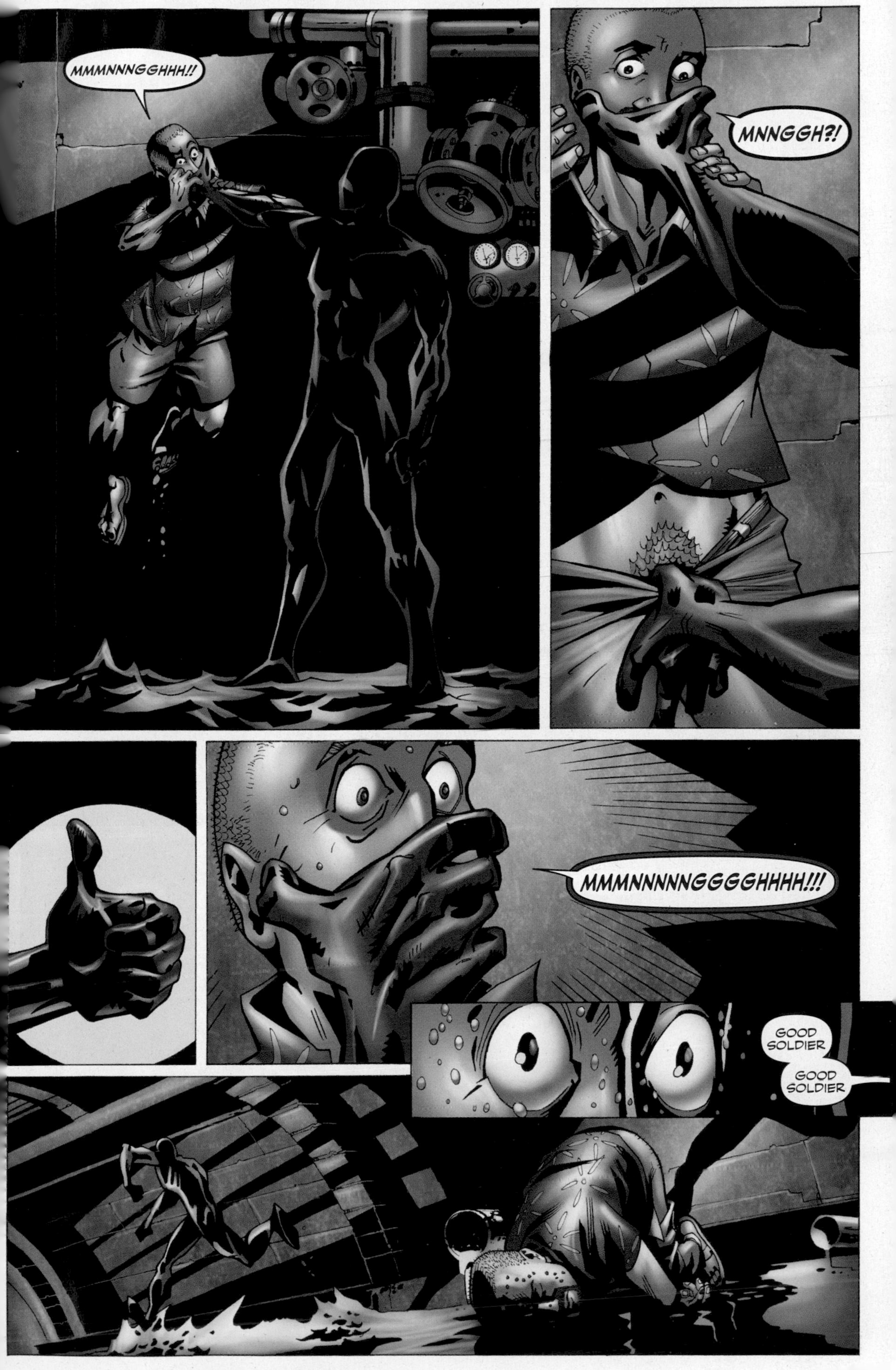
MMMNNNGGHHH!!
MNNGGH?!
MMMNNNNNGGGGHHHH!!!
GOOD SOLDIER
GOOD SOLDIER

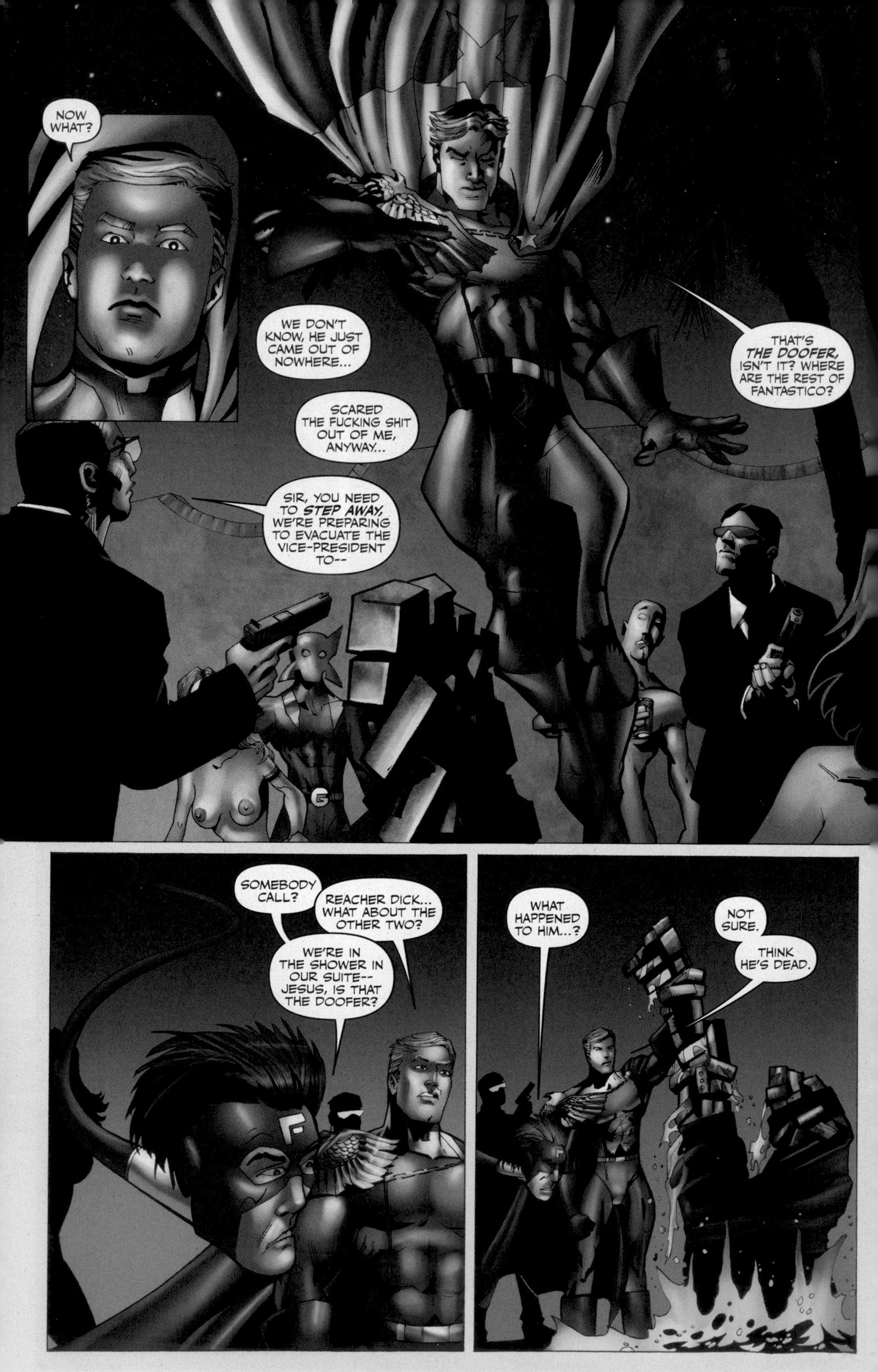
NOW WHAT?
WE DON'T KNOW, HE JUST CAME OUT OF NOWHERE...
SCARED THE FUCKING SHIT OUT OF ME, ANYWAY...
THAT'S THE DOOFER, ISN'T IT? WHERE ARE THE REST OF FANTASTICO?
SIR, YOU NEED TO STEP AWAY, WE'RE PREPARING TO EVACUATE THE VICE-PRESIDENT TO--
SOMEBODY CALL?
REACHER DICK... WHAT ABOUT THE OTHER TWO?
WE'RE IN THE SHOWER IN OUR SUITE-- JESUS, IS THAT THE DOOFER?
WHAT HAPPENED TO HIM...?
NOT SURE.
THINK HE'S DEAD.

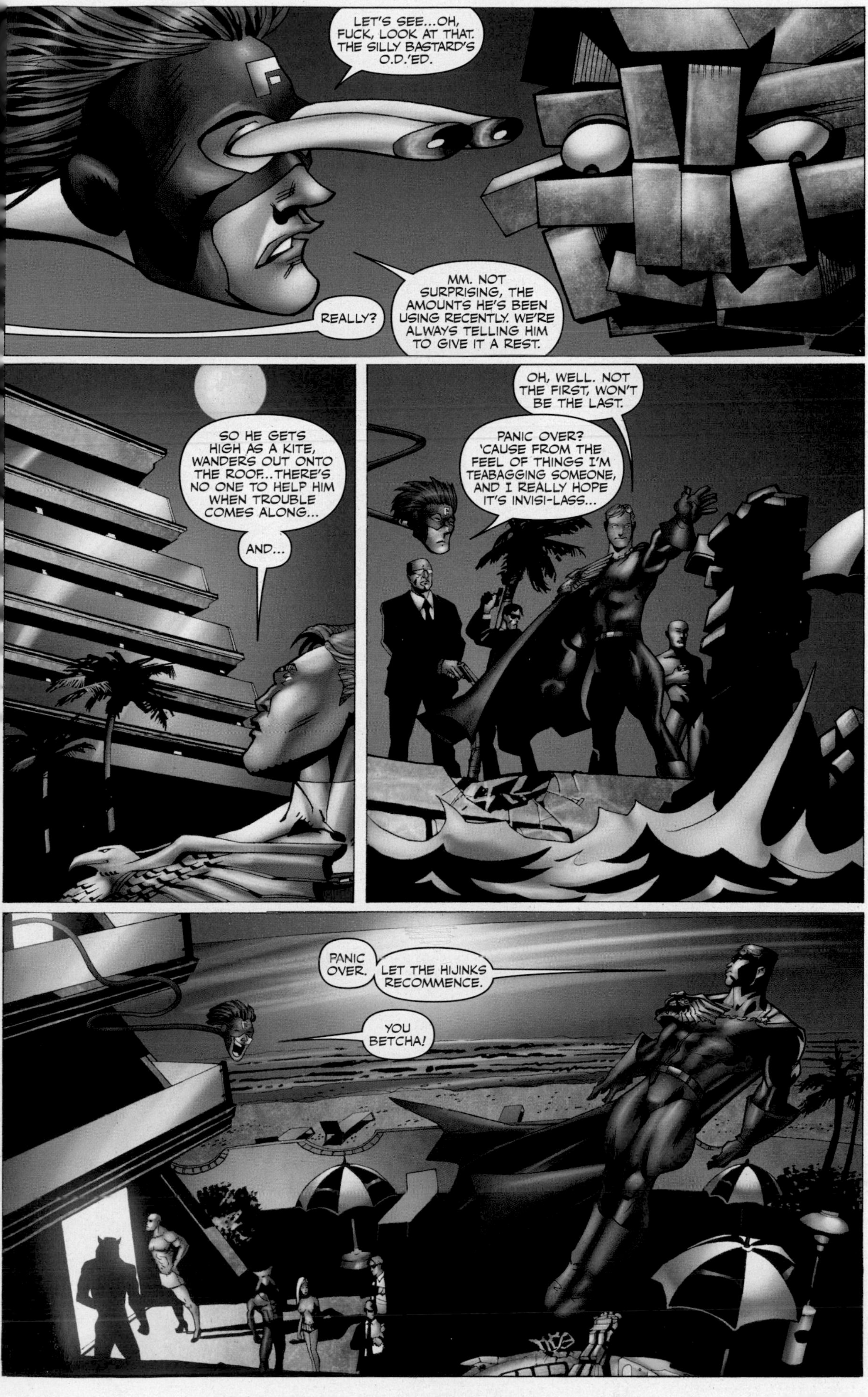
LET'S SEE...OH, FUCK, LOOK AT THAT. THE SILLY BASTARD'S O.D.'ED.
REALLY?
MM. NOT SURPRISING, THE AMOUNTS HE'S BEEN USING RECENTLY. WE'RE ALWAYS TELLING HIM TO GIVE IT A REST.
SO HE GETS HIGH AS A KITE, WANDERS OUT ONTO THE ROOF...THERE'S NO ONE TO HELP HIM WHEN TROUBLE COMES ALONG...
AND...
OH, WELL. NOT THE FIRST, WON'T BE THE LAST.
PANIC OVER? 'CAUSE FROM THE FEEL OF THINGS I'M TEABAGGING SOMEONE, AND I REALLY HOPE IT'S INVISI-LASS...
PANIC OVER.
LET THE HIJINKS RECOMMENCE.
YOU BETCHA!

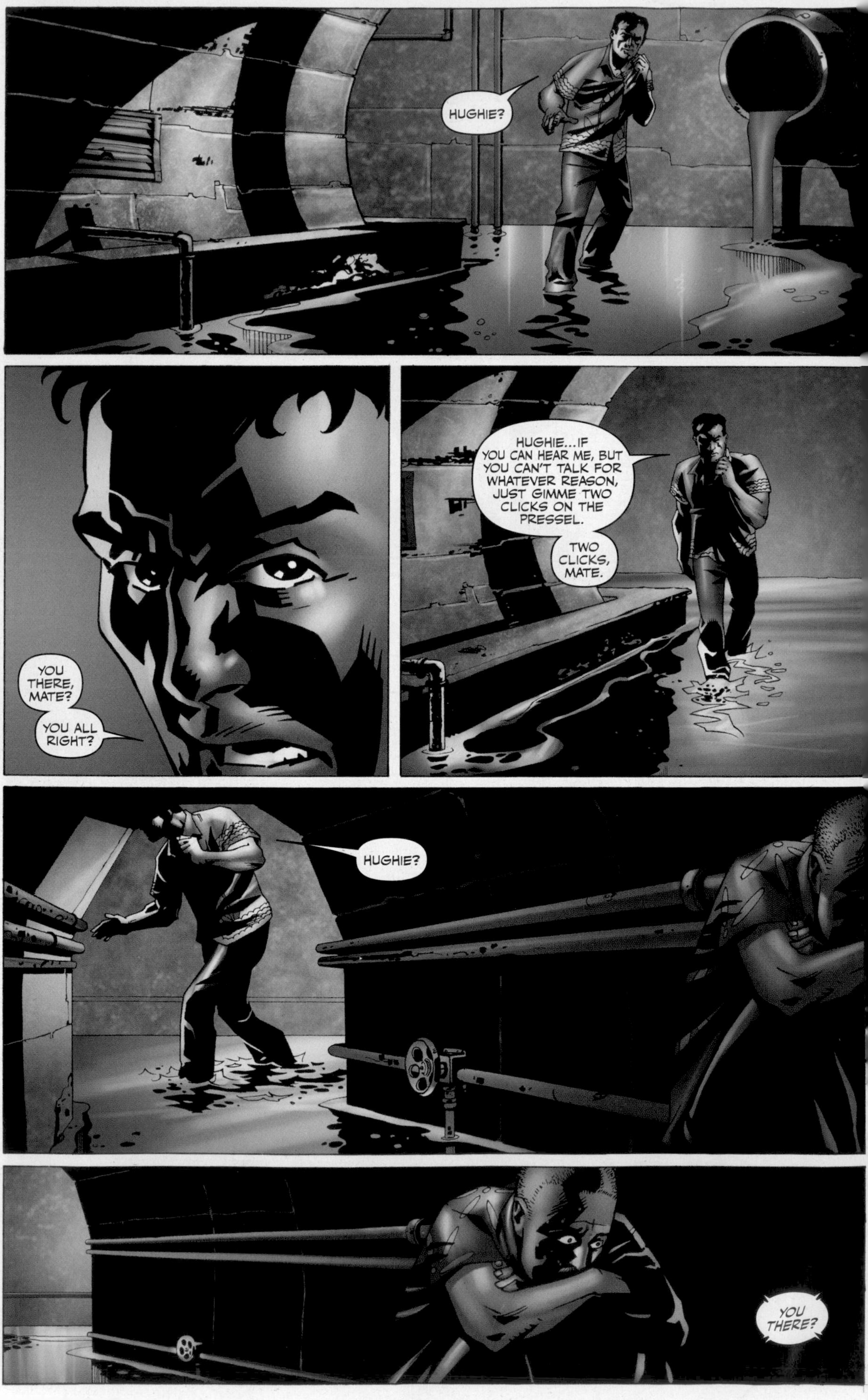
HUGHIE?
YOU THERE, MATE?
YOU ALL RIGHT?
HUGHIE...IF YOU CAN HEAR ME, BUT YOU CAN'T TALK FOR WHATEVER REASON, JUST GIMME TWO CLICKS ON THE PRESSEL.
TWO CLICKS, MATE.
HUGHIE?
YOU THERE?

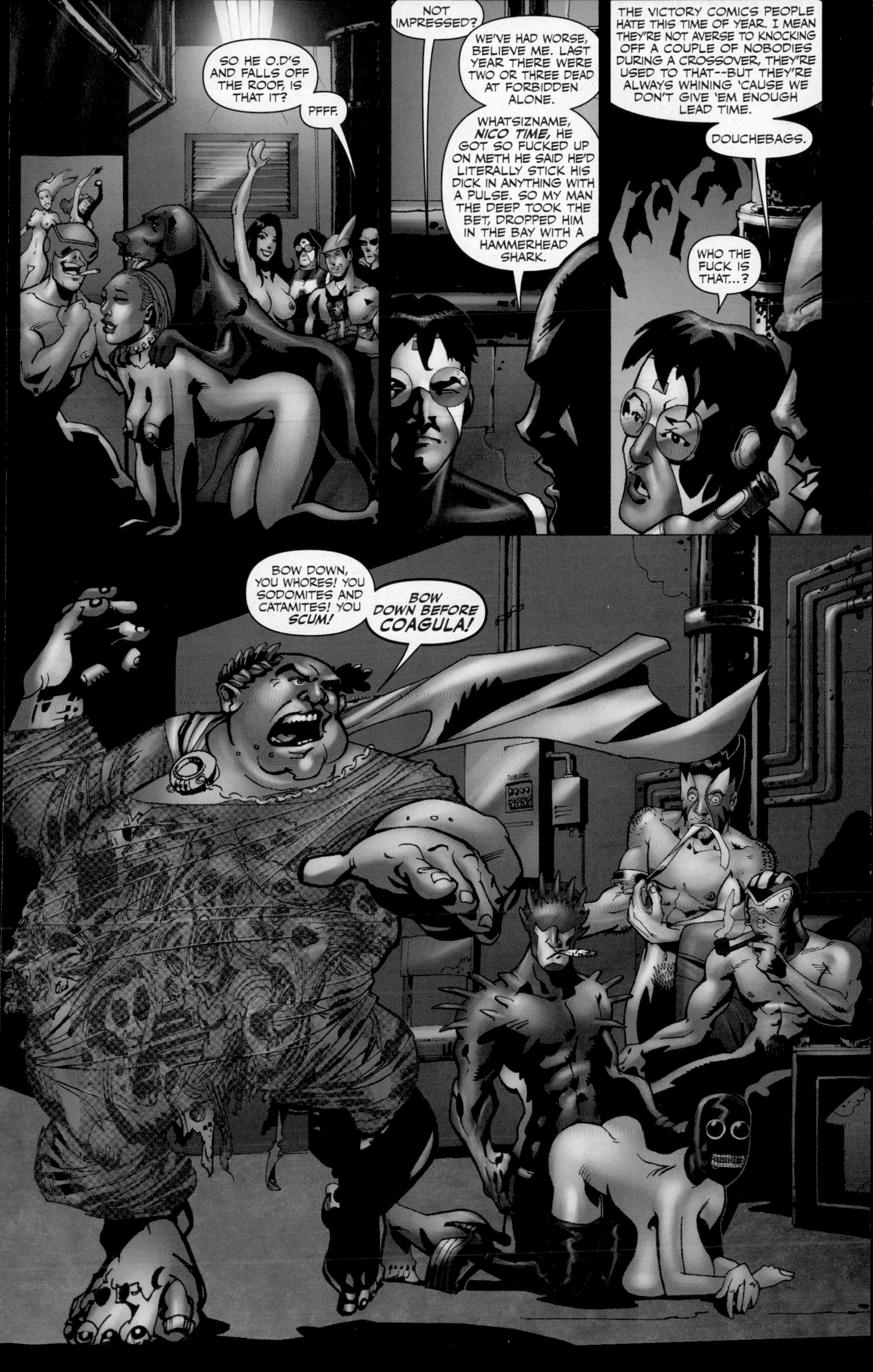

SO HE O.D'S AND FALLS OFF THE ROOF, IS THAT IT?
PFFF.
NOT IMPRESSED?
WE'VE HAD WORSE, BELIEVE ME. LAST YEAR THERE WERE TWO OR THREE DEAD AT FORBIDDEN ALONE.
WHATSIZNAME, NICO TIME, HE GOT SO FUCKED UP ON METH HE SAID HE'D LITERALLY STICK HIS DICK IN ANYTHING WITH A PULSE. SO MY MAN THE DEEP TOOK THE BET, DROPPED HIM IN THE BAY WITH A HAMMERHEAD SHARK.
THE VICTORY COMICS PEOPLE HATE THIS TIME OF YEAR. I MEAN THEY'RE NOT AVERSE TO KNOCKING OFF A COUPLE OF NOBODIES DURING A CROSSOVER, THEY'RE USED TO THAT--BUT THEY'RE ALWAYS WHINING 'CAUSE WE DON'T GIVE 'EM ENOUGH LEAD TIME.
DOUCHEBAGS.
WHO THE FUCK IS THAT...?
BOW DOWN, YOU WHORES! YOU SODOMITES AND CATAMITES! YOU SCUM!
BOW DOWN BEFORE COAGULA!

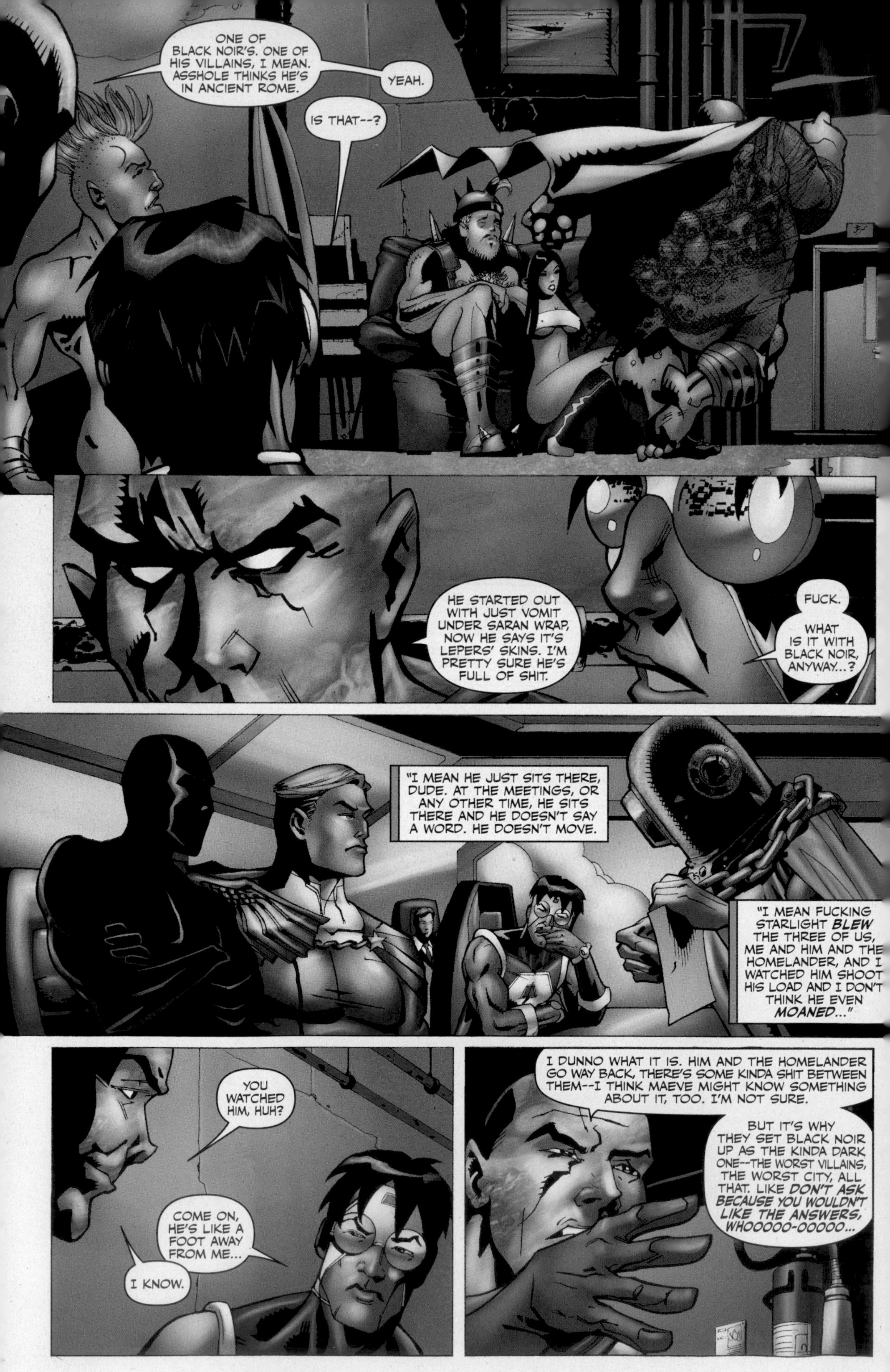
ONE OF BLACK NOIR'S. ONE OF HIS VILLAINS, I MEAN. ASSHOLE THINKS HE'S IN ANCIENT ROME.
YEAH.
IS THAT--?
HE STARTED OUT WITH JUST VOMIT UNDER SARAN WRAP, NOW HE SAYS IT'S LEPERS' SKINS. I'M PRETTY SURE HE'S FULL OF SHIT.
FUCK.
WHAT IS IT WITH BLACK NOIR, ANYWAY...?
"I MEAN HE JUST SITS THERE, DUDE. AT THE MEETINGS, OR ANY OTHER TIME, HE SITS THERE AND HE DOESN'T SAY A WORD. HE DOESN'T MOVE.
"I MEAN FUCKING STARLIGHT BLEW THE THREE OF US, ME AND HIM AND THE HOMELANDER, AND I WATCHED HIM SHOOT HIS LOAD AND I DON'T THINK HE EVEN MOANED..."
YOU WATCHED HIM, HUH?
COME ON, HE'S LIKE A FOOT AWAY FROM ME...
I KNOW.
I DUNNO WHAT IT IS. HIM AND THE HOMELANDER GO WAY BACK, THERE'S SOME KINDA SHIT BETWEEN THEM--I THINK MAEVE MIGHT KNOW SOMETHING ABOUT IT, TOO. I'M NOT SURE.
BUT IT'S WHY THEY SET BLACK NOIR UP AS THE KINDA DARK ONE--THE WORST VILLAINS, THE WORST CITY, ALL THAT. LIKE DON'T ASK BECAUSE YOU WOULDN'T LIKE THE ANSWERS, WHOOOOO-OOOOO...

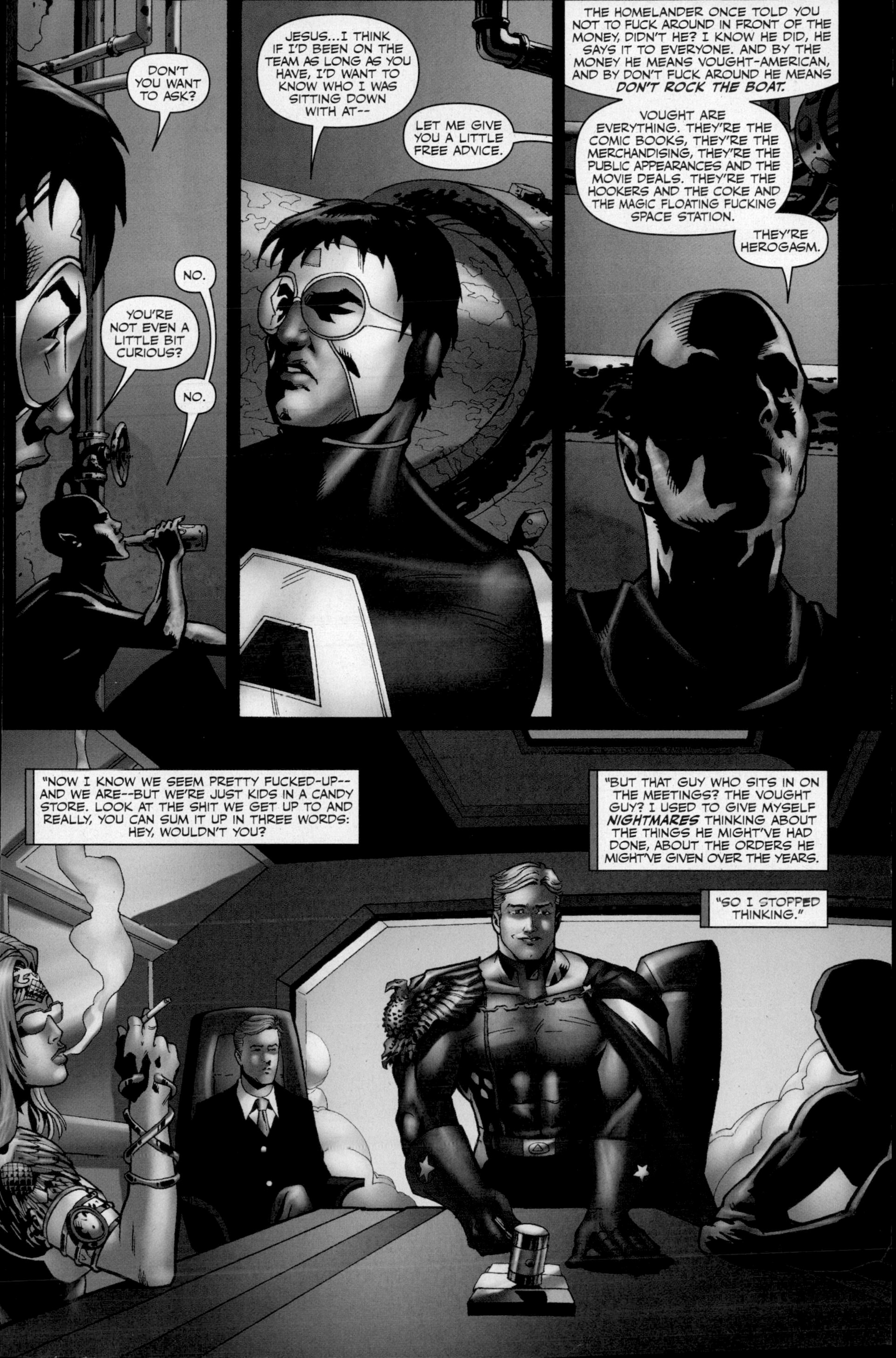
DON'T YOU WANT TO ASK?
NO.
YOU'RE NOT EVEN A LITTLE BIT CURIOUS?
NO.
JESUS...I THINK IF I'D BEEN ON THE TEAM AS LONG AS YOU HAVE, I'D WANT TO KNOW WHO I WAS SITTING DOWN WITH AT--
LET ME GIVE YOU A LITTLE FREE ADVICE.
THE HOMELANDER ONCE TOLD YOU NOT TO FUCK AROUND IN FRONT OF THE MONEY, DIDN'T HE? I KNOW HE DID, HE SAYS IT TO EVERYONE. AND BY THE MONEY HE MEANS VOUGHT-AMERICAN, AND BY DON'T FUCK AROUND HE MEANS DON'T ROCK THE BOAT.
VOUGHT ARE EVERYTHING. THEY'RE THE COMIC BOOKS, THEY'RE THE MERCHANDISING, THEY'RE THE PUBLIC APPEARANCES AND THE MOVIE DEALS. THEY'RE THE HOOKERS AND THE COKE AND THE MAGIC FLOATING FUCKING SPACE STATION.
THEY'RE HEROGASM.
"NOW I KNOW WE SEEM PRETTY FUCKED-UP--AND WE ARE--BUT WE'RE JUST KIDS IN A CANDY STORE. LOOK AT THE SHIT WE GET UP TO AND REALLY, YOU CAN SUM IT UP IN THREE WORDS: HEY, WOULDN'T YOU?
"BUT THAT GUY WHO SITS IN ON THE MEETINGS? THE VOUGHT GUY? I USED TO GIVE MYSELF NIGHTMARES THINKING ABOUT THE THINGS HE MIGHT'VE HAD DONE, ABOUT THE ORDERS HE MIGHT'VE GIVEN OVER THE YEARS.
"SO I STOPPED THINKING."

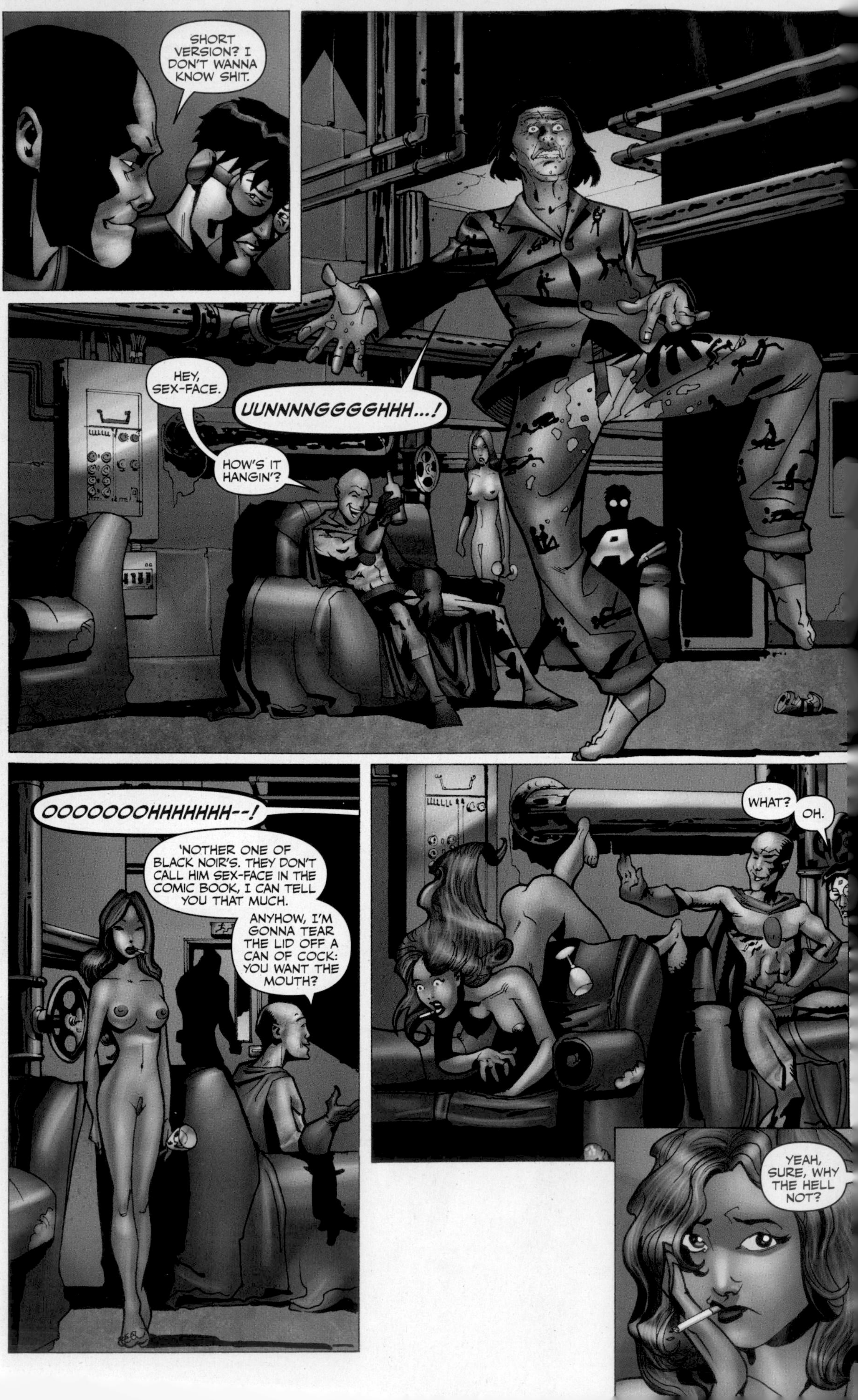
SHORT VERSION? I DON'T WANNA KNOW SHIT.
HEY, SEX-FACE.
UUNNNNGGGGHHH...!
HOW'S IT HANGIN'?
OOOOOOOHHHHHHH--!
'NOTHER ONE OF BLACK NOIR'S. THEY DON'T CALL HIM SEX-FACE IN THE COMIC BOOK, I CAN TELL YOU THAT MUCH.
ANYHOW, I'M GONNA TEAR THE LID OFF A CAN OF COCK: YOU WANT THE MOUTH?
WHAT?
OH.
YEAH, SURE, WHY THE HELL NOT?

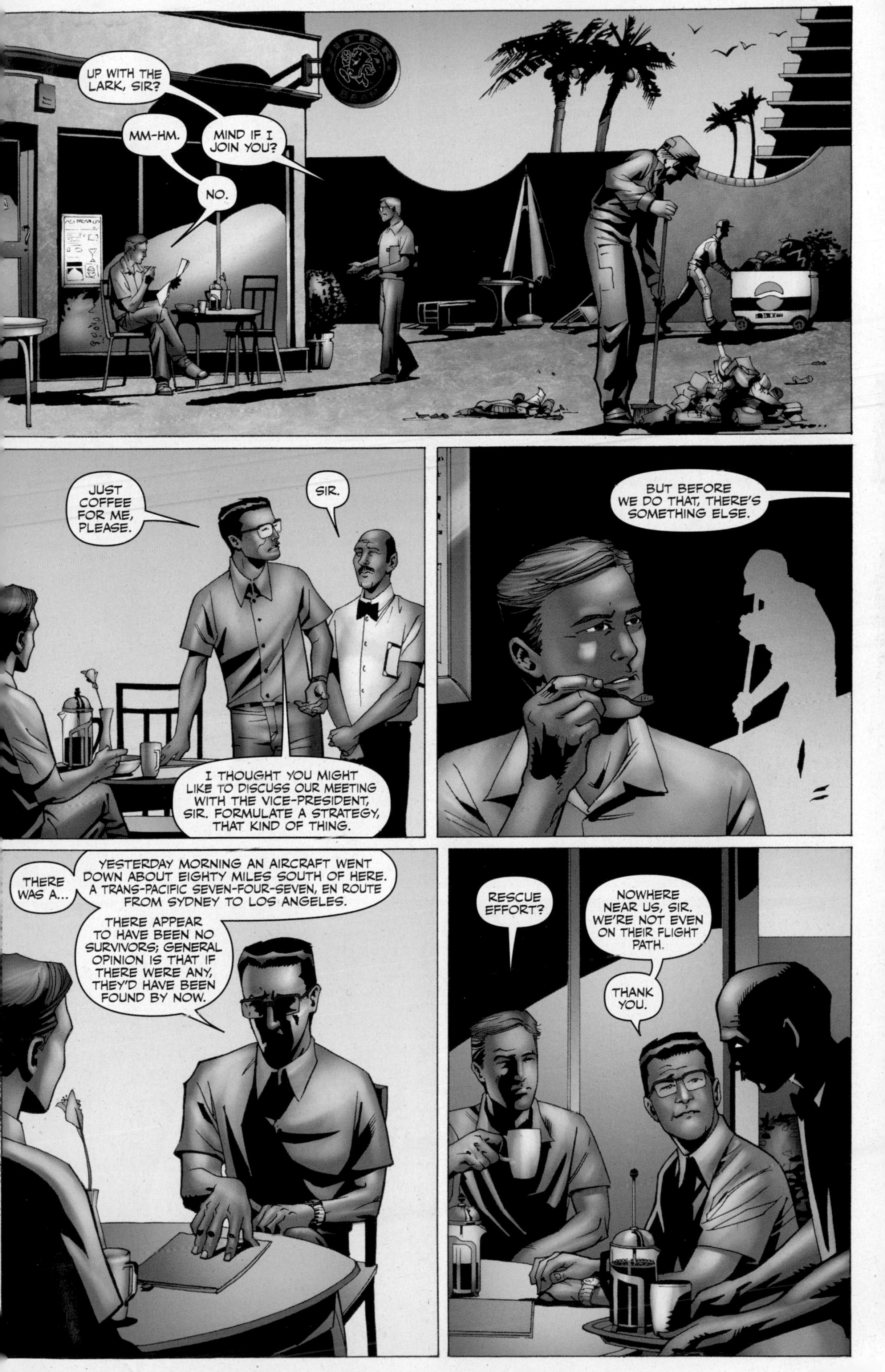
UP WITH THE LARK, SIR?
MM-HM.
MIND IF I JOIN YOU?
NO.
JUST COFFEE FOR ME, PLEASE.
SIR.
I THOUGHT YOU MIGHT LIKE TO DISCUSS OUR MEETING WITH THE VICE-PRESIDENT, SIR. FORMULATE A STRATEGY, THAT KIND OF THING.
BUT BEFORE WE DO THAT, THERE'S SOMETHING ELSE.
THERE WAS A...
YESTERDAY MORNING AN AIRCRAFT WENT DOWN ABOUT EIGHTY MILES SOUTH OF HERE. A TRANS-PACIFIC SEVEN-FOUR-SEVEN, EN ROUTE FROM SYDNEY TO LOS ANGELES.
THERE APPEAR TO HAVE BEEN NO SURVIVORS; GENERAL OPINION IS THAT IF THERE WERE ANY, THEY'D HAVE BEEN FOUND BY NOW.
RESCUE EFFORT?
NOWHERE NEAR US, SIR. WE'RE NOT EVEN ON THEIR FLIGHT PATH.
THANK YOU.

IN THAT CASE...?

I HAVE A PIECE OF CARD TAPED TO MY COMPUTER MONITOR BACK HOME, SIR. FOUR INCHES BY TWO.

SIMPLY SAYS, "EVERYTHING".

YOU ALMOST CERTAINLY WON'T REMEMBER THIS, BUT ABOUT SIX YEARS AGO, YOU SPOKE AT A SEMINAR FOR JUNIOR EXECUTIVES IN ATLANTA. ANYONE WHO'S GOTTEN A BUMP UP IN THE LAST YEAR WAS WELCOME TO COME ALONG.

THERE WAS A Q AND A AFTERWARDS, AND SOMEONE ASKED YOU WHAT THE MOST IMPORTANT ELEMENT WAS IN PREPARING AN OPERATION. TAKEOVER, SALE, HOSTILE OR OTHERWISE. WHATEVER.

AND YOU SAID EVERYTHING.

YOU SAID YOU NEVER RESTED UNTIL YOU'D CHECKED EVERYTHING; YOU NEVER WENT AHEAD UNTIL YOU'D LOOKED AT EVERY POSSIBLE CONTINGENCY AND THEN LOOKED AGAIN. NOTHING WASN'T IMPORTANT, IT WAS AS SIMPLE AS THAT.

WHICH IS WHY I CALLED A FRIEND ON THE TRANS-PACIFIC BOARD, AND ASKED HIM TO GET ME THIS AS QUICKLY AND QUIETLY AS POSSIBLE.

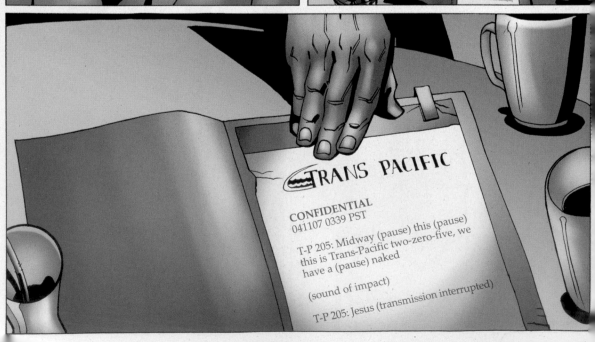

TRANS PACIFIC

CONFIDENTIAL
041107 0339 PST

T-P 205: Midway (pause) this (pause) this is Trans-Pacific two-zero-five, we have a (pause) naked

(sound of impact)

T-P 205: Jesus (transmission interrupted)

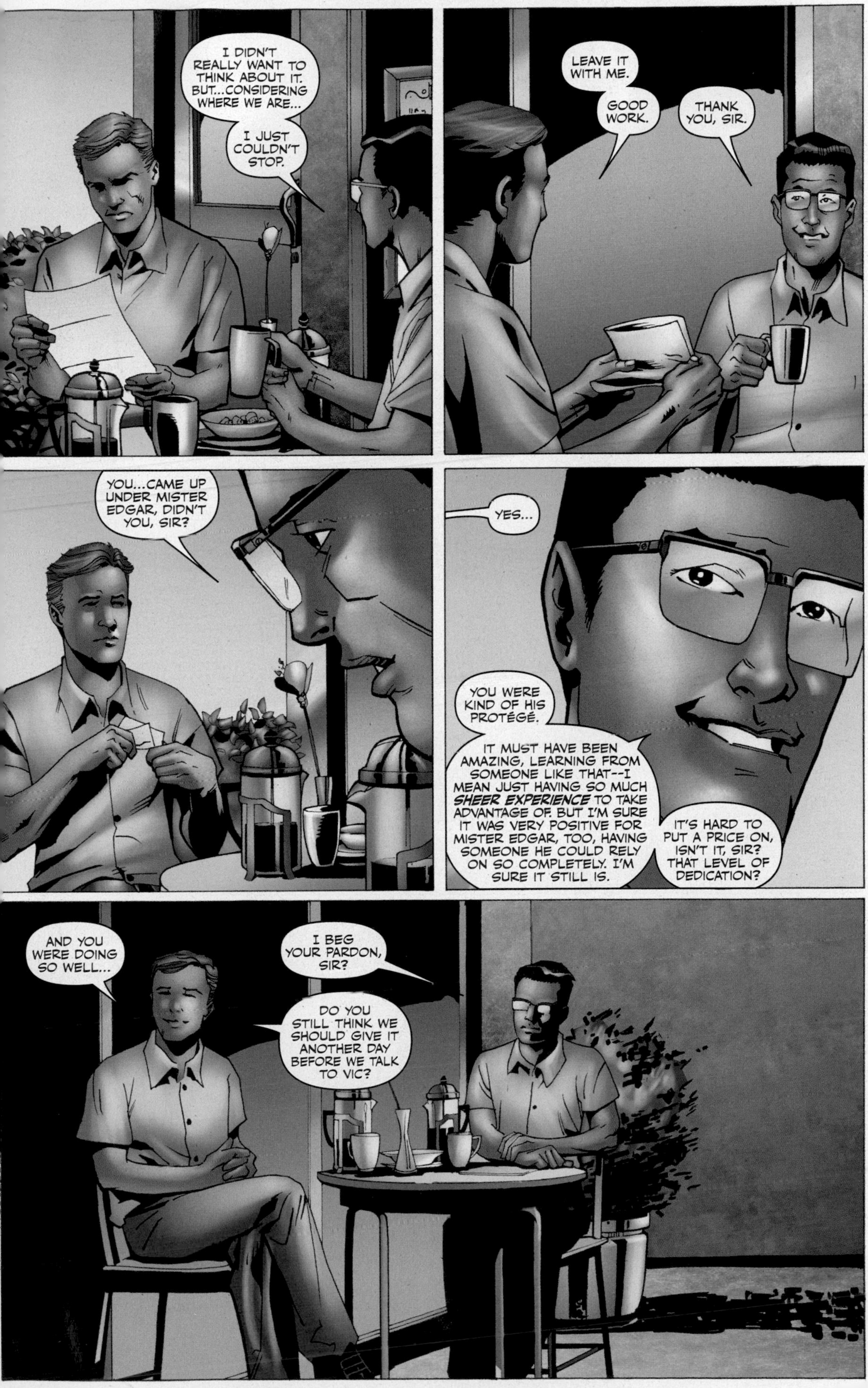
I DIDN'T REALLY WANT TO THINK ABOUT IT. BUT...CONSIDERING WHERE WE ARE...
I JUST COULDN'T STOP.
LEAVE IT WITH ME.
GOOD WORK.
THANK YOU, SIR.
YOU...CAME UP UNDER MISTER EDGAR, DIDN'T YOU, SIR?
YES...
YOU WERE KIND OF HIS PROTÉGÉ.
IT MUST HAVE BEEN AMAZING, LEARNING FROM SOMEONE LIKE THAT--I MEAN JUST HAVING SO MUCH SHEER EXPERIENCE TO TAKE ADVANTAGE OF. BUT I'M SURE IT WAS VERY POSITIVE FOR MISTER EDGAR, TOO, HAVING SOMEONE HE COULD RELY ON SO COMPLETELY. I'M SURE IT STILL IS.
IT'S HARD TO PUT A PRICE ON, ISN'T IT, SIR? THAT LEVEL OF DEDICATION?
AND YOU WERE DOING SO WELL...
I BEG YOUR PARDON, SIR?
DO YOU STILL THINK WE SHOULD GIVE IT ANOTHER DAY BEFORE WE TALK TO VIC?

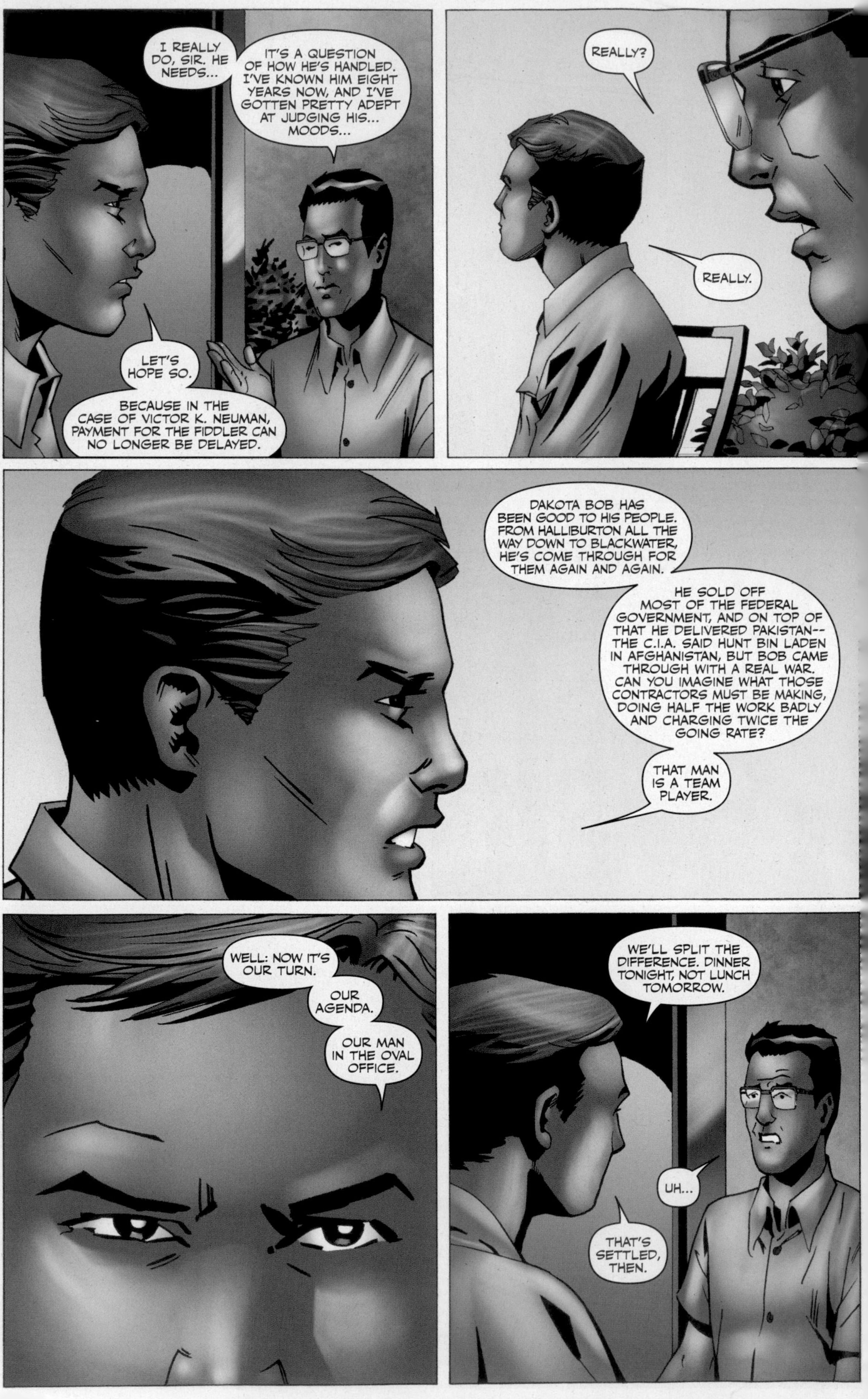
I REALLY DO, SIR. HE NEEDS...
IT'S A QUESTION OF HOW HE'S HANDLED. I'VE KNOWN HIM EIGHT YEARS NOW, AND I'VE GOTTEN PRETTY ADEPT AT JUDGING HIS... MOODS...
LET'S HOPE SO.
BECAUSE IN THE CASE OF VICTOR K. NEUMAN, PAYMENT FOR THE FIDDLER CAN NO LONGER BE DELAYED.
REALLY?
REALLY.
DAKOTA BOB HAS BEEN GOOD TO HIS PEOPLE. FROM HALLIBURTON ALL THE WAY DOWN TO BLACKWATER, HE'S COME THROUGH FOR THEM AGAIN AND AGAIN.
HE SOLD OFF MOST OF THE FEDERAL GOVERNMENT, AND ON TOP OF THAT HE DELIVERED PAKISTAN-- THE C.I.A. SAID HUNT BIN LADEN IN AFGHANISTAN, BUT BOB CAME THROUGH WITH A REAL WAR. CAN YOU IMAGINE WHAT THOSE CONTRACTORS MUST BE MAKING, DOING HALF THE WORK BADLY AND CHARGING TWICE THE GOING RATE?
THAT MAN IS A TEAM PLAYER.
WELL: NOW IT'S OUR TURN.
OUR AGENDA.
OUR MAN IN THE OVAL OFFICE.
WE'LL SPLIT THE DIFFERENCE. DINNER TONIGHT, NOT LUNCH TOMORROW.
UH...
THAT'S SETTLED, THEN.

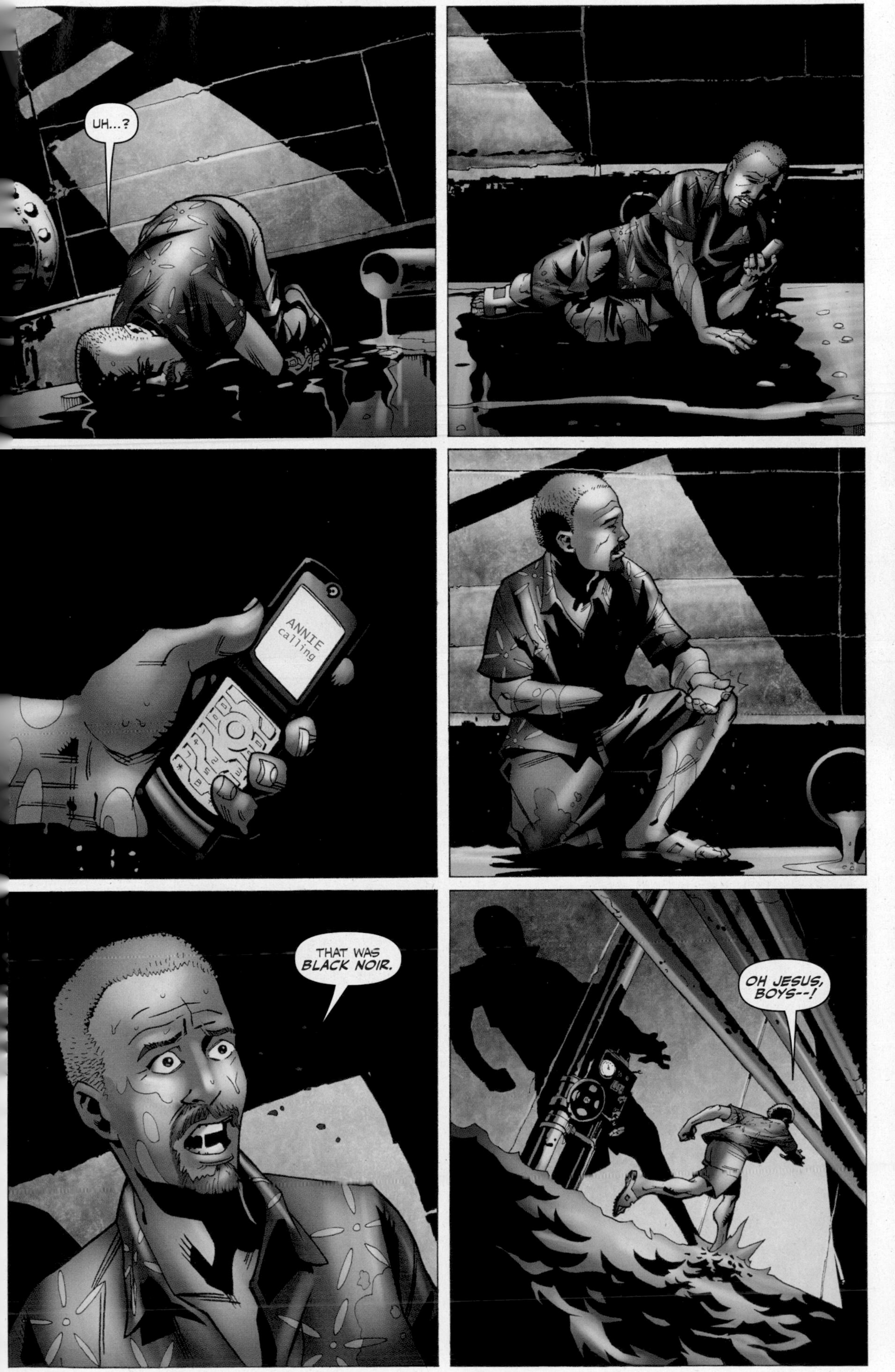
UH...?
ANNIE
calling
THAT WAS BLACK NOIR.
OH JESUS, BOYS--!

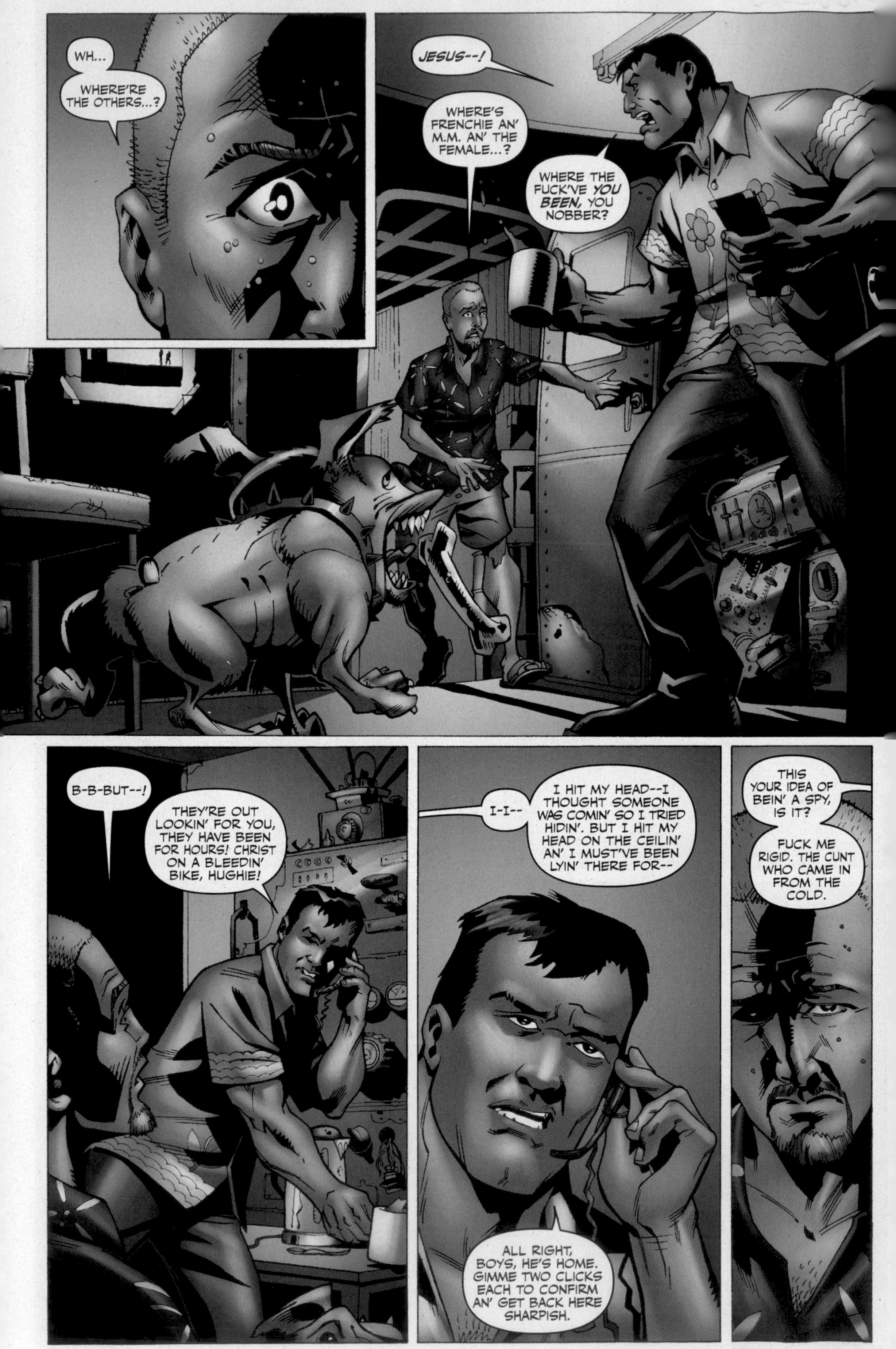
WH...
WHERE'RE THE OTHERS...?
JESUS--!
WHERE'S FRENCHIE AN' M.M. AN' THE FEMALE...?
WHERE THE FUCK'VE *YOU BEEN,* YOU NOBBER?
B-B-BUT--!
THEY'RE OUT LOOKIN' FOR YOU, THEY HAVE BEEN FOR HOURS! CHRIST ON A BLEEDIN' BIKE, HUGHIE!
I-I--
I HIT MY HEAD--I THOUGHT SOMEONE WAS COMIN' SO I TRIED HIDIN'. BUT I HIT MY HEAD ON THE CEILIN' AN' I MUST'VE BEEN LYIN' THERE FOR--
ALL RIGHT, BOYS, HE'S HOME. GIMME TWO CLICKS EACH TO CONFIRM AN' GET BACK HERE SHARPISH.
THIS YOUR IDEA OF BEIN' A SPY, IS IT?
FUCK ME RIGID. THE CUNT WHO CAME IN FROM THE COLD.

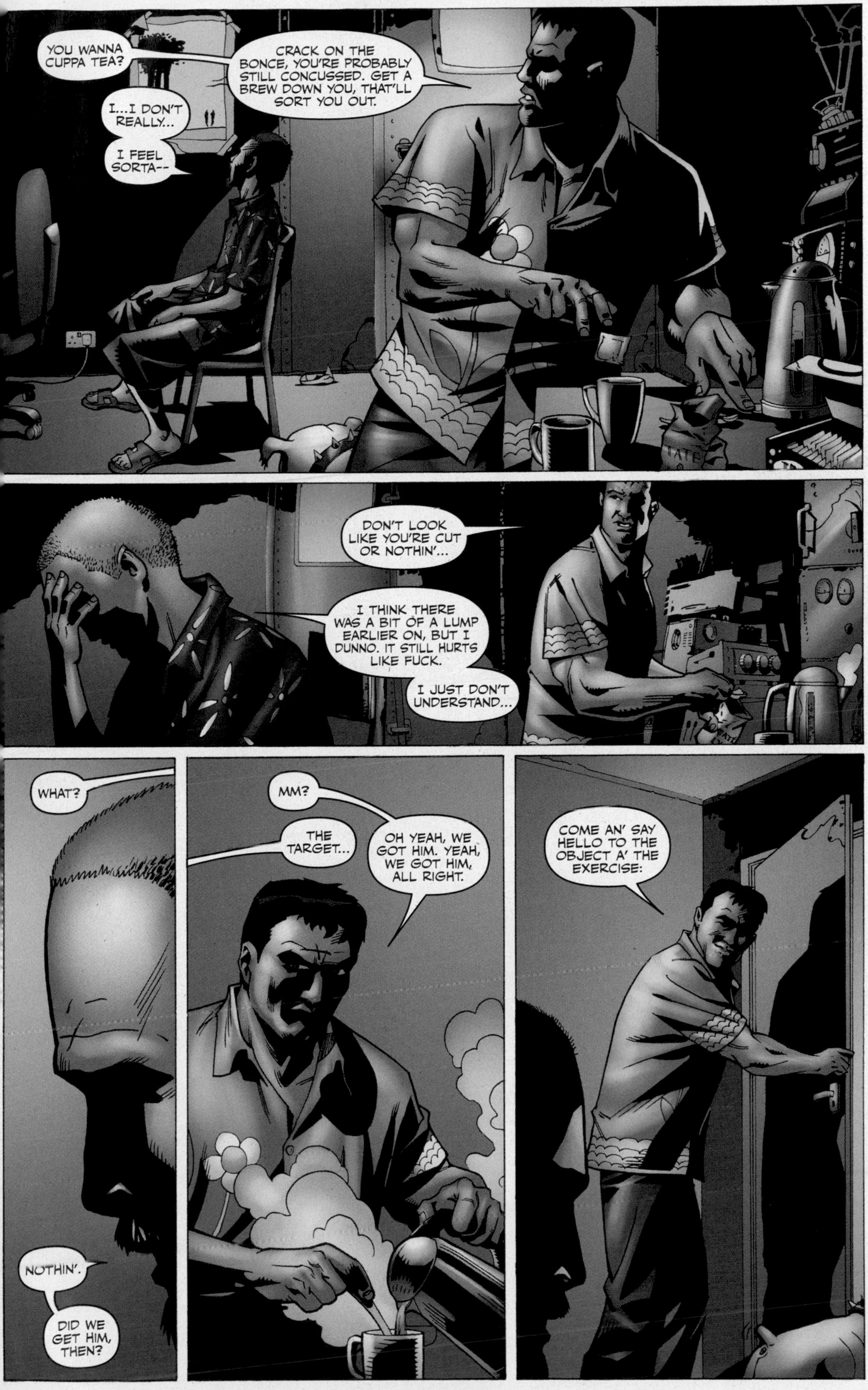

YOU WANNA CUPPA TEA?
CRACK ON THE BONCE, YOU'RE PROBABLY STILL CONCUSSED. GET A BREW DOWN YOU, THAT'LL SORT YOU OUT.
I...I DON'T REALLY...
I FEEL SORTA--
DON'T LOOK LIKE YOU'RE CUT OR NOTHIN'...
I THINK THERE WAS A BIT OF A LUMP EARLIER ON, BUT I DUNNO. IT STILL HURTS LIKE FUCK.
I JUST DON'T UNDERSTAND...
WHAT?
NOTHIN'.
DID WE GET HIM, THEN?
MM?
THE TARGET...
OH YEAH, WE GOT HIM. YEAH, WE GOT HIM, ALL RIGHT.
COME AN' SAY HELLO TO THE OBJECT A' THE EXERCISE:

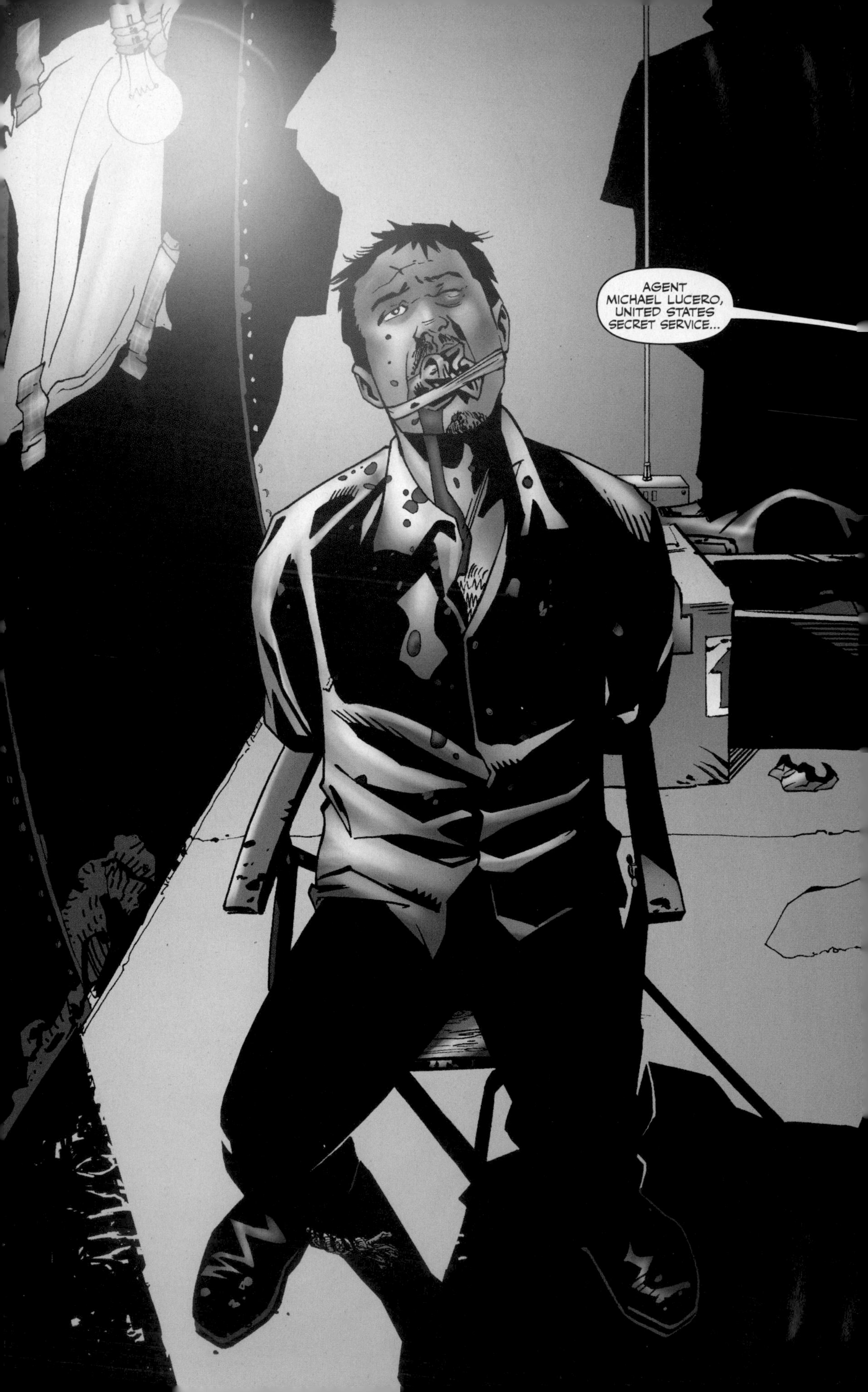
AGENT MICHAEL LUCERO, UNITED STATES SECRET SERVICE...

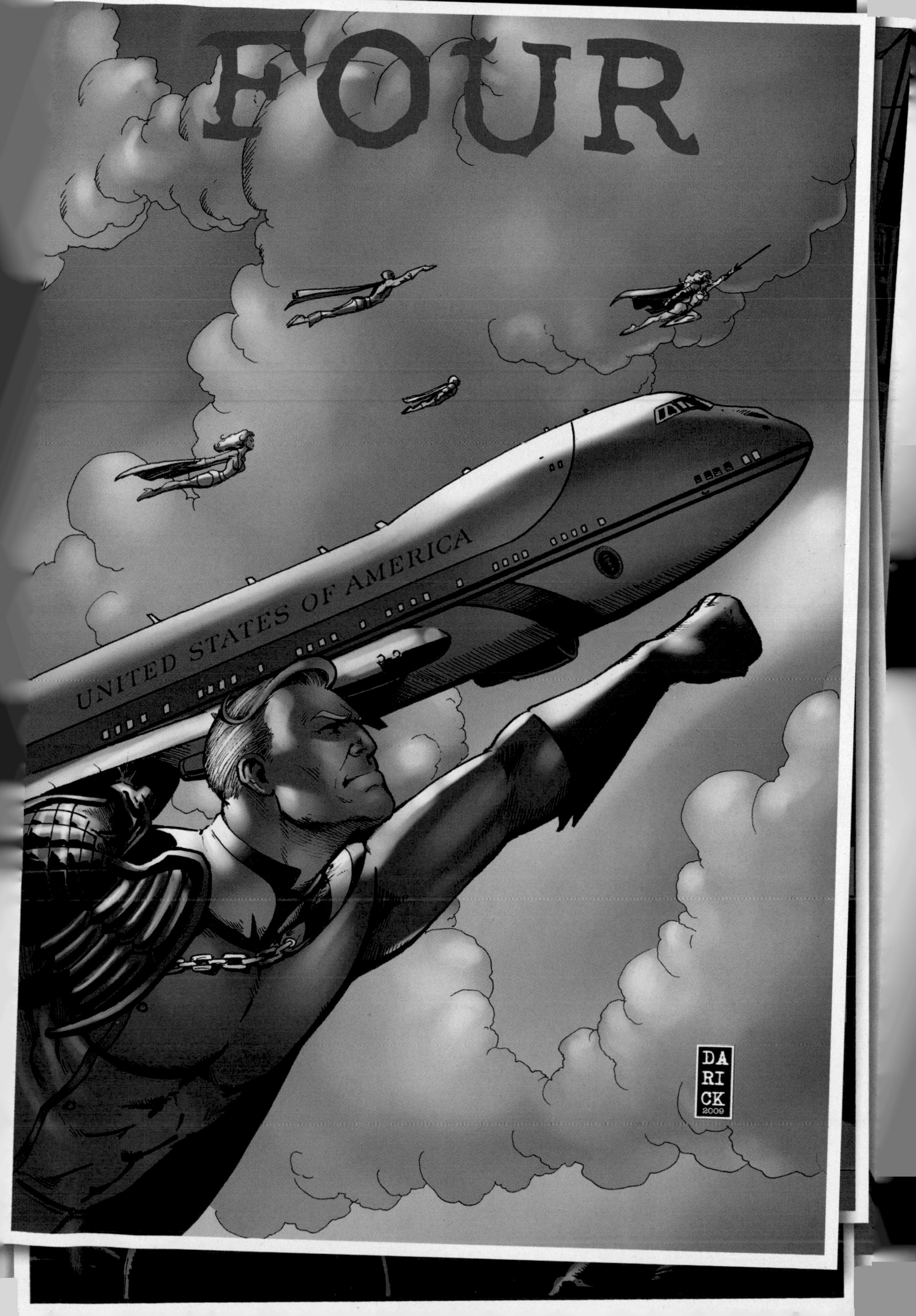
FOUR
UNITED STATES OF AMERICA
DA
RI
CK
2009

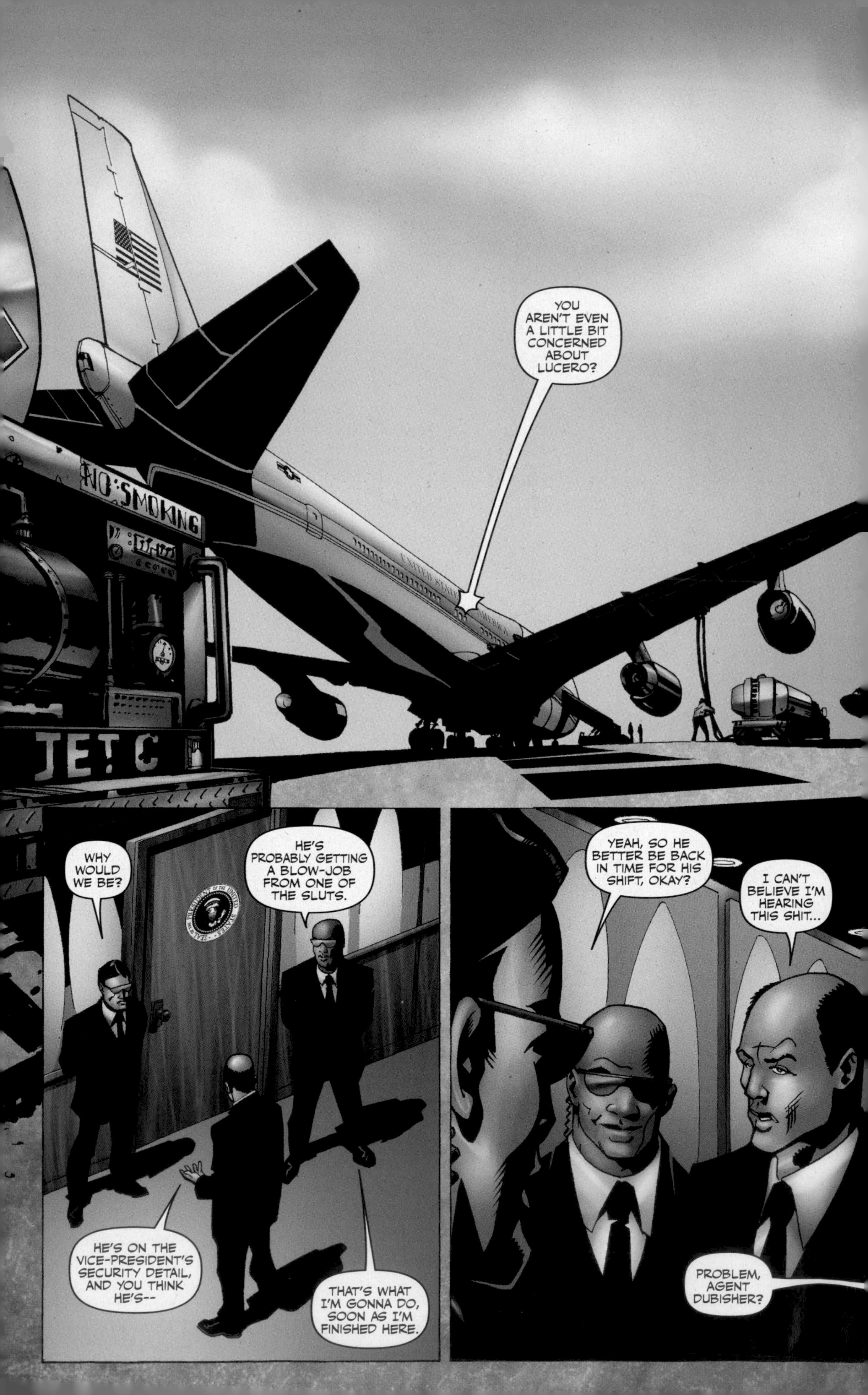
NO SMOKING
JET C
YOU AREN'T EVEN A LITTLE BIT CONCERNED ABOUT LUCERO?
WHY WOULD WE BE?
HE'S PROBABLY GETTING A BLOW-JOB FROM ONE OF THE SLUTS.
HE'S ON THE VICE-PRESIDENT'S SECURITY DETAIL, AND YOU THINK HE'S--
THAT'S WHAT I'M GONNA DO, SOON AS I'M FINISHED HERE.
YEAH, SO HE BETTER BE BACK IN TIME FOR HIS SHIFT, OKAY?
I CAN'T BELIEVE I'M HEARING THIS SHIT...
PROBLEM, AGENT DUBISHER?

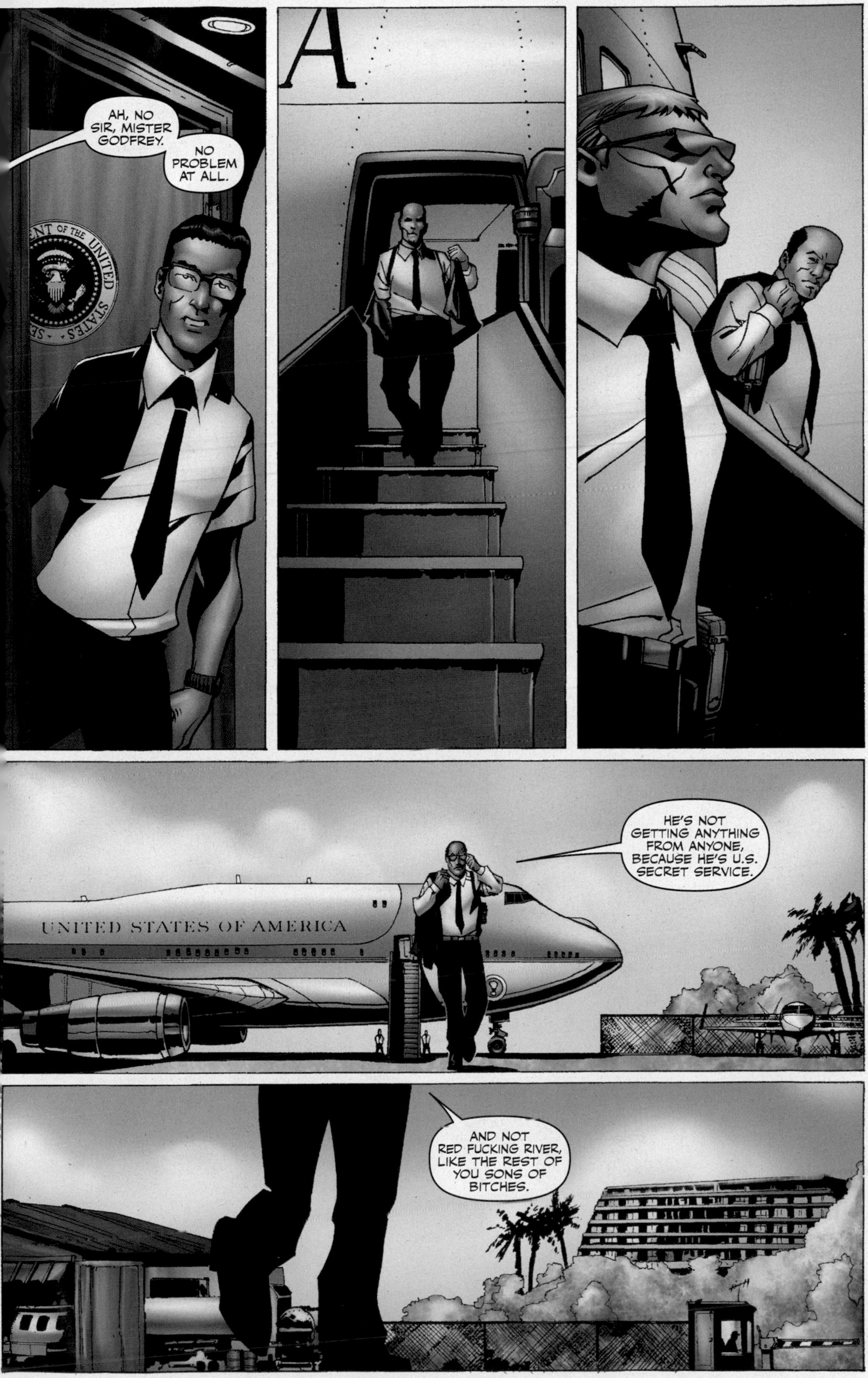
AH, NO SIR, MISTER GODFREY.
NO PROBLEM AT ALL.
HE'S NOT GETTING ANYTHING FROM ANYONE, BECAUSE HE'S U.S. SECRET SERVICE.
UNITED STATES OF AMERICA
AND NOT RED FUCKING RIVER, LIKE THE REST OF YOU SONS OF BITCHES.

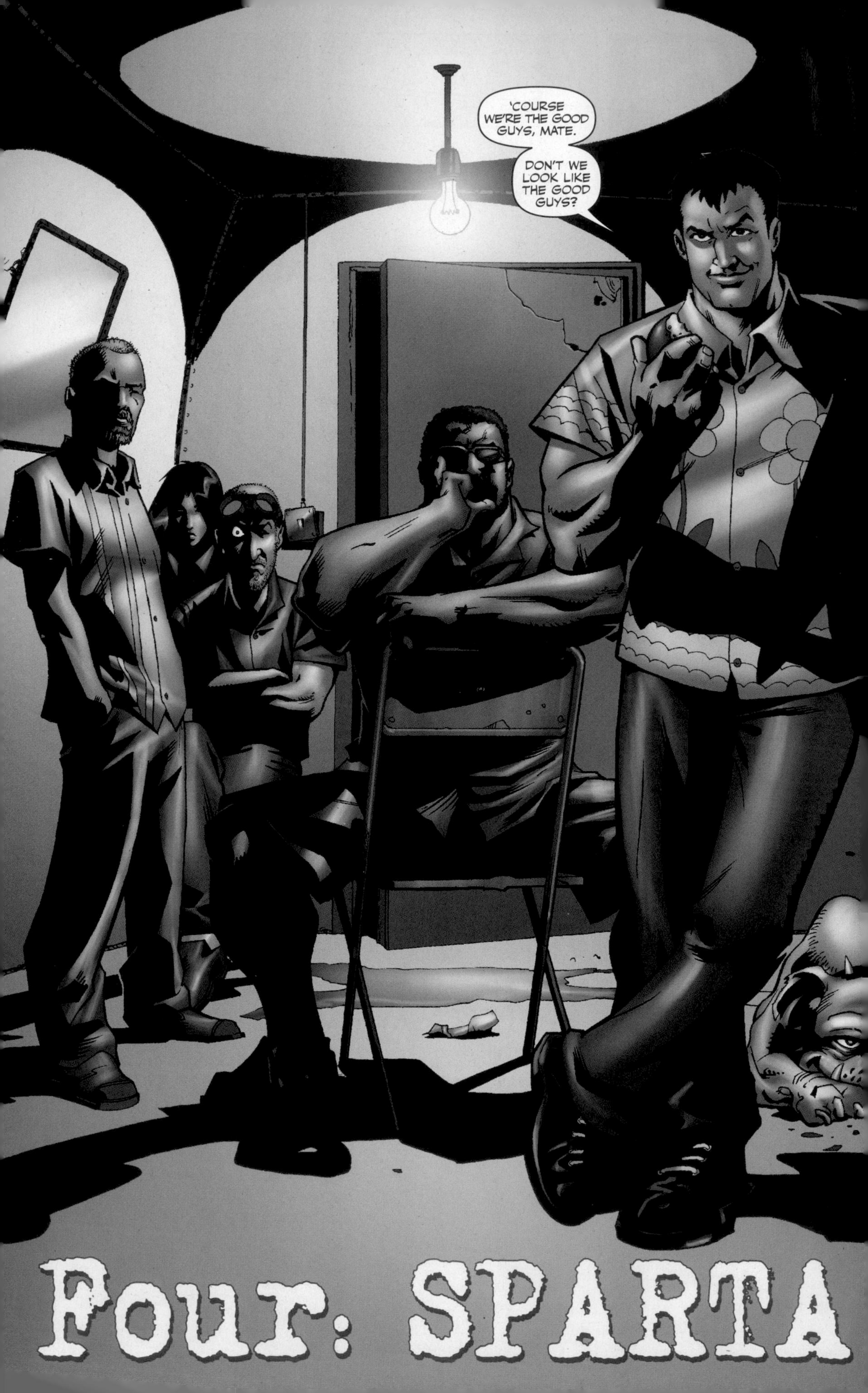
'COURSE WE'RE THE GOOD GUYS, MATE.
DON'T WE LOOK LIKE THE GOOD GUYS?
Four: SPARTA

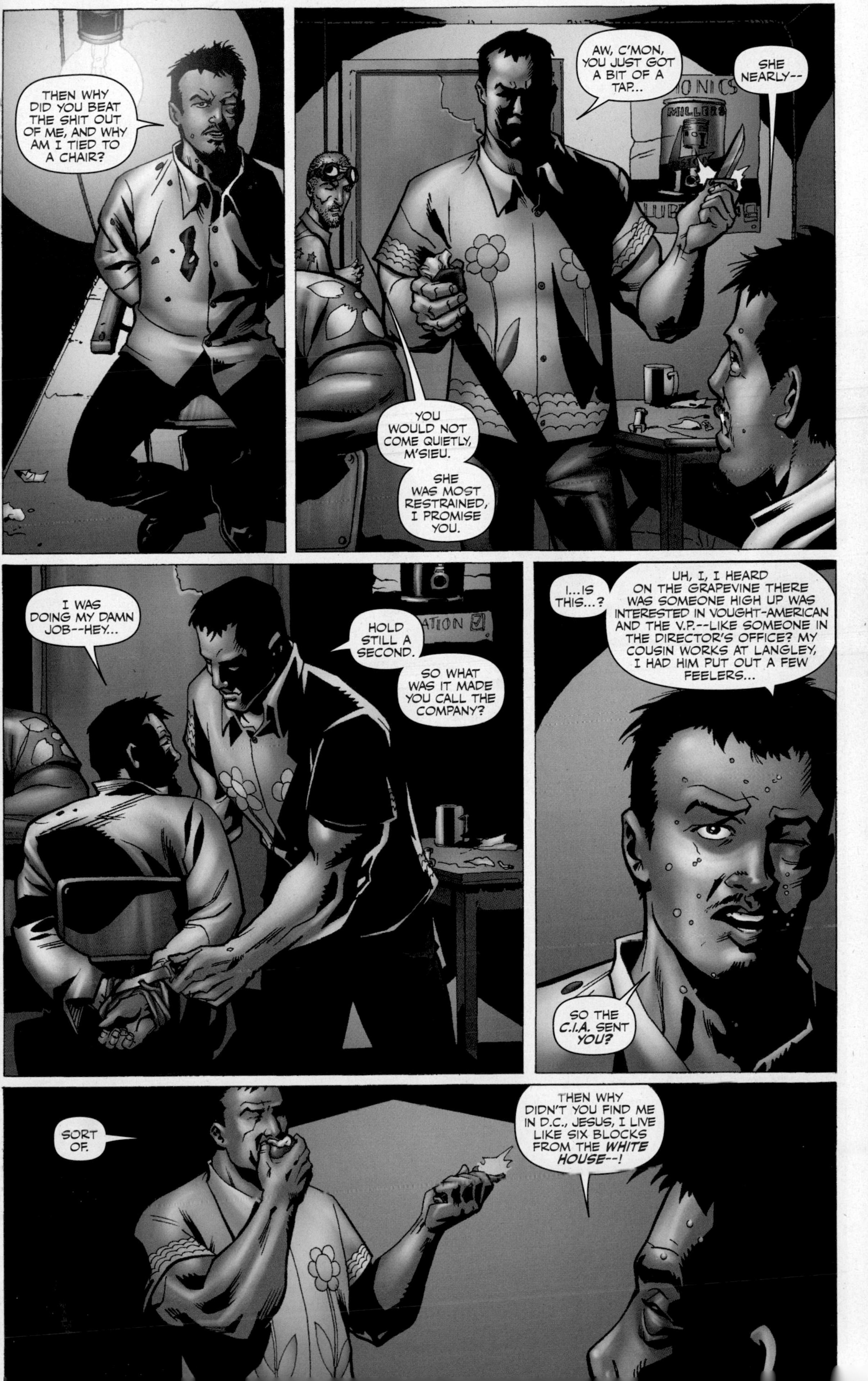
THEN WHY DID YOU BEAT THE SHIT OUT OF ME, AND WHY AM I TIED TO A CHAIR?
AW, C'MON, YOU JUST GOT A BIT OF A TAP...
SHE NEARLY--
YOU WOULD NOT COME QUIETLY, M'SIEU.
SHE WAS MOST RESTRAINED, I PROMISE YOU.
I WAS DOING MY DAMN JOB--HEY...
HOLD STILL A SECOND.
SO WHAT WAS IT MADE YOU CALL THE COMPANY?
I...IS THIS...?
UH, I, I HEARD ON THE GRAPEVINE THERE WAS SOMEONE HIGH UP WAS INTERESTED IN VOUGHT-AMERICAN AND THE V.P.--LIKE SOMEONE IN THE DIRECTOR'S OFFICE? MY COUSIN WORKS AT LANGLEY, I HAD HIM PUT OUT A FEW FEELERS...
SO THE C.I.A. SENT YOU?
SORT OF.
THEN WHY DIDN'T YOU FIND ME IN D.C., JESUS, I LIVE LIKE SIX BLOCKS FROM THE WHITE HOUSE--!

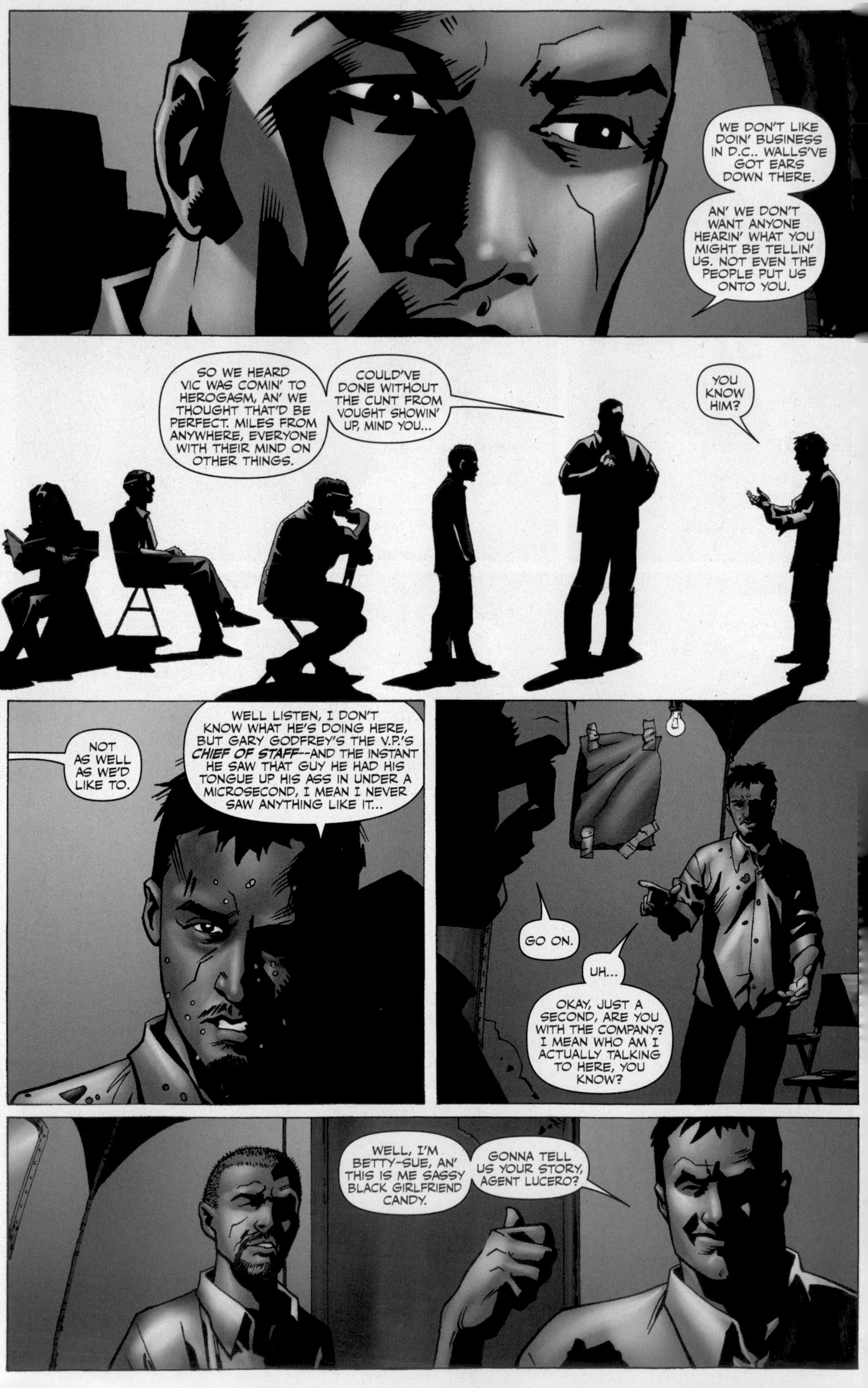

WE DON'T LIKE DOIN' BUSINESS IN D.C.. WALLS'VE GOT EARS DOWN THERE.
AN' WE DON'T WANT ANYONE HEARIN' WHAT YOU MIGHT BE TELLIN' US. NOT EVEN THE PEOPLE PUT US ONTO YOU.
SO WE HEARD VIC WAS COMIN' TO HEROGASM, AN' WE THOUGHT THAT'D BE PERFECT. MILES FROM ANYWHERE, EVERYONE WITH THEIR MIND ON OTHER THINGS.
COULD'VE DONE WITHOUT THE CUNT FROM VOUGHT SHOWIN' UP, MIND YOU...
YOU KNOW HIM?
NOT AS WELL AS WE'D LIKE TO.
WELL LISTEN, I DON'T KNOW WHAT HE'S DOING HERE, BUT GARY GODFREY'S THE V.P.'S *CHIEF OF STAFF*--AND THE INSTANT HE SAW THAT GUY HE HAD HIS TONGUE UP HIS ASS IN UNDER A MICROSECOND, I MEAN I NEVER SAW ANYTHING LIKE IT...
GO ON.
UH...
OKAY, JUST A SECOND, ARE YOU WITH THE COMPANY? I MEAN WHO AM I ACTUALLY TALKING TO HERE, YOU KNOW?
WELL, I'M BETTY-SUE, AN' THIS IS ME SASSY BLACK GIRLFRIEND CANDY.
GONNA TELL US YOUR STORY, AGENT LUCERO?

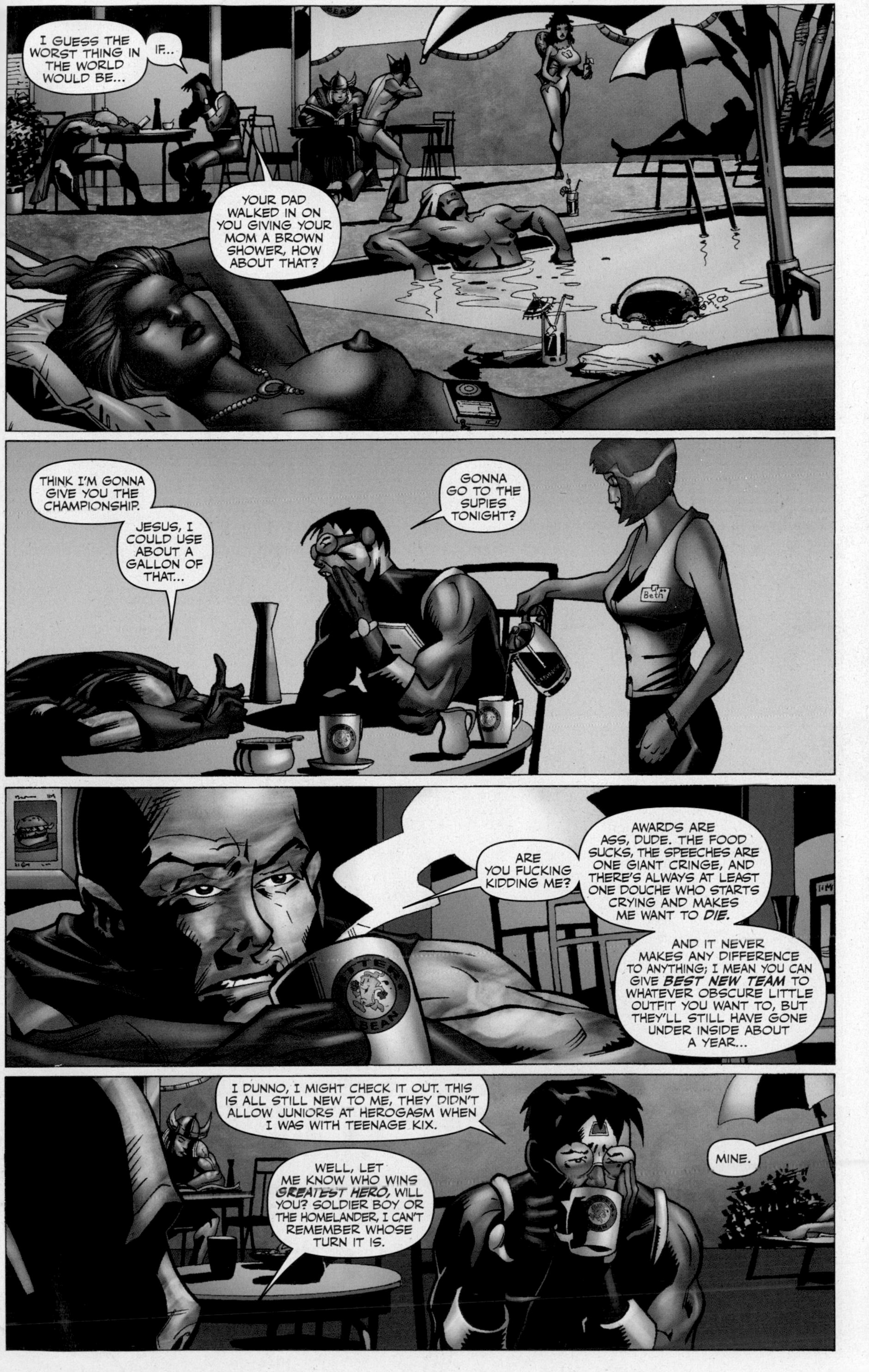
I GUESS THE WORST THING IN THE WORLD WOULD BE...
IF...
YOUR DAD WALKED IN ON YOU GIVING YOUR MOM A BROWN SHOWER, HOW ABOUT THAT?
THINK I'M GONNA GIVE YOU THE CHAMPIONSHIP.
JESUS, I COULD USE ABOUT A GALLON OF THAT...
GONNA GO TO THE SUPIES TONIGHT?
Beth
ARE YOU FUCKING KIDDING ME?
AWARDS ARE ASS, DUDE. THE FOOD SUCKS, THE SPEECHES ARE ONE GIANT CRINGE, AND THERE'S ALWAYS AT LEAST ONE DOUCHE WHO STARTS CRYING AND MAKES ME WANT TO *DIE.*
AND IT NEVER MAKES ANY DIFFERENCE TO ANYTHING; I MEAN YOU CAN GIVE ***BEST NEW TEAM*** TO WHATEVER OBSCURE LITTLE OUTFIT YOU WANT TO, BUT THEY'LL STILL HAVE GONE UNDER INSIDE ABOUT A YEAR...
I DUNNO, I MIGHT CHECK IT OUT. THIS IS ALL STILL NEW TO ME, THEY DIDN'T ALLOW JUNIORS AT HEROGASM WHEN I WAS WITH TEENAGE KIX.
WELL, LET ME KNOW WHO WINS *GREATEST HERO,* WILL YOU? SOLDIER BOY OR THE HOMELANDER, I CAN'T REMEMBER WHOSE TURN IT IS.
MINE.

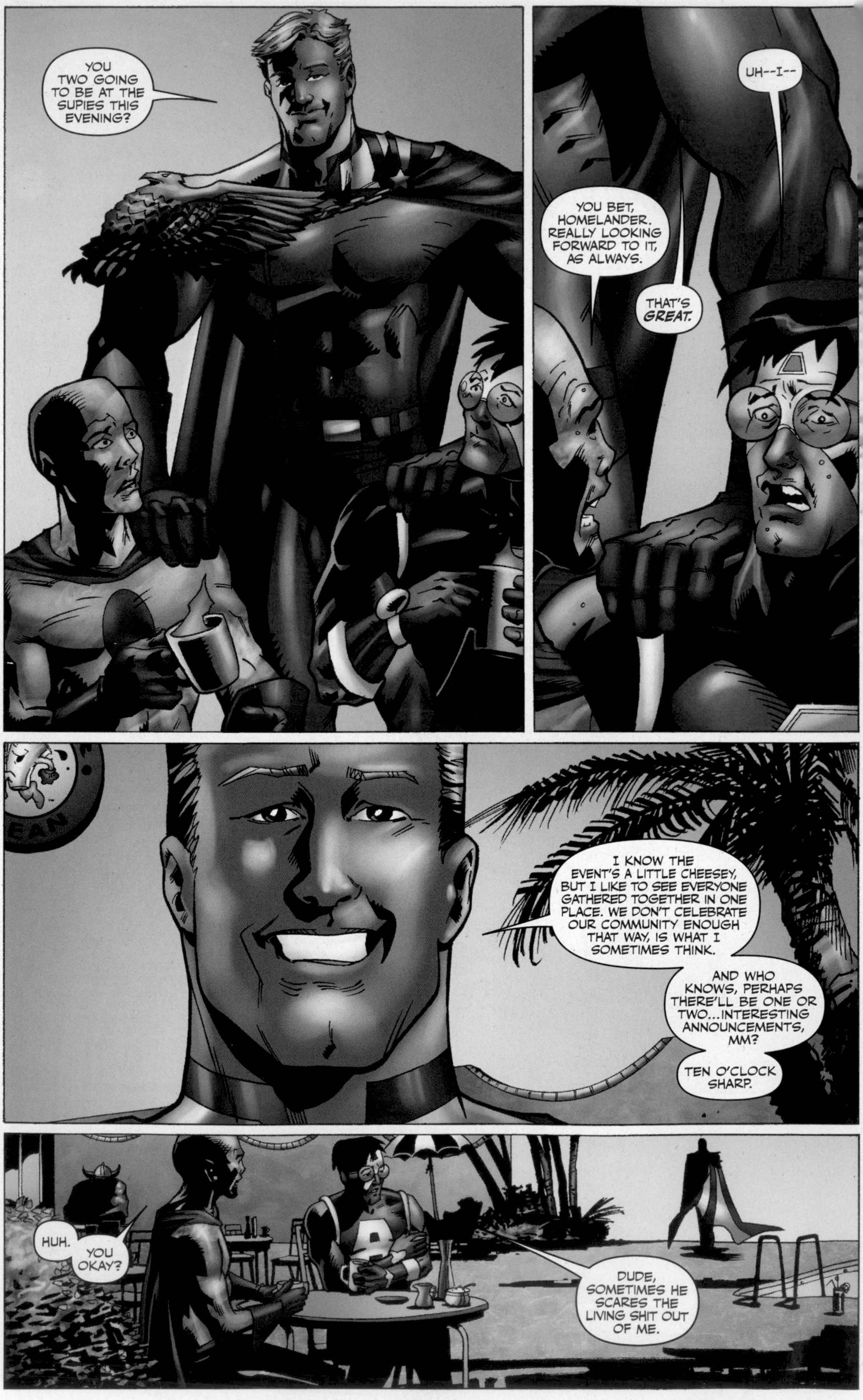

YOU TWO GOING TO BE AT THE SUPIES THIS EVENING?
UH--I--
YOU BET, HOMELANDER. REALLY LOOKING FORWARD TO IT, AS ALWAYS.
THAT'S *GREAT.*
I KNOW THE EVENT'S A LITTLE CHEESEY, BUT I LIKE TO SEE EVERYONE GATHERED TOGETHER IN ONE PLACE. WE DON'T CELEBRATE OUR COMMUNITY ENOUGH THAT WAY, IS WHAT I SOMETIMES THINK.
AND WHO KNOWS, PERHAPS THERE'LL BE ONE OR TWO...INTERESTING ANNOUNCEMENTS, MM?
TEN O'CLOCK SHARP.
HUH.
YOU OKAY?
DUDE, SOMETIMES HE SCARES THE LIVING SHIT OUT OF ME.

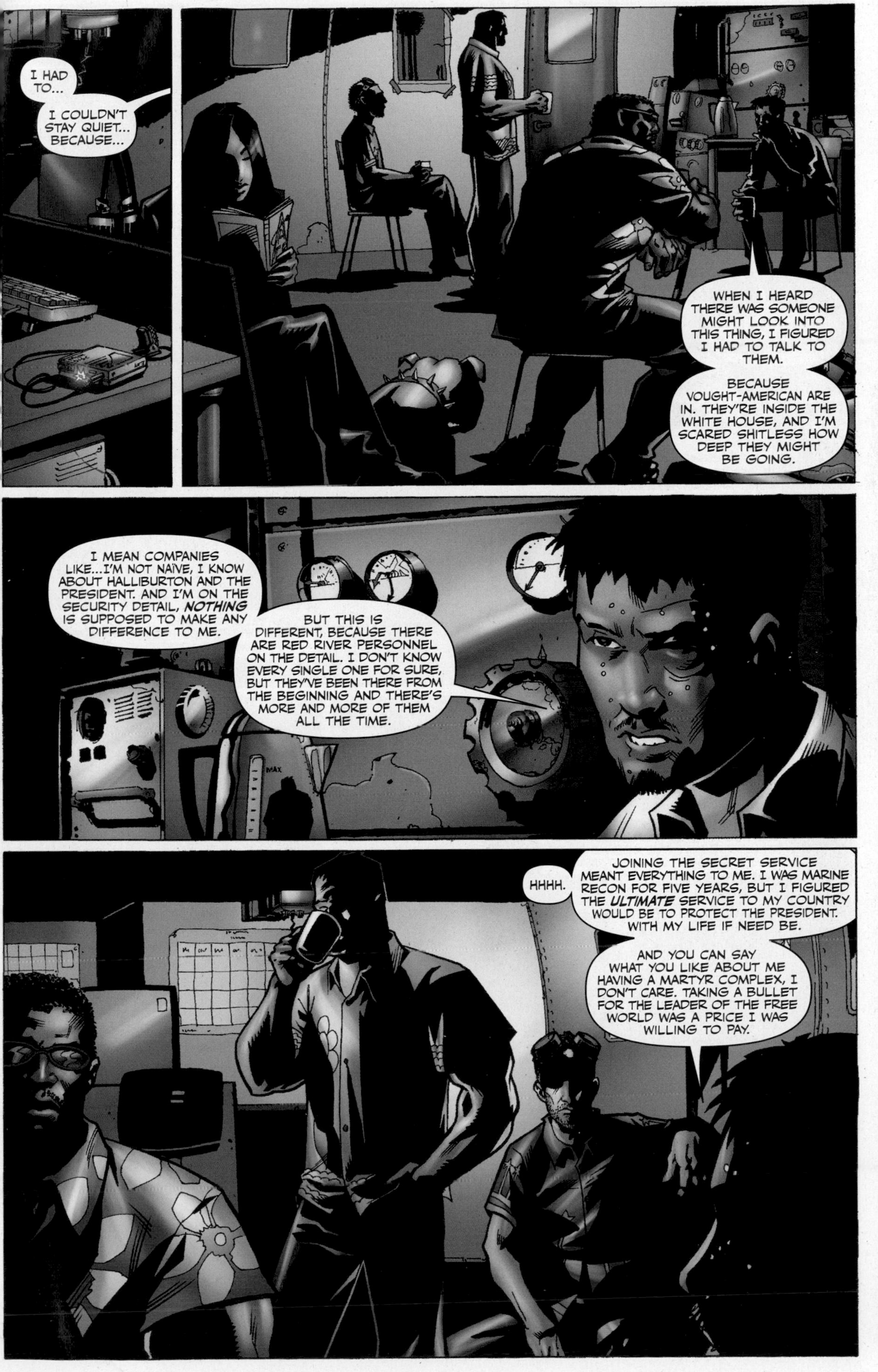

I HAD TO...
I COULDN'T STAY QUIET... BECAUSE...
WHEN I HEARD THERE WAS SOMEONE MIGHT LOOK INTO THIS THING, I FIGURED I HAD TO TALK TO THEM.
BECAUSE VOUGHT-AMERICAN ARE IN. THEY'RE INSIDE THE WHITE HOUSE, AND I'M SCARED SHITLESS HOW DEEP THEY MIGHT BE GOING.
I MEAN COMPANIES LIKE...I'M NOT NAÏVE, I KNOW ABOUT HALLIBURTON AND THE PRESIDENT. AND I'M ON THE SECURITY DETAIL, *NOTHING* IS SUPPOSED TO MAKE ANY DIFFERENCE TO ME.
BUT THIS IS DIFFERENT, BECAUSE THERE ARE RED RIVER PERSONNEL ON THE DETAIL. I DON'T KNOW EVERY SINGLE ONE FOR SURE, BUT THEY'VE BEEN THERE FROM THE BEGINNING AND THERE'S MORE AND MORE OF THEM ALL THE TIME.
HHHH.
JOINING THE SECRET SERVICE MEANT EVERYTHING TO ME. I WAS MARINE RECON FOR FIVE YEARS, BUT I FIGURED THE *ULTIMATE* SERVICE TO MY COUNTRY WOULD BE TO PROTECT THE PRESIDENT. WITH MY LIFE IF NEED BE.
AND YOU CAN SAY WHAT YOU LIKE ABOUT ME HAVING A MARTYR COMPLEX, I DON'T CARE. TAKING A BULLET FOR THE LEADER OF THE FREE WORLD WAS A PRICE I WAS WILLING TO PAY.

...BUT I GOT ASSIGNED TO *VIC THE VEEP*...

IT-- SEEMED OKAY AT FIRST.

"I JOINED THE DETAIL RIGHT AFTER THEY WON IN TWO THOUSAND. I MEAN YOU MEET HIM AND YOU THINK, OKAY, SOMETHING'S NOT RIGHT HERE, BUT..."

"YOU TELL YOURSELF IT'S ABOUT THE OFFICE OF THE VICE-PRESIDENT, NOT THE MAN HIMSELF. YOU DO YOUR JOB."

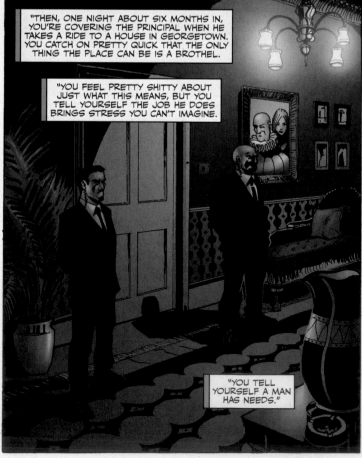

"THEN, ONE NIGHT ABOUT SIX MONTHS IN, YOU'RE COVERING THE PRINCIPAL WHEN HE TAKES A RIDE TO A HOUSE IN GEORGETOWN. YOU CATCH ON PRETTY QUICK THAT THE ONLY THING THE PLACE CAN BE IS A BROTHEL.

"YOU FEEL PRETTY SHITTY ABOUT JUST WHAT THIS MEANS, BUT YOU TELL YOURSELF THE JOB HE DOES BRINGS STRESS YOU CAN'T IMAGINE."

"YOU TELL YOURSELF A MAN HAS NEEDS."

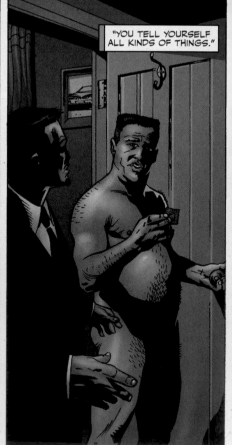

"YOU TELL YOURSELF ALL KINDS OF THINGS."

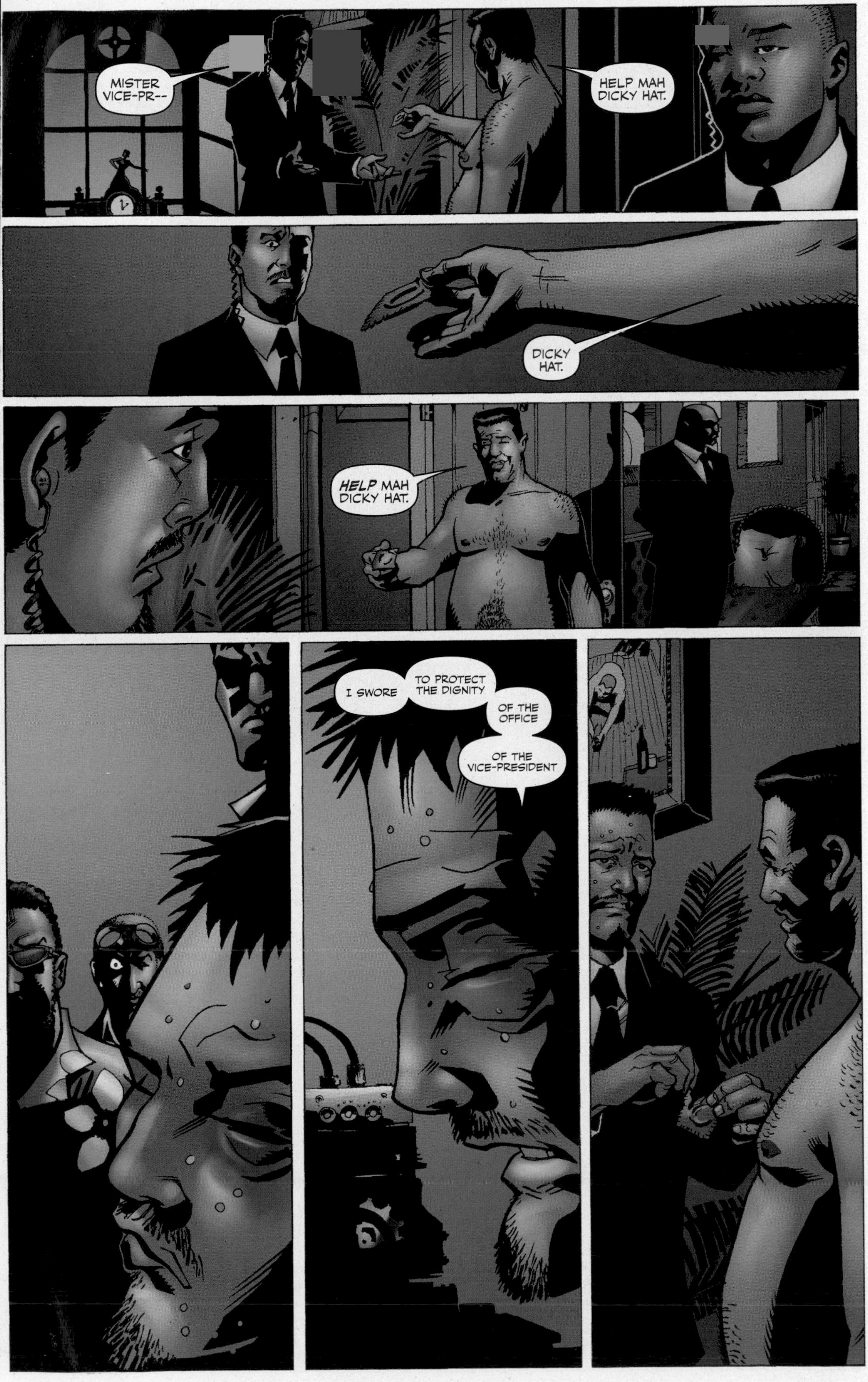
MISTER VICE-PR--
HELP MAH DICKY HAT.
DICKY HAT.
HELP MAH DICKY HAT.
I SWORE
TO PROTECT THE DIGNITY
OF THE OFFICE
OF THE VICE-PRESIDENT

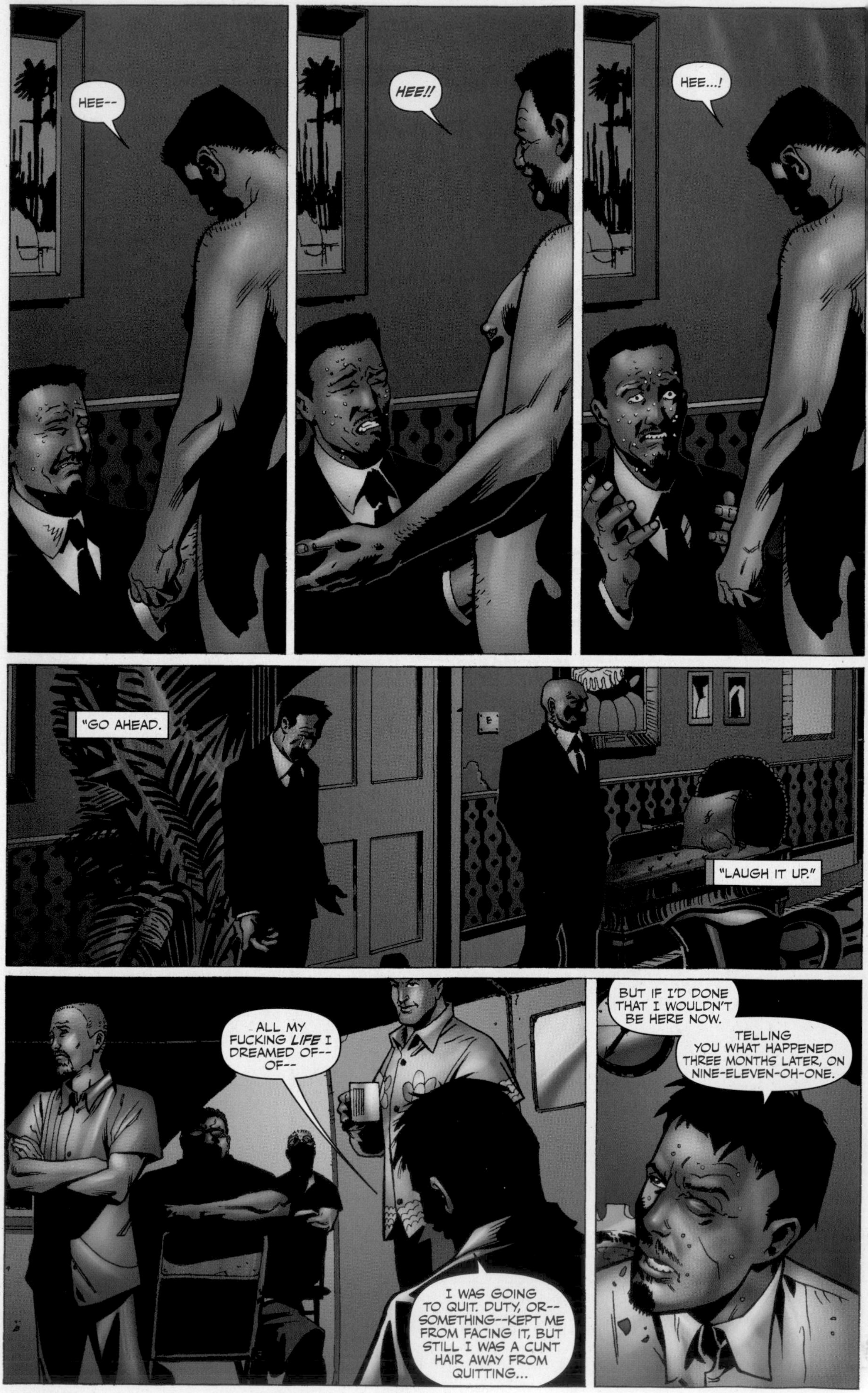
HEE--
HEE!!
HEE...!
"GO AHEAD.
"LAUGH IT UP."
ALL MY FUCKING LIFE I DREAMED OF--OF--
I WAS GOING TO QUIT. DUTY, OR--SOMETHING--KEPT ME FROM FACING IT, BUT STILL I WAS A CUNT HAIR AWAY FROM QUITTING...
BUT IF I'D DONE THAT I WOULDN'T BE HERE NOW.
TELLING YOU WHAT HAPPENED THREE MONTHS LATER, ON NINE-ELEVEN-OH-ONE.

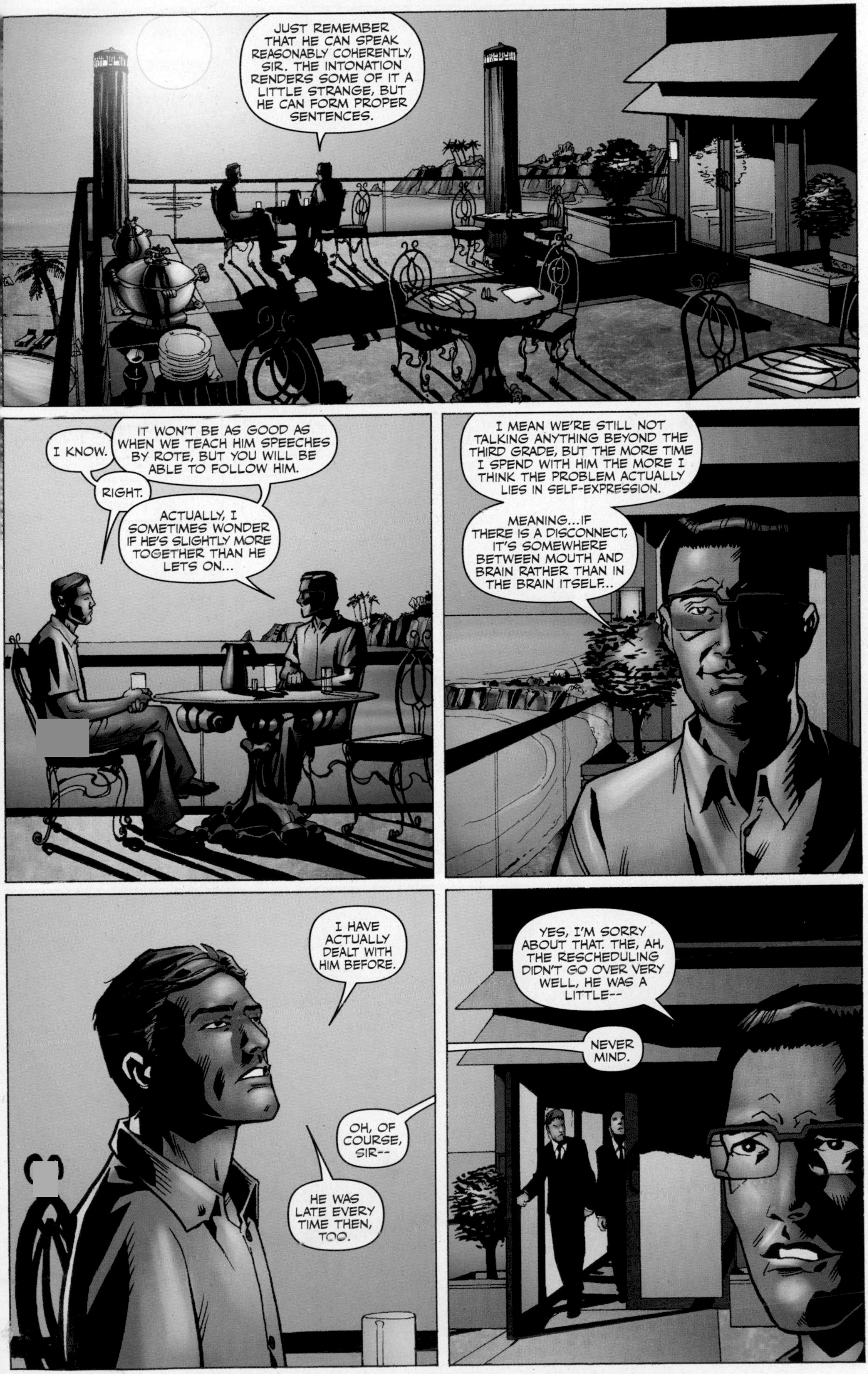
JUST REMEMBER THAT HE CAN SPEAK REASONABLY COHERENTLY, SIR. THE INTONATION RENDERS SOME OF IT A LITTLE STRANGE, BUT HE CAN FORM PROPER SENTENCES.
I KNOW.
IT WON'T BE AS GOOD AS WHEN WE TEACH HIM SPEECHES BY ROTE, BUT YOU WILL BE ABLE TO FOLLOW HIM.
RIGHT.
ACTUALLY, I SOMETIMES WONDER IF HE'S SLIGHTLY MORE TOGETHER THAN HE LETS ON...
I MEAN WE'RE STILL NOT TALKING ANYTHING BEYOND THE THIRD GRADE, BUT THE MORE TIME I SPEND WITH HIM THE MORE I THINK THE PROBLEM ACTUALLY LIES IN SELF-EXPRESSION.
MEANING...IF THERE IS A DISCONNECT, IT'S SOMEWHERE BETWEEN MOUTH AND BRAIN RATHER THAN IN THE BRAIN ITSELF...
I HAVE ACTUALLY DEALT WITH HIM BEFORE.
OH, OF COURSE, SIR--
HE WAS LATE EVERY TIME THEN, TOO.
YES, I'M SORRY ABOUT THAT. THE, AH, THE RESCHEDULING DIDN'T GO OVER VERY WELL, HE WAS A LITTLE--
NEVER MIND.

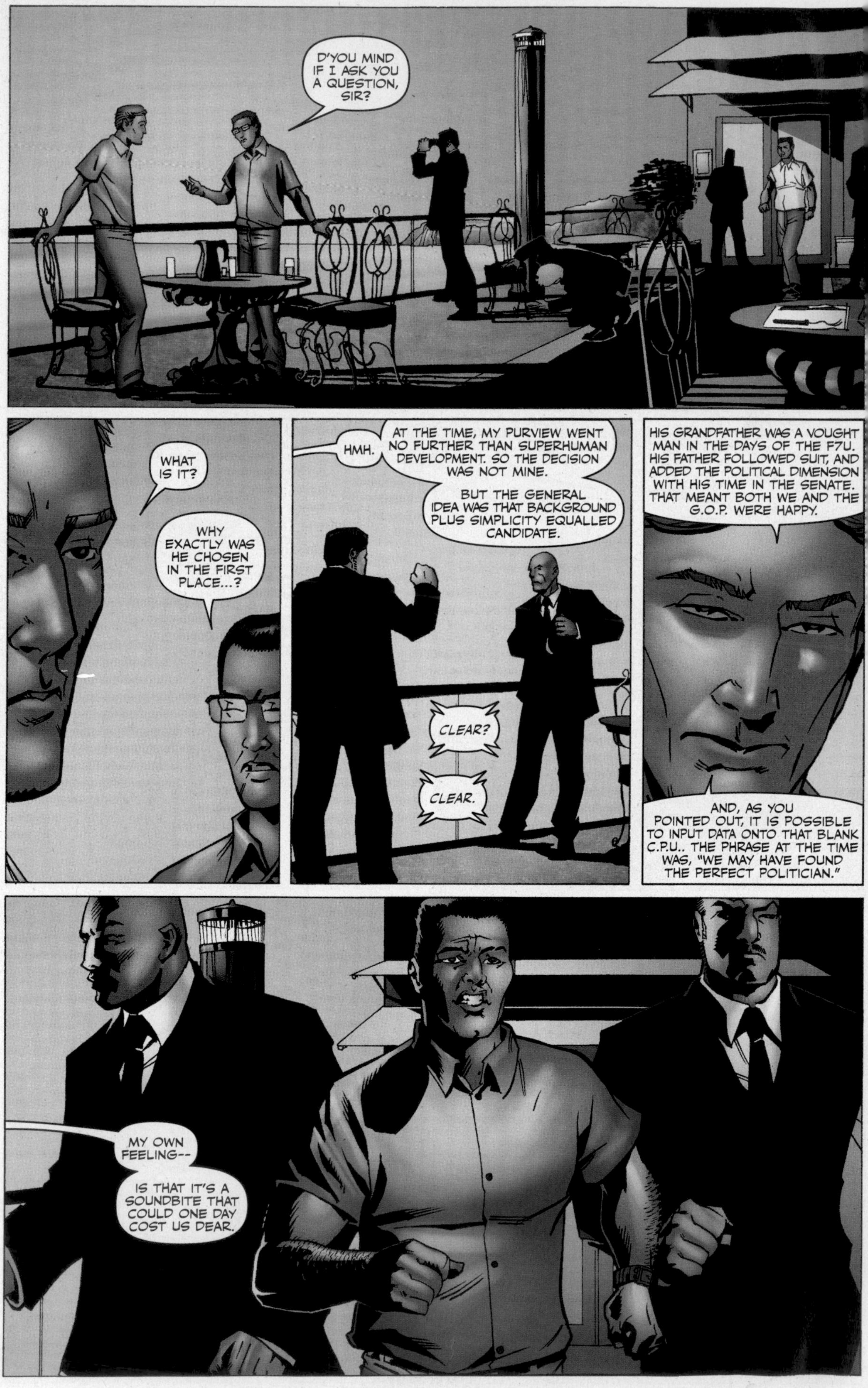
D'YOU MIND IF I ASK YOU A QUESTION, SIR?
WHAT IS IT?
WHY EXACTLY WAS HE CHOSEN IN THE FIRST PLACE...?
HMH.
AT THE TIME, MY PURVIEW WENT NO FURTHER THAN SUPERHUMAN DEVELOPMENT. SO THE DECISION WAS NOT MINE.
BUT THE GENERAL IDEA WAS THAT BACKGROUND PLUS SIMPLICITY EQUALLED CANDIDATE.
CLEAR?
CLEAR.
HIS GRANDFATHER WAS A VOUGHT MAN IN THE DAYS OF THE F7U. HIS FATHER FOLLOWED SUIT, AND ADDED THE POLITICAL DIMENSION WITH HIS TIME IN THE SENATE. THAT MEANT BOTH WE AND THE G.O.P. WERE HAPPY.
AND, AS YOU POINTED OUT, IT IS POSSIBLE TO INPUT DATA ONTO THAT BLANK C.P.U.. THE PHRASE AT THE TIME WAS, "WE MAY HAVE FOUND THE PERFECT POLITICIAN."
MY OWN FEELING--
IS THAT IT'S A SOUNDBITE THAT COULD ONE DAY COST US DEAR.

DAKOTA BOB.

WHY COULDN'T I HAVE GOTTEN HIM.

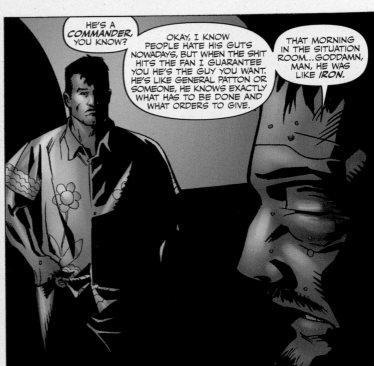

HE'S A *COMMANDER*, YOU KNOW?

OKAY, I KNOW PEOPLE HATE HIS GUTS NOWADAYS, BUT WHEN THE SHIT HITS THE FAN I GUARANTEE YOU HE'S THE GUY YOU WANT. HE'S LIKE GENERAL PATTON OR SOMEONE, HE KNOWS EXACTLY WHAT HAS TO BE DONE AND WHAT ORDERS TO GIVE.

THAT MORNING IN THE SITUATION ROOM...GODDAMN, MAN, HE WAS LIKE *IRON*.

...NORAD HAS THE TWO F-16S CLOSING ON AMERICAN ONE-ONE, MISTER PRESIDENT. SHOULD HAVE VISUAL ANY SECOND.

RIGHT.

SIR, NEWARK TOWER HAS HELD UNITED NINETY-THREE AS ORDERED. STILL NO RESPONSE FROM THE AIRCRAFT SINCE THE SUSPICIOUS TRANSMISSION.

UNDERSTOOD.

MISTER PRESIDENT, A NAVY F-14 FROM THE *JAKE FOSS* JUST INTERCEPTED AMERICAN SEVENTY-SEVEN. PILOT'S REQUESTING CLARIFICATION OF ORDERS.

PUT HIM ON.

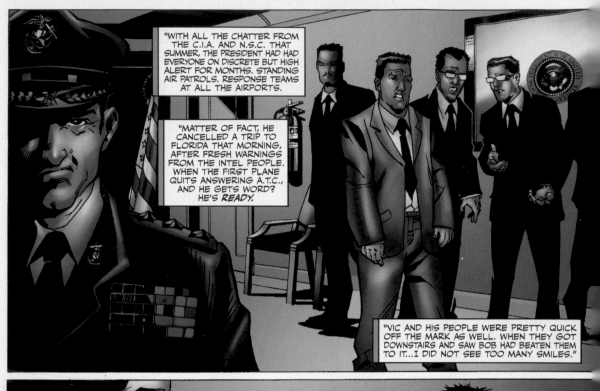

"WITH ALL THE CHATTER FROM THE C.I.A. AND N.S.C. THAT SUMMER, THE PRESIDENT HAD HAD EVERYONE ON DISCRETE BUT HIGH ALERT FOR MONTHS. STANDING AIR PATROLS. RESPONSE TEAMS AT ALL THE AIRPORTS.

"MATTER OF FACT, HE CANCELLED A TRIP TO FLORIDA THAT MORNING, AFTER FRESH WARNINGS FROM THE INTEL PEOPLE. WHEN THE FIRST PLANE QUITS ANSWERING A.T.C., AND HE GETS WORD? HE'S *READY.*

"VIC AND HIS PEOPLE WERE PRETTY QUICK OFF THE MARK AS WELL. WHEN THEY GOT DOWNSTAIRS AND SAW BOB HAD BEATEN THEM TO IT...I DID NOT SEE TOO MANY SMILES."

YOU MEAN...

I THINK THE PRESIDENT WAS MEANT TO BE IN FLORIDA.

SAY AGAIN THIS IS GREEN OCEAN ONE, GREEN OCEAN ONE, NORAD, REPEAT YOUR LAST--

GREEN OCEAN ONE, DO YOU RECOGNIZE MY VOICE?

AH-- SIR?

GREEN OCEAN ONE, YOU ARE ORDERED TO ENGAGE AND DESTROY THE TARGET.

BUT-- SIR, IT'S A--

IT'S A COMMERCIAL AIRLINER FULL OF INNOCENT CIVILIANS, AND BY THE HIGHEST AUTHORITY ON GOD'S EARTH I AM ORDERING YOU TO SHOOT IT DOWN.

SIR...!

SON, WE BELIEVE SOMEONE'S TAKING A SHOT AT US TODAY, SOMEONE WE'VE BEEN EXPECTING. WHAT THAT MEANS IS THIS IS WAR.

AND IN WAR WE DO UNSPEAKABLE THINGS.

MY CALL, GREEN OCEAN ONE. ENGAGE AND DESTROY.

...YES SIR.

TAKE HIM OFF SPEAKER.

DONE.

SIR, ARCHER LEADER HAS AMERICAN ONE-ONE LOCKED UP, NORAD ARE REQUESTING AUTHORISATION...

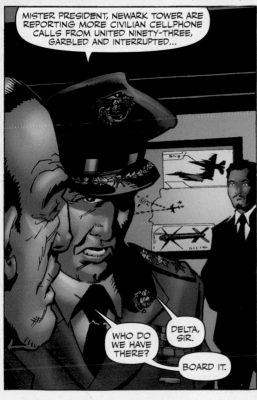

MISTER PRESIDENT, NEWARK TOWER ARE REPORTING MORE CIVILIAN CELLPHONE CALLS FROM UNITED NINETY-THREE, GARBLED AND INTERRUPTED...

WHO DO WE HAVE THERE?

DELTA, SIR.

BOARD IT.

"THERE'D BEEN OTHER SHIT SINCE... IT HAPPENED. NOWHERE NEAR AS BAD, BUT IT MEANT I COULD HARDLY LOOK AT VIC--WHICH WASN'T GOOD, HIM BEING THE GUY I WAS MEANT TO BE PROTECTING.

"WHO I COULD SEE WAS GODFREY, AND ALAN BLAKE, WHO HE REPLACED LATER ON AS CHIEF OF STAFF. THEY WEREN'T HAPPY--I MEAN NOBODY WAS, THAT MORNING, BUT THEY WERE REALLY FREAKING OUT..."

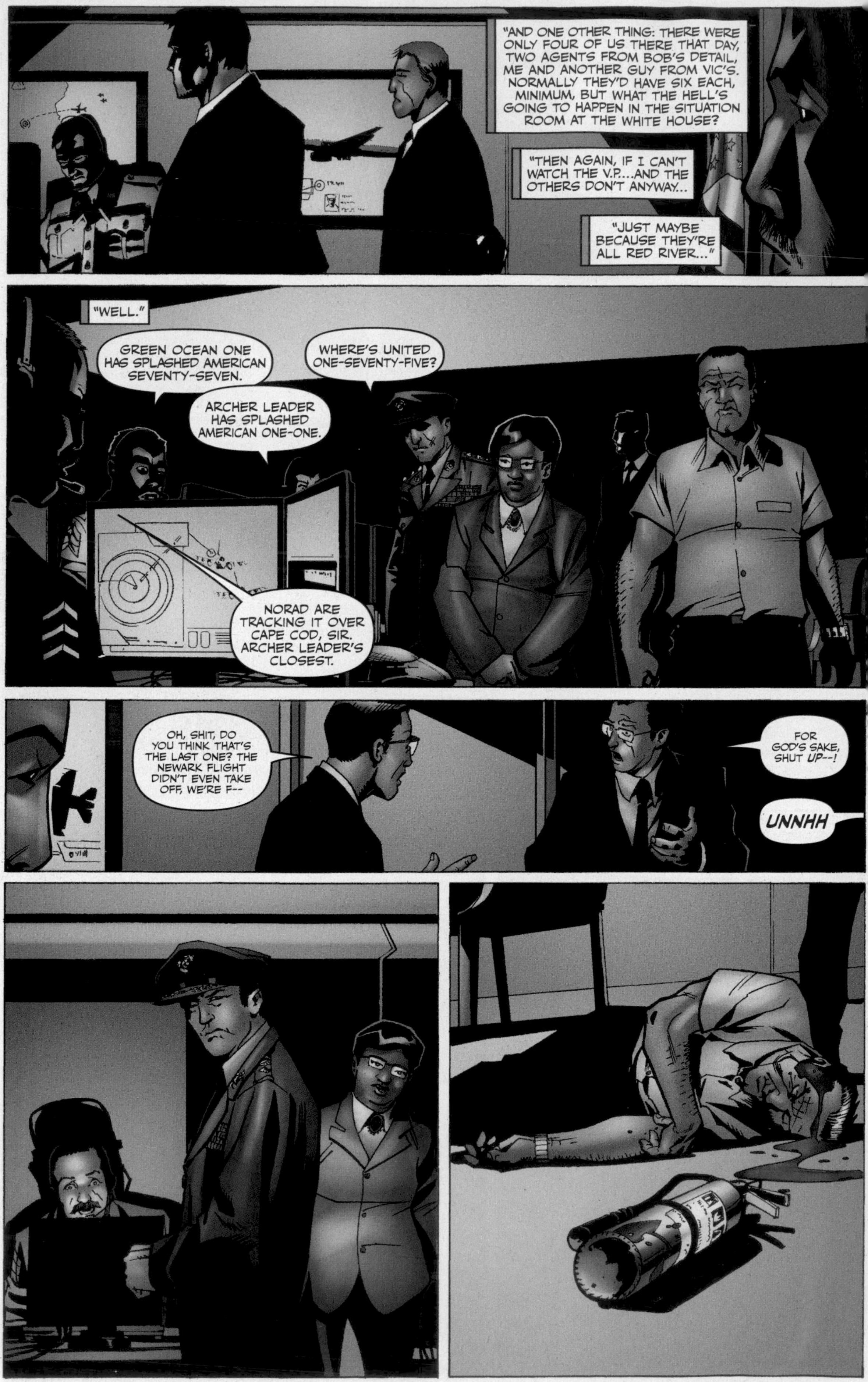
"AND ONE OTHER THING: THERE WERE ONLY FOUR OF US THERE THAT DAY, TWO AGENTS FROM BOB'S DETAIL, ME AND ANOTHER GUY FROM VIC'S. NORMALLY THEY'D HAVE SIX EACH, MINIMUM, BUT WHAT THE HELL'S GOING TO HAPPEN IN THE SITUATION ROOM AT THE WHITE HOUSE?
"THEN AGAIN, IF I CAN'T WATCH THE V.P....AND THE OTHERS DON'T ANYWAY...
"JUST MAYBE BECAUSE THEY'RE ALL RED RIVER..."
"WELL."
GREEN OCEAN ONE HAS SPLASHED AMERICAN SEVENTY-SEVEN.
ARCHER LEADER HAS SPLASHED AMERICAN ONE-ONE.
WHERE'S UNITED ONE-SEVENTY-FIVE?
NORAD ARE TRACKING IT OVER CAPE COD, SIR. ARCHER LEADER'S CLOSEST.
OH, SHIT, DO YOU THINK THAT'S THE LAST ONE? THE NEWARK FLIGHT DIDN'T EVEN TAKE OFF, WE'RE F--
FOR GOD'S SAKE, SHUT UP--!
UNNHH

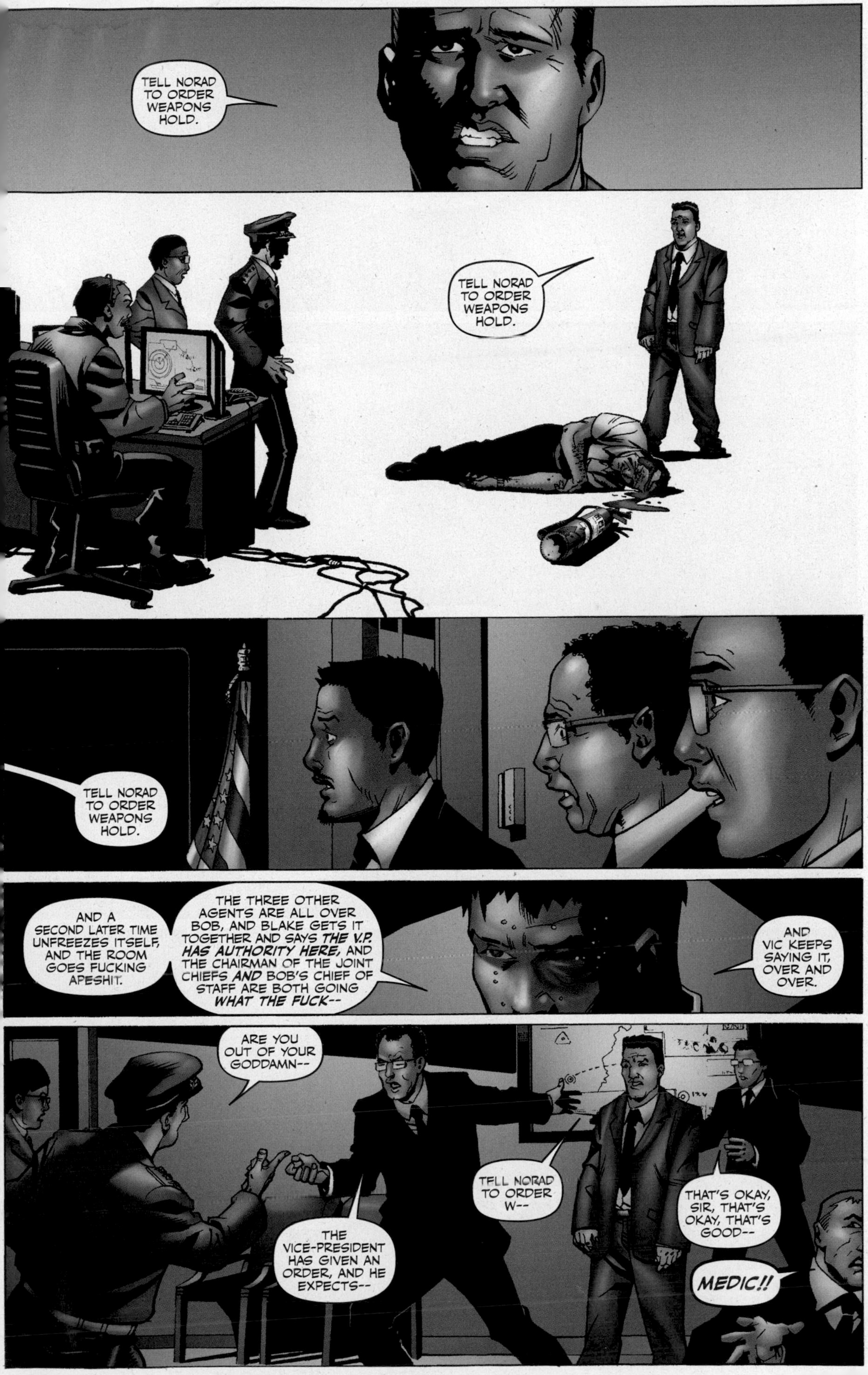
TELL NORAD TO ORDER WEAPONS HOLD.
TELL NORAD TO ORDER WEAPONS HOLD.
TELL NORAD TO ORDER WEAPONS HOLD.
AND A SECOND LATER TIME UNFREEZES ITSELF, AND THE ROOM GOES FUCKING APESHIT.
THE THREE OTHER AGENTS ARE ALL OVER BOB, AND BLAKE GETS IT TOGETHER AND SAYS *THE V.P. HAS AUTHORITY HERE,* AND THE CHAIRMAN OF THE JOINT CHIEFS *AND* BOB'S CHIEF OF STAFF ARE BOTH GOING *WHAT THE FUCK--*
AND VIC KEEPS SAYING IT, OVER AND OVER.
ARE YOU OUT OF YOUR GODDAMN--
THE VICE-PRESIDENT HAS GIVEN AN ORDER, AND HE EXPECTS--
TELL NORAD TO ORDER W--
THAT'S OKAY, SIR, THAT'S OKAY, THAT'S GOOD--
MEDIC!!

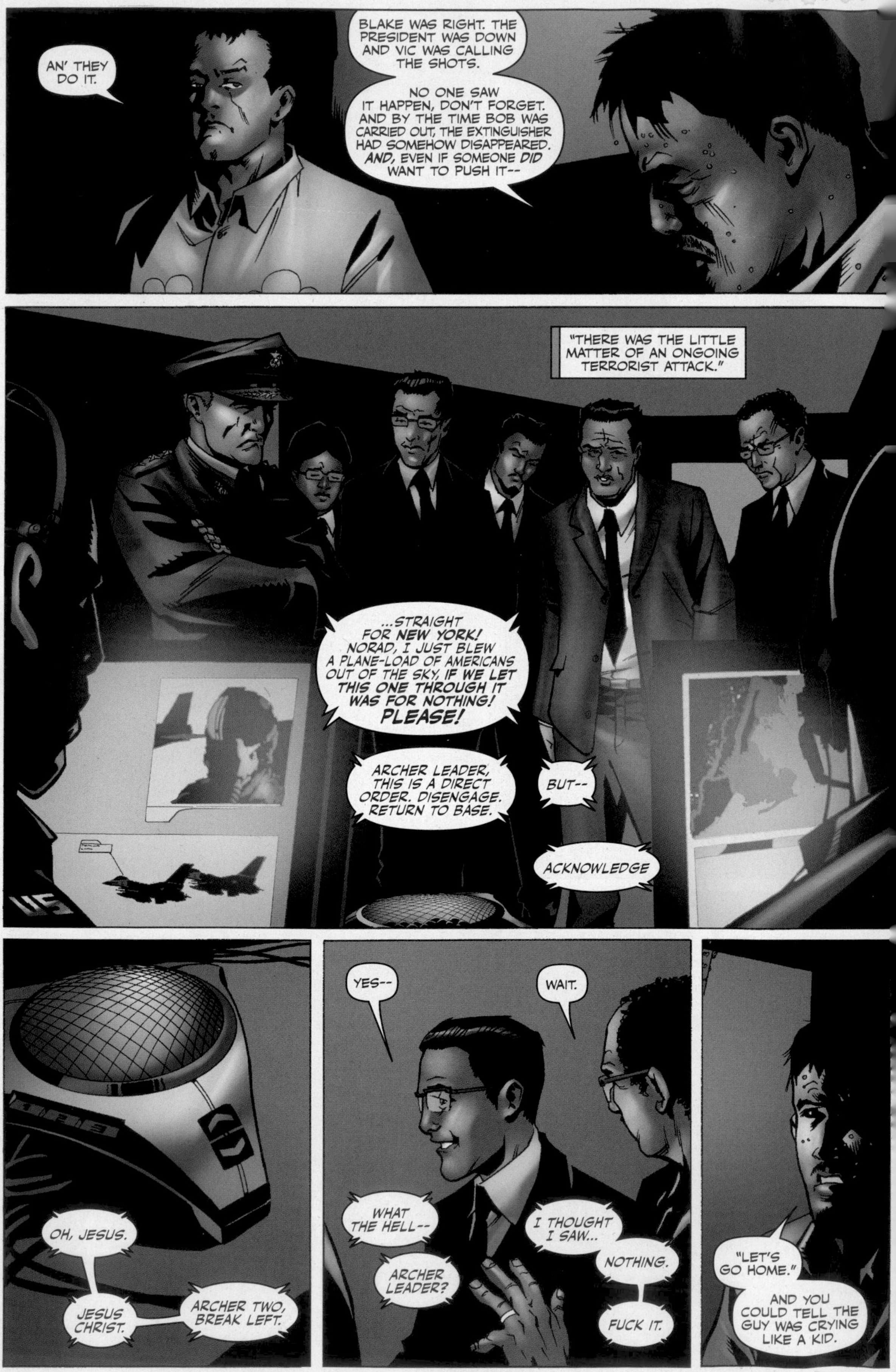
AN' THEY DO IT.
BLAKE WAS RIGHT. THE PRESIDENT WAS DOWN AND VIC WAS CALLING THE SHOTS.
NO ONE SAW IT HAPPEN, DON'T FORGET. AND BY THE TIME BOB WAS CARRIED OUT, THE EXTINGUISHER HAD SOMEHOW DISAPPEARED. AND, EVEN IF SOMEONE DID WANT TO PUSH IT--
"THERE WAS THE LITTLE MATTER OF AN ONGOING TERRORIST ATTACK."
...STRAIGHT FOR NEW YORK! NORAD, I JUST BLEW A PLANE-LOAD OF AMERICANS OUT OF THE SKY, IF WE LET THIS ONE THROUGH IT WAS FOR NOTHING! PLEASE!
ARCHER LEADER, THIS IS A DIRECT ORDER. DISENGAGE. RETURN TO BASE.
BUT--
ACKNOWLEDGE
OH, JESUS.
JESUS CHRIST.
ARCHER TWO, BREAK LEFT.
YES--
WAIT.
WHAT THE HELL--
ARCHER LEADER?
I THOUGHT I SAW...
NOTHING.
FUCK IT.
"LET'S GO HOME."
AND YOU COULD TELL THE GUY WAS CRYING LIKE A KID.

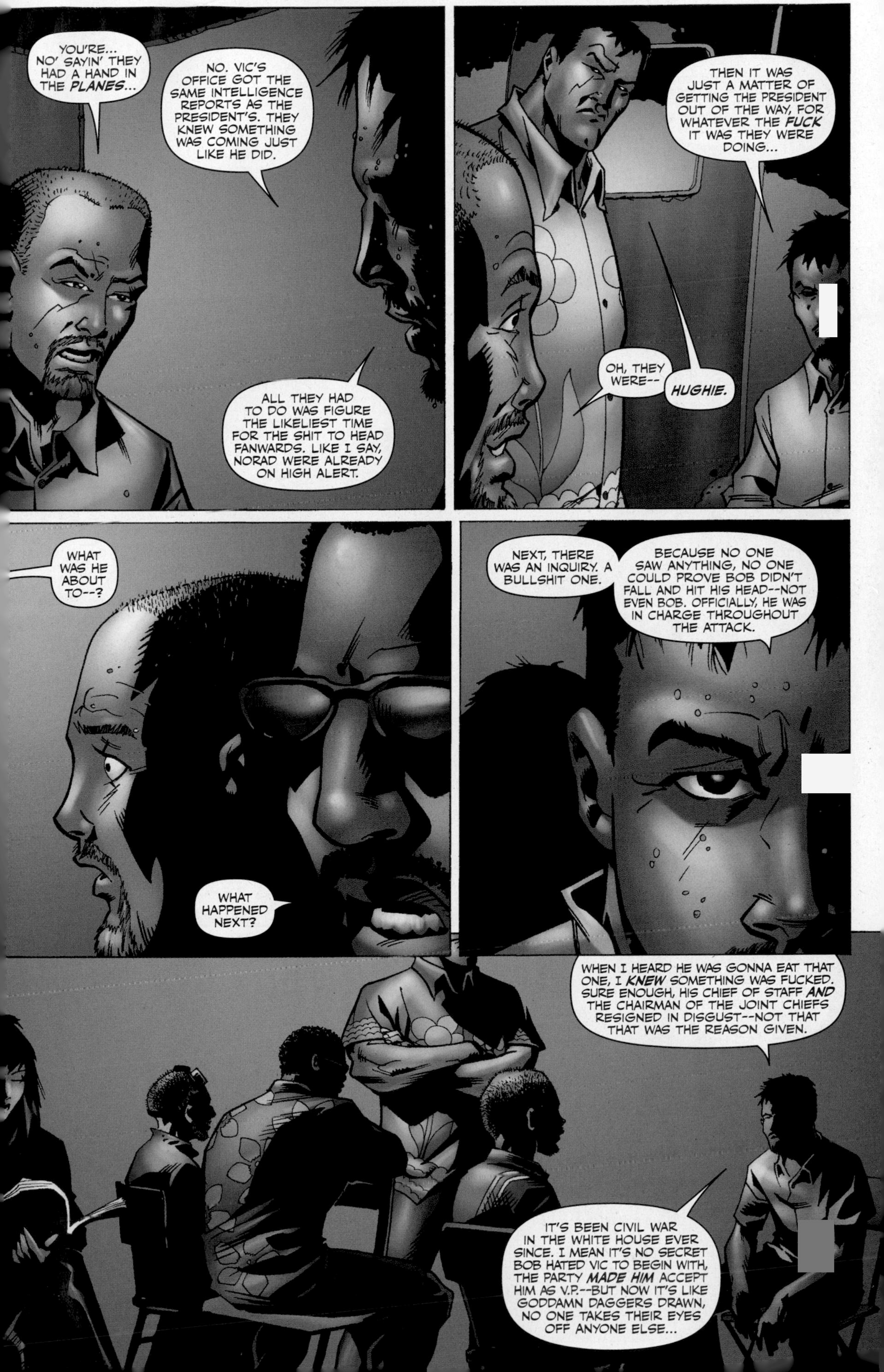
YOU'RE... NO' SAYIN' THEY HAD A HAND IN THE PLANES...
NO. VIC'S OFFICE GOT THE SAME INTELLIGENCE REPORTS AS THE PRESIDENT'S. THEY KNEW SOMETHING WAS COMING JUST LIKE HE DID.
ALL THEY HAD TO DO WAS FIGURE THE LIKELIEST TIME FOR THE SHIT TO HEAD FANWARDS. LIKE I SAY, NORAD WERE ALREADY ON HIGH ALERT.
THEN IT WAS JUST A MATTER OF GETTING THE PRESIDENT OUT OF THE WAY, FOR WHATEVER THE FUCK IT WAS THEY WERE DOING...
OH, THEY WERE--
HUGHIE.
WHAT WAS HE ABOUT TO--?
WHAT HAPPENED NEXT?
NEXT, THERE WAS AN INQUIRY. A BULLSHIT ONE.
BECAUSE NO ONE SAW ANYTHING, NO ONE COULD PROVE BOB DIDN'T FALL AND HIT HIS HEAD--NOT EVEN BOB. OFFICIALLY, HE WAS IN CHARGE THROUGHOUT THE ATTACK.
WHEN I HEARD HE WAS GONNA EAT THAT ONE, I KNEW SOMETHING WAS FUCKED. SURE ENOUGH, HIS CHIEF OF STAFF AND THE CHAIRMAN OF THE JOINT CHIEFS RESIGNED IN DISGUST--NOT THAT THAT WAS THE REASON GIVEN.
IT'S BEEN CIVIL WAR IN THE WHITE HOUSE EVER SINCE. I MEAN IT'S NO SECRET BOB HATED VIC TO BEGIN WITH, THE PARTY MADE HIM ACCEPT HIM AS V.P.--BUT NOW IT'S LIKE GODDAMN DAGGERS DRAWN, NO ONE TAKES THEIR EYES OFF ANYONE ELSE...

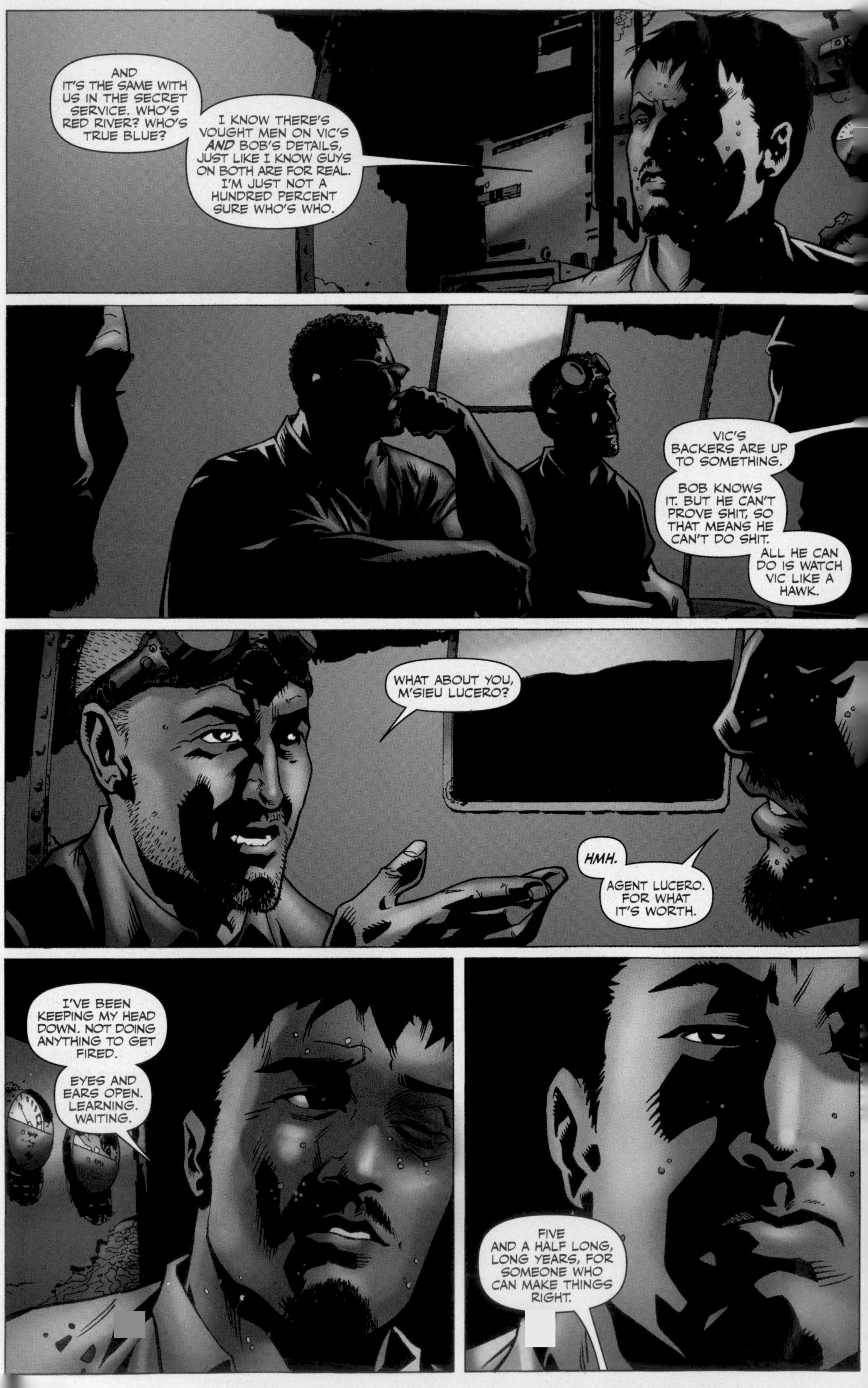
AND IT'S THE SAME WITH US IN THE SECRET SERVICE. WHO'S RED RIVER? WHO'S TRUE BLUE?
I KNOW THERE'S VOUGHT MEN ON VIC'S AND BOB'S DETAILS, JUST LIKE I KNOW GUYS ON BOTH ARE FOR REAL. I'M JUST NOT A HUNDRED PERCENT SURE WHO'S WHO.
VIC'S BACKERS ARE UP TO SOMETHING.
BOB KNOWS IT. BUT HE CAN'T PROVE SHIT, SO THAT MEANS HE CAN'T DO SHIT.
ALL HE CAN DO IS WATCH VIC LIKE A HAWK.
WHAT ABOUT YOU, M'SIEU LUCERO?
HMH.
AGENT LUCERO. FOR WHAT IT'S WORTH.
I'VE BEEN KEEPING MY HEAD DOWN. NOT DOING ANYTHING TO GET FIRED.
EYES AND EARS OPEN. LEARNING. WAITING.
FIVE AND A HALF LONG, LONG YEARS, FOR SOMEONE WHO CAN MAKE THINGS RIGHT.

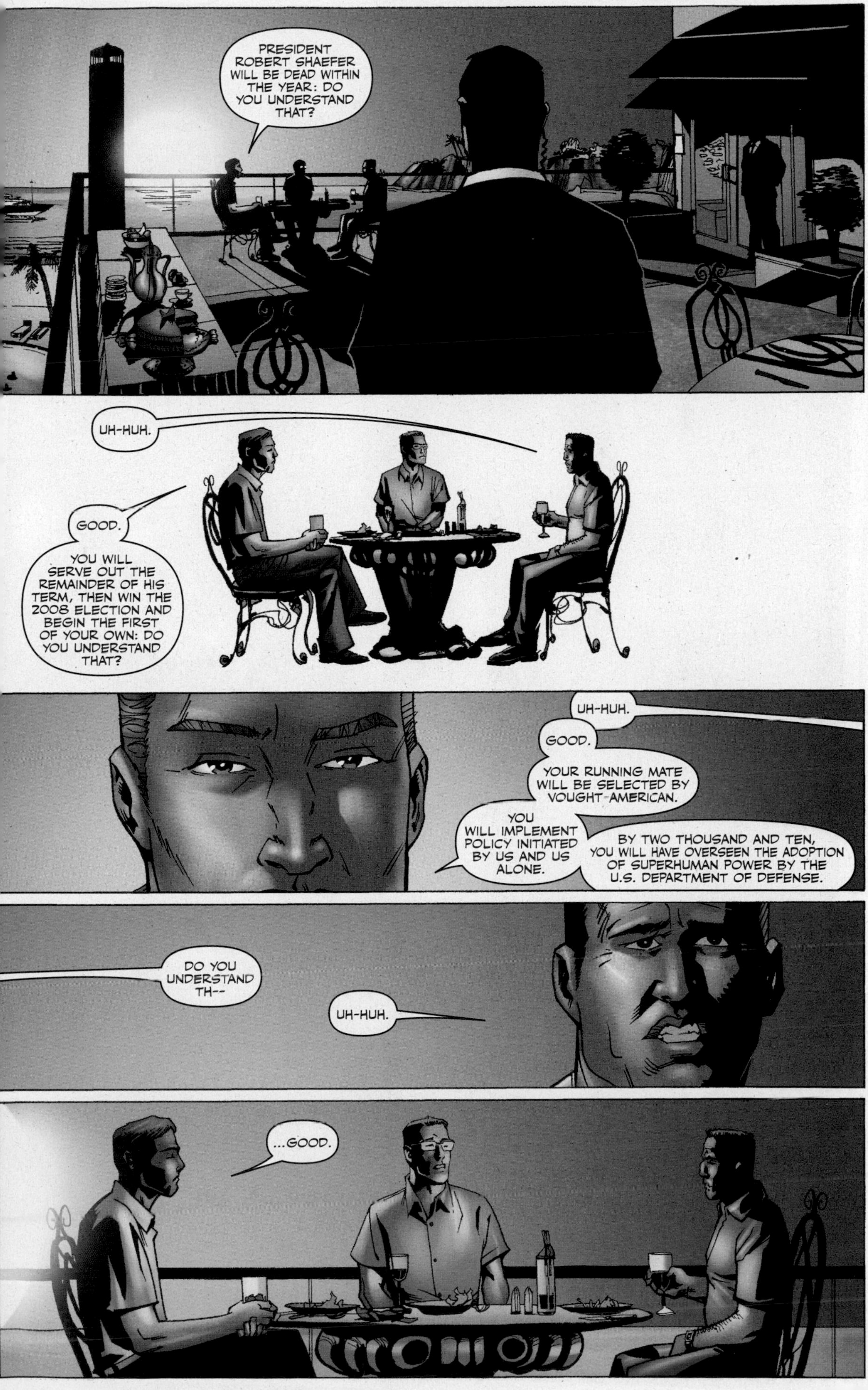
PRESIDENT ROBERT SHAEFER WILL BE DEAD WITHIN THE YEAR: DO YOU UNDERSTAND THAT?
UH-HUH.
GOOD.
YOU WILL SERVE OUT THE REMAINDER OF HIS TERM, THEN WIN THE 2008 ELECTION AND BEGIN THE FIRST OF YOUR OWN: DO YOU UNDERSTAND THAT?
UH-HUH.
GOOD.
YOUR RUNNING MATE WILL BE SELECTED BY VOUGHT-AMERICAN.
YOU WILL IMPLEMENT POLICY INITIATED BY US AND US ALONE.
BY TWO THOUSAND AND TEN, YOU WILL HAVE OVERSEEN THE ADOPTION OF SUPERHUMAN POWER BY THE U.S. DEPARTMENT OF DEFENSE.
DO YOU UNDERSTAND TH--
UH-HUH.
...GOOD.

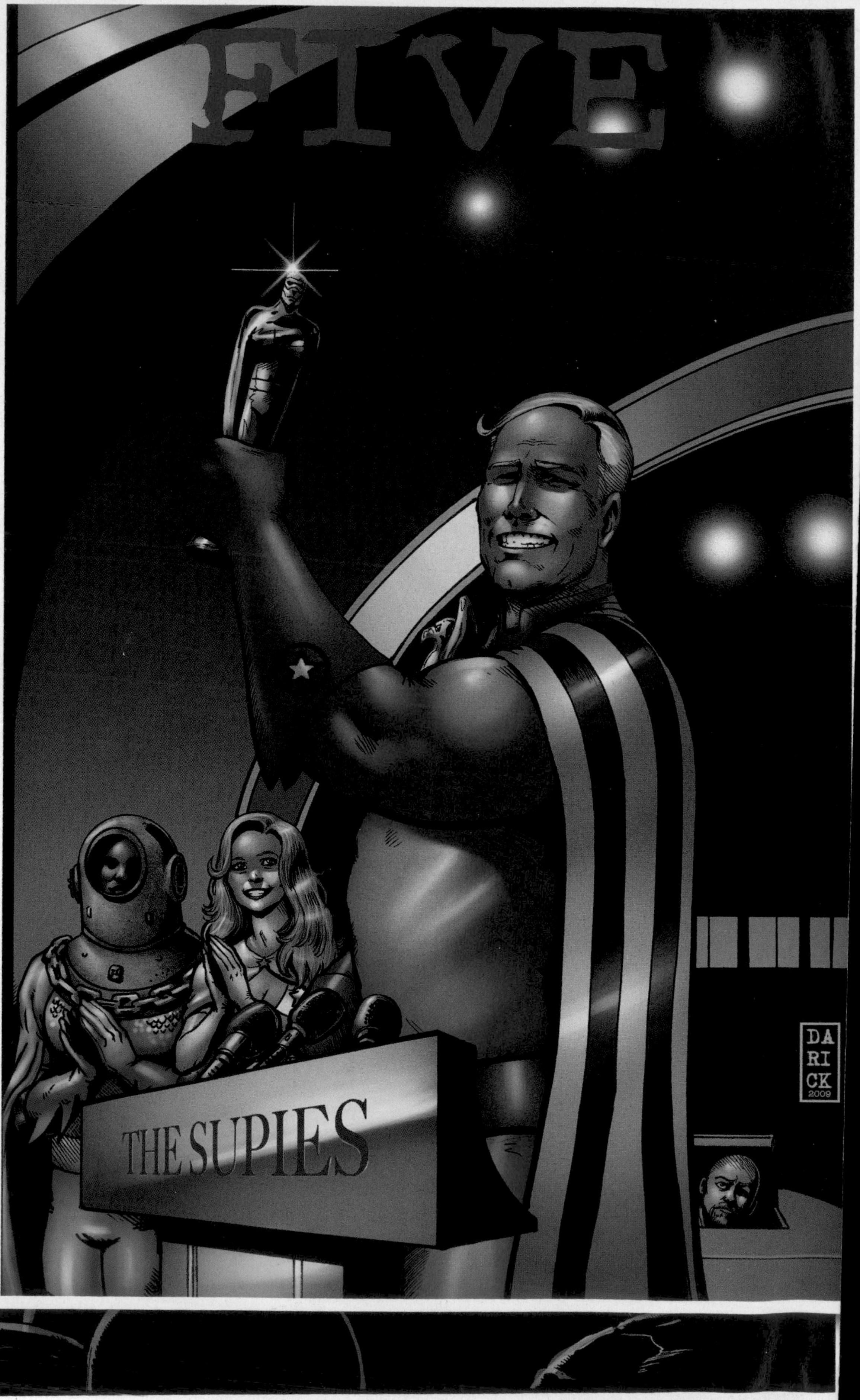
FIVE
THE SUPIES
DA
RI
CK
2009

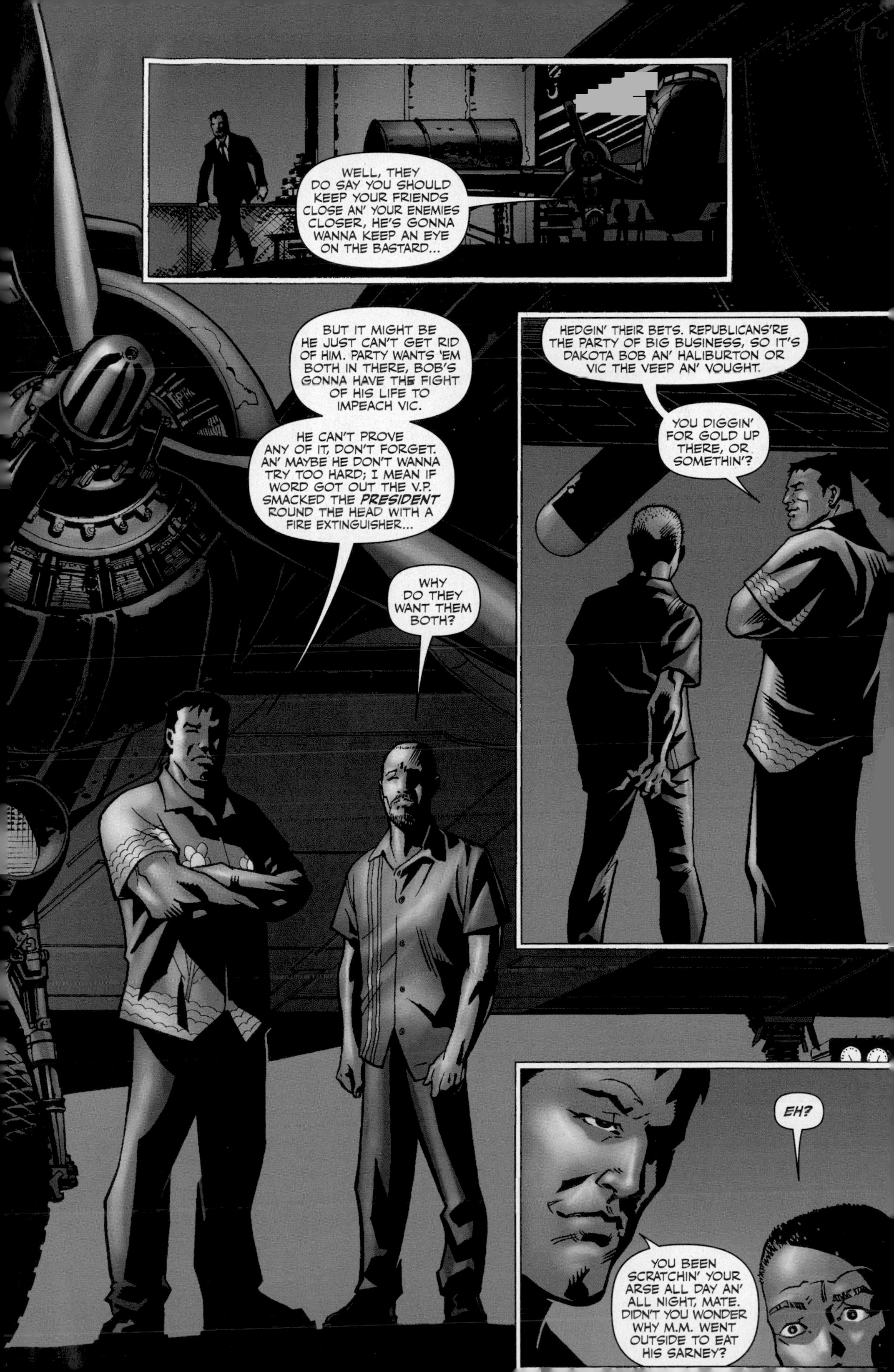
WELL, THEY DO SAY YOU SHOULD KEEP YOUR FRIENDS CLOSE AN' YOUR ENEMIES CLOSER, HE'S GONNA WANNA KEEP AN EYE ON THE BASTARD...
BUT IT MIGHT BE HE JUST CAN'T GET RID OF HIM. PARTY WANTS 'EM BOTH IN THERE, BOB'S GONNA HAVE THE FIGHT OF HIS LIFE TO IMPEACH VIC.
HE CAN'T PROVE ANY OF IT, DON'T FORGET. AN' MAYBE HE DON'T WANNA TRY TOO HARD; I MEAN IF WORD GOT OUT THE V.P. SMACKED THE *PRESIDENT* ROUND THE HEAD WITH A FIRE EXTINGUISHER...
WHY DO THEY WANT THEM BOTH?
HEDGIN' THEIR BETS. REPUBLICANS'RE THE PARTY OF BIG BUSINESS, SO IT'S DAKOTA BOB AN' HALIBURTON OR VIC THE VEEP AN' VOUGHT.
YOU DIGGIN' FOR GOLD UP THERE, OR SOMETHIN'?
EH?
YOU BEEN SCRATCHIN' YOUR ARSE ALL DAY AN' ALL NIGHT, MATE. DIDN'T YOU WONDER WHY M.M. WENT OUTSIDE TO EAT HIS SARNEY?

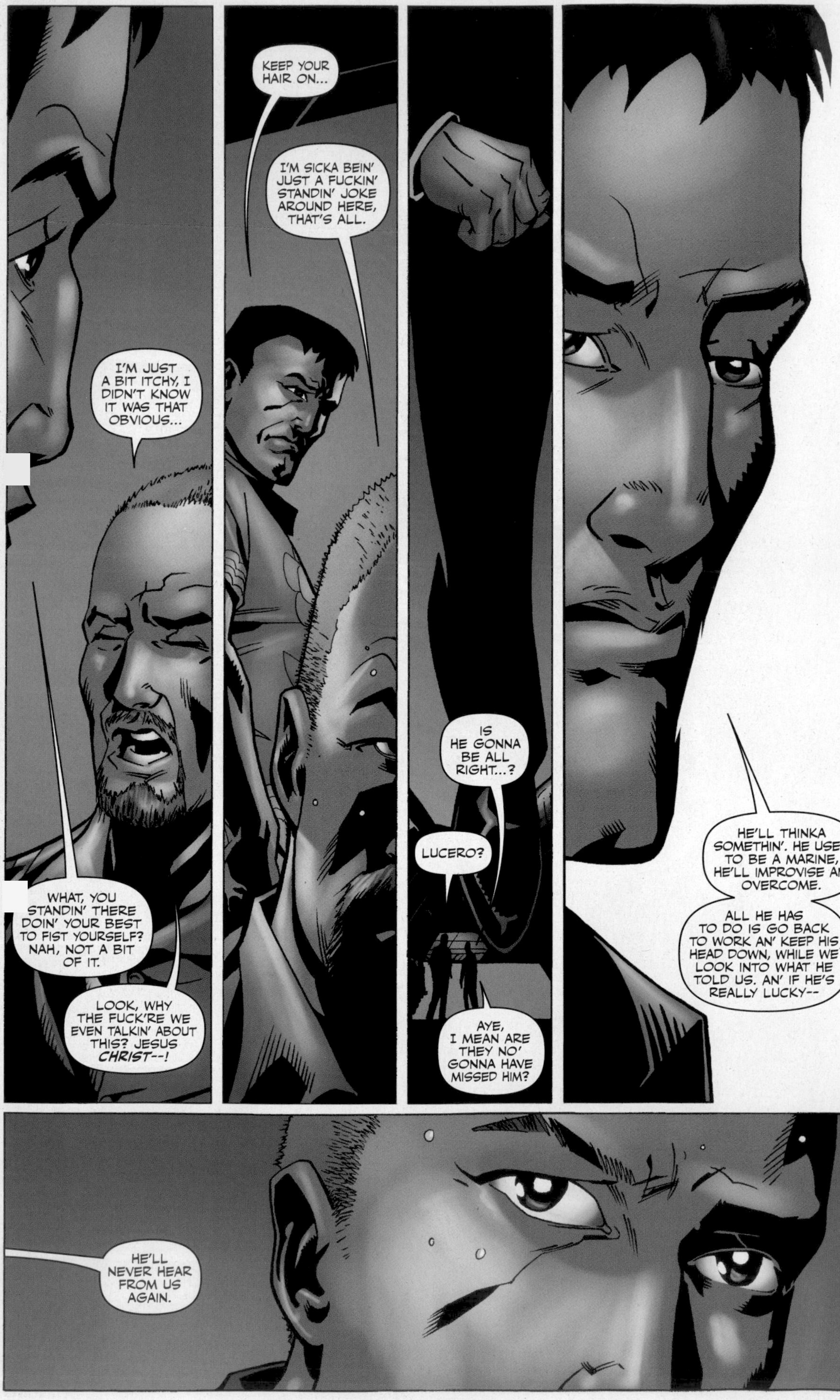
KEEP YOUR HAIR ON...
I'M SICKA BEIN' JUST A FUCKIN' STANDIN' JOKE AROUND HERE, THAT'S ALL.
I'M JUST A BIT ITCHY, I DIDN'T KNOW IT WAS THAT OBVIOUS...
WHAT, YOU STANDIN' THERE DOIN' YOUR BEST TO FIST YOURSELF? NAH, NOT A BIT OF IT.
LOOK, WHY THE FUCK'RE WE EVEN TALKIN' ABOUT THIS? JESUS *CHRIST*--!
IS HE GONNA BE ALL RIGHT...?
LUCERO?
AYE, I MEAN ARE THEY NO' GONNA HAVE MISSED HIM?
HE'LL THINKA SOMETHIN'. HE USED TO BE A MARINE, HE'LL IMPROVISE AN' OVERCOME.
ALL HE HAS TO DO IS GO BACK TO WORK AN' KEEP HIS HEAD DOWN, WHILE WE LOOK INTO WHAT HE TOLD US. AN' IF HE'S REALLY LUCKY--
HE'LL NEVER HEAR FROM US AGAIN.

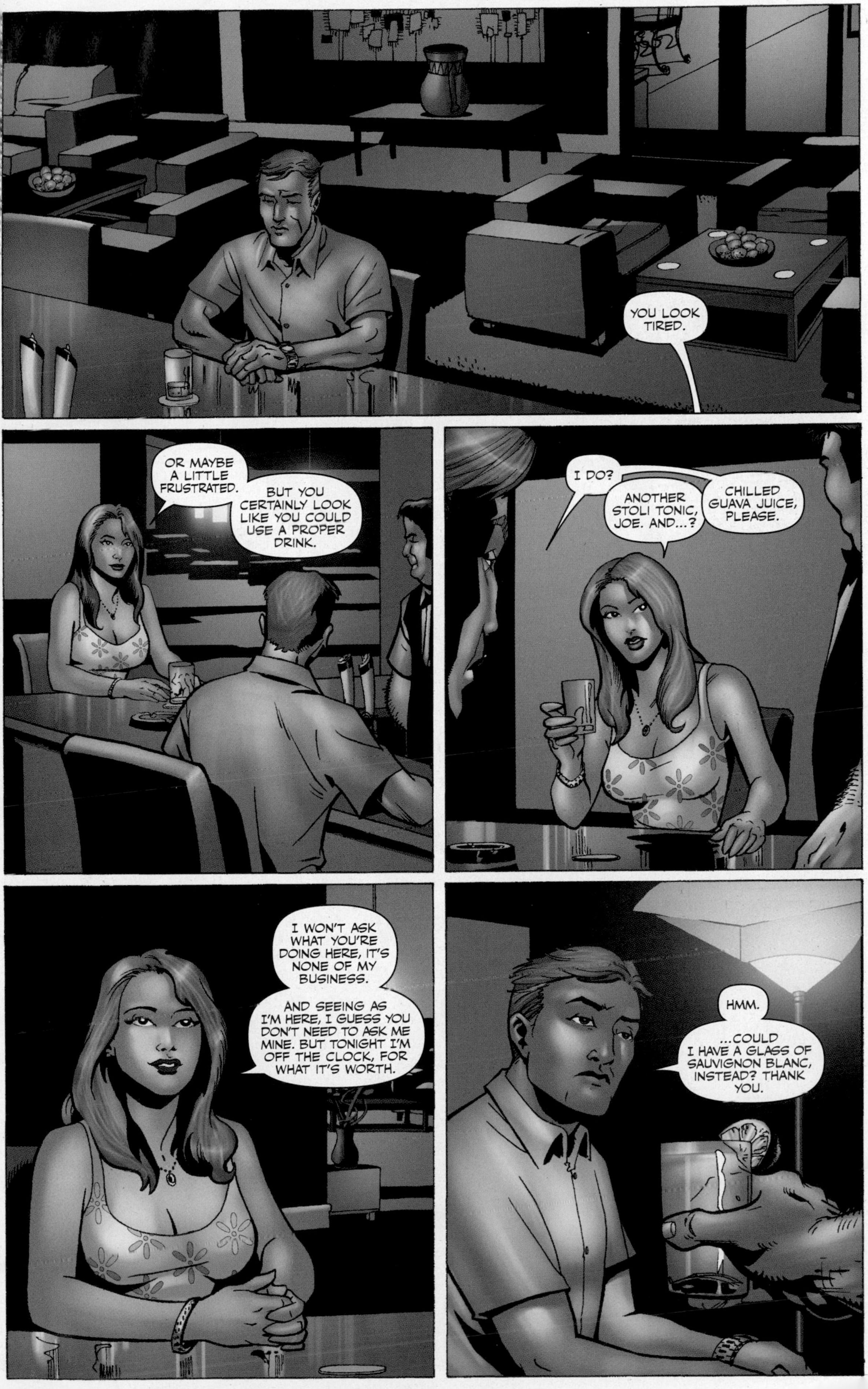
YOU LOOK TIRED.
OR MAYBE A LITTLE FRUSTRATED.
BUT YOU CERTAINLY LOOK LIKE YOU COULD USE A PROPER DRINK.
I DO?
ANOTHER STOLI TONIC, JOE. AND...?
CHILLED GUAVA JUICE, PLEASE.
I WON'T ASK WHAT YOU'RE DOING HERE, IT'S NONE OF MY BUSINESS.
AND SEEING AS I'M HERE, I GUESS YOU DON'T NEED TO ASK ME MINE. BUT TONIGHT I'M OFF THE CLOCK, FOR WHAT IT'S WORTH.
HMM.
...COULD I HAVE A GLASS OF SAUVIGNON BLANC, INSTEAD? THANK YOU.

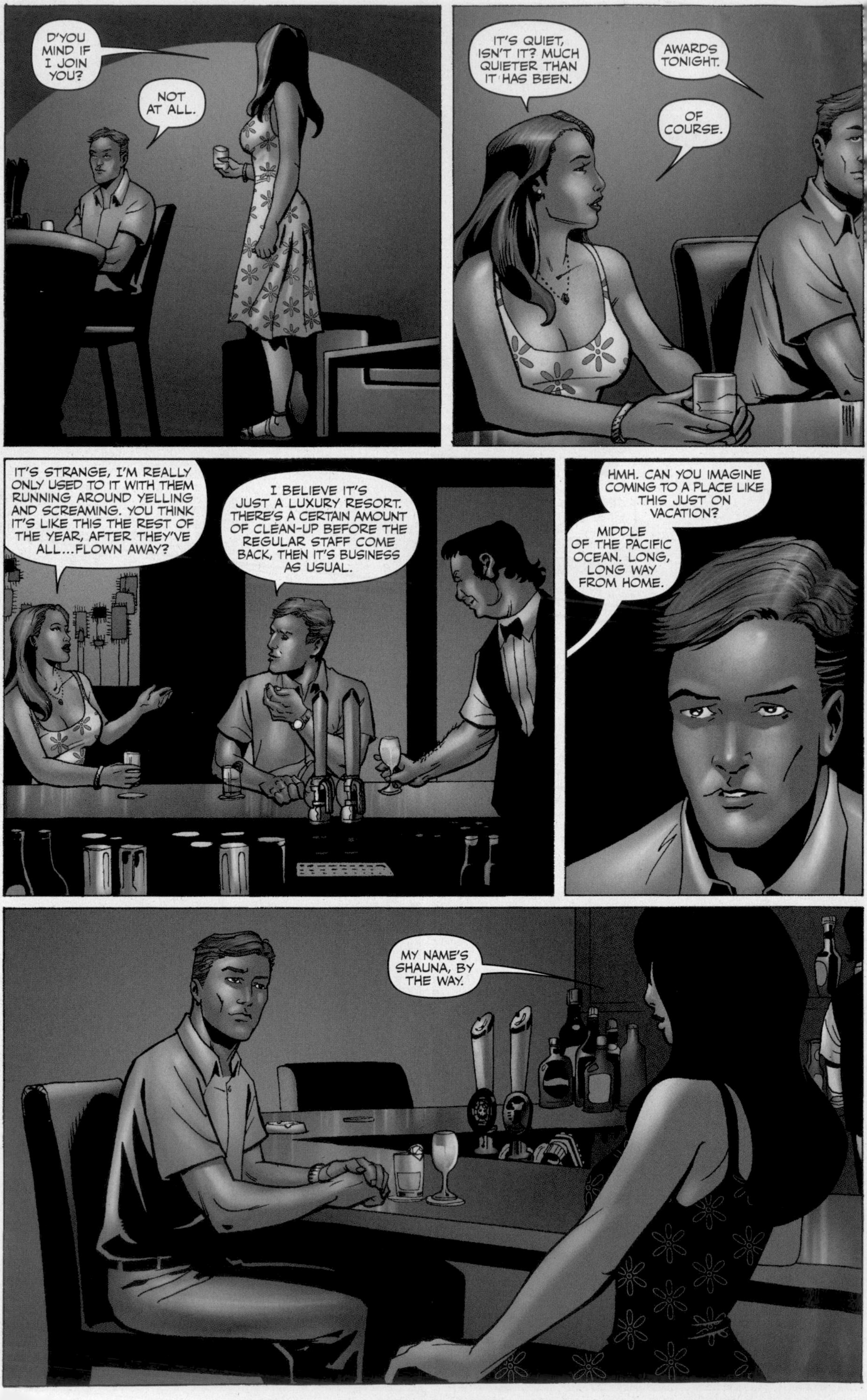
D'YOU MIND IF I JOIN YOU?
NOT AT ALL.
IT'S QUIET, ISN'T IT? MUCH QUIETER THAN IT HAS BEEN.
AWARDS TONIGHT.
OF COURSE.
IT'S STRANGE, I'M REALLY ONLY USED TO IT WITH THEM RUNNING AROUND YELLING AND SCREAMING. YOU THINK IT'S LIKE THIS THE REST OF THE YEAR, AFTER THEY'VE ALL...FLOWN AWAY?
I BELIEVE IT'S JUST A LUXURY RESORT. THERE'S A CERTAIN AMOUNT OF CLEAN-UP BEFORE THE REGULAR STAFF COME BACK, THEN IT'S BUSINESS AS USUAL.
HMH. CAN YOU IMAGINE COMING TO A PLACE LIKE THIS JUST ON VACATION?
MIDDLE OF THE PACIFIC OCEAN. LONG, LONG WAY FROM HOME.
MY NAME'S SHAUNA, BY THE WAY.

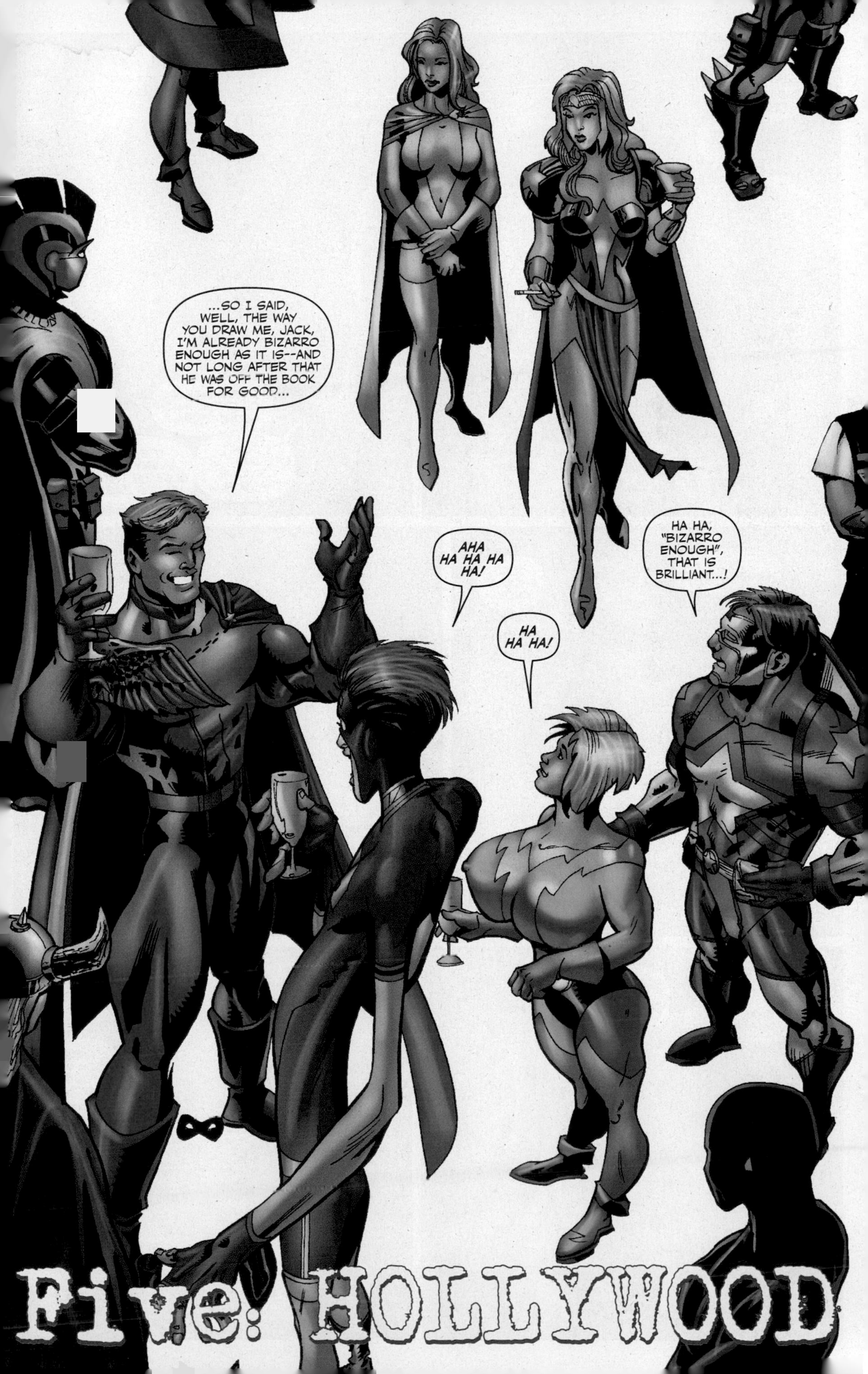
...SO I SAID, WELL, THE WAY YOU DRAW ME, JACK, I'M ALREADY BIZARRO ENOUGH AS IT IS--AND NOT LONG AFTER THAT HE WAS OFF THE BOOK FOR GOOD...
AHA HA HA HA HA!
HA HA HA!
HA HA, "BIZARRO ENOUGH", THAT IS BRILLIANT...!
Five: HOLLYWOOD

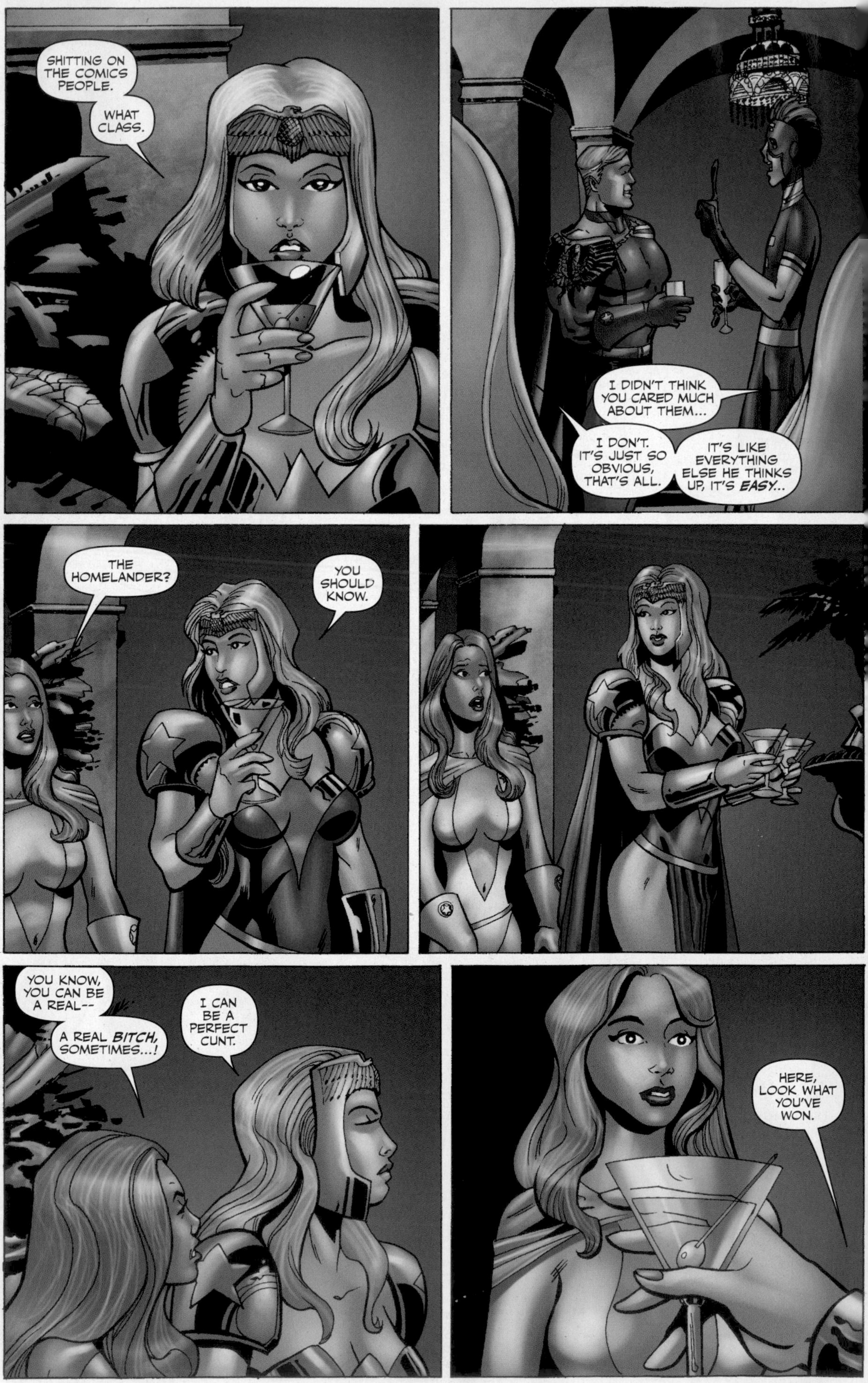
SHITTING ON THE COMICS PEOPLE.
WHAT CLASS.
I DIDN'T THINK YOU CARED MUCH ABOUT THEM...
I DON'T. IT'S JUST SO OBVIOUS, THAT'S ALL.
IT'S LIKE EVERYTHING ELSE HE THINKS UP, IT'S *EASY*...
THE HOMELANDER?
YOU SHOULD KNOW.
YOU KNOW, YOU CAN BE A REAL--
A REAL *BITCH*, SOMETIMES...!
I CAN BE A PERFECT CUNT.
HERE, LOOK WHAT YOU'VE WON.

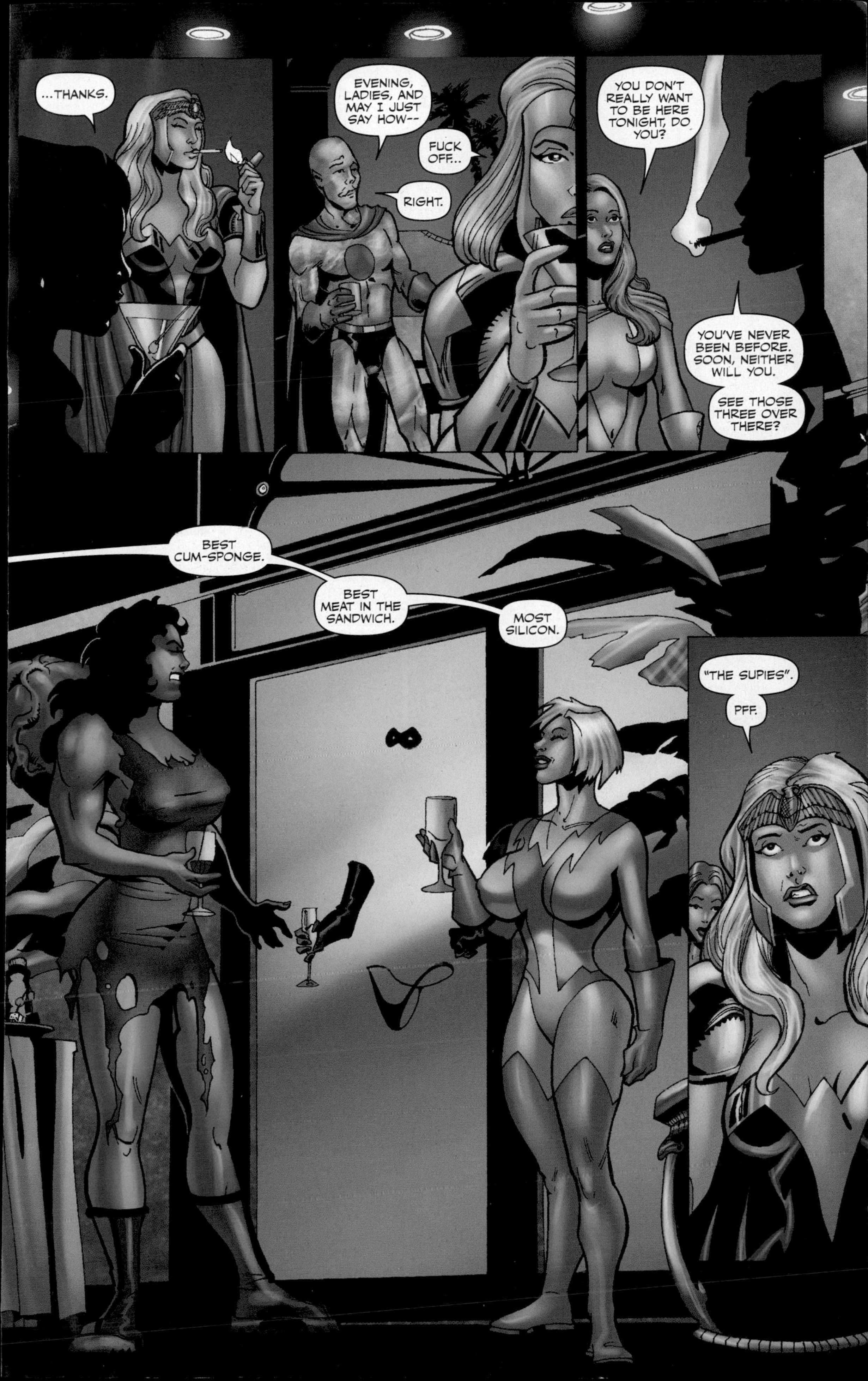
...THANKS.
EVENING, LADIES, AND MAY I JUST SAY HOW--
FUCK OFF...
RIGHT.
YOU DON'T REALLY WANT TO BE HERE TONIGHT, DO YOU?
YOU'VE NEVER BEEN BEFORE. SOON, NEITHER WILL YOU.
SEE THOSE THREE OVER THERE?
BEST CUM-SPONGE.
BEST MEAT IN THE SANDWICH.
MOST SILICON.
"THE SUPIES".
PFF.

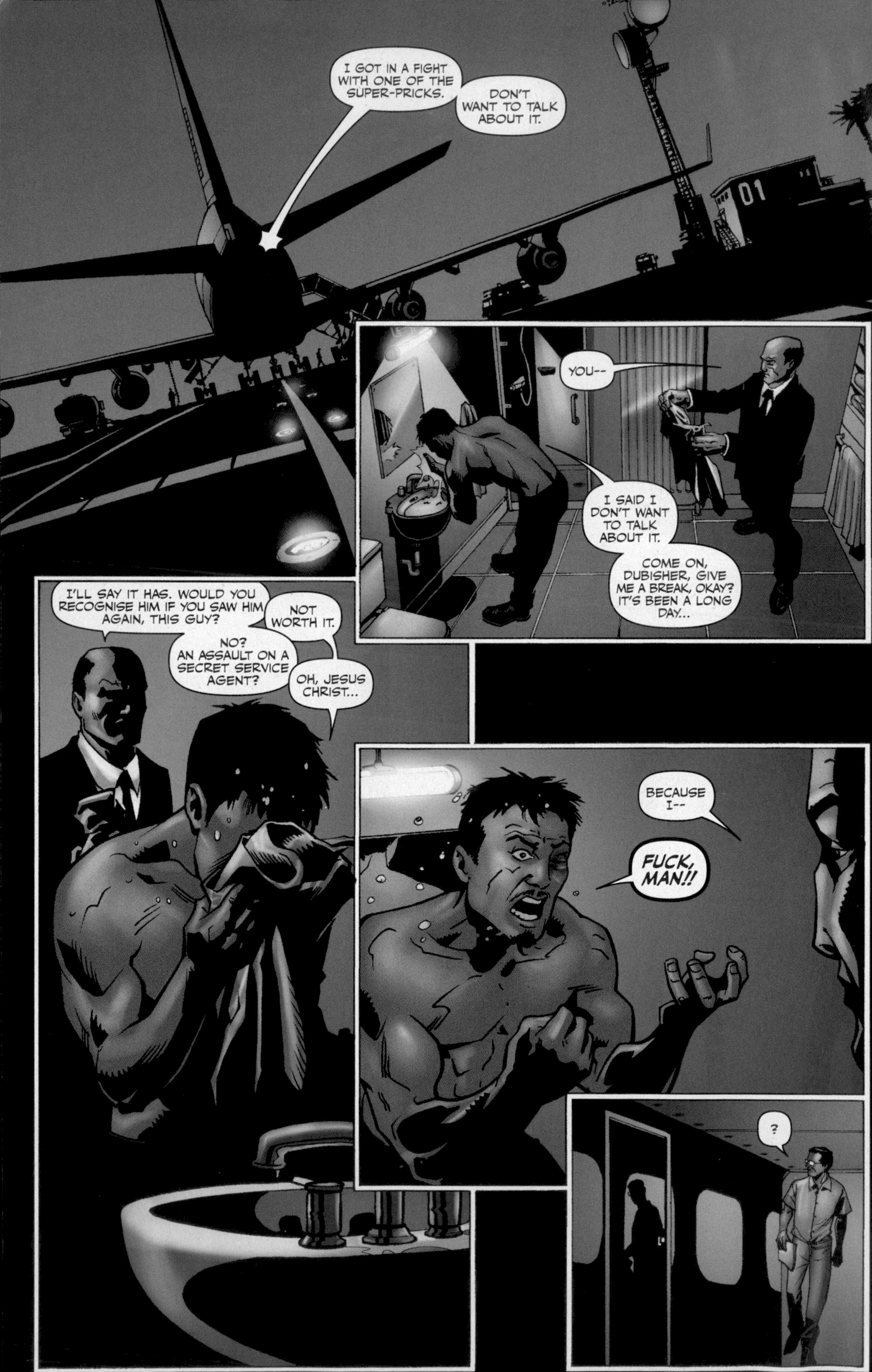
I GOT IN A FIGHT WITH ONE OF THE SUPER-PRICKS.
DON'T WANT TO TALK ABOUT IT.
YOU--
I SAID I DON'T WANT TO TALK ABOUT IT.
COME ON, DUBISHER, GIVE ME A BREAK, OKAY? IT'S BEEN A LONG DAY...
I'LL SAY IT HAS. WOULD YOU RECOGNISE HIM IF YOU SAW HIM AGAIN, THIS GUY?
NOT WORTH IT.
NO? AN ASSAULT ON A SECRET SERVICE AGENT?
OH, JESUS CHRIST...
BECAUSE I--
FUCK, MAN!!
?

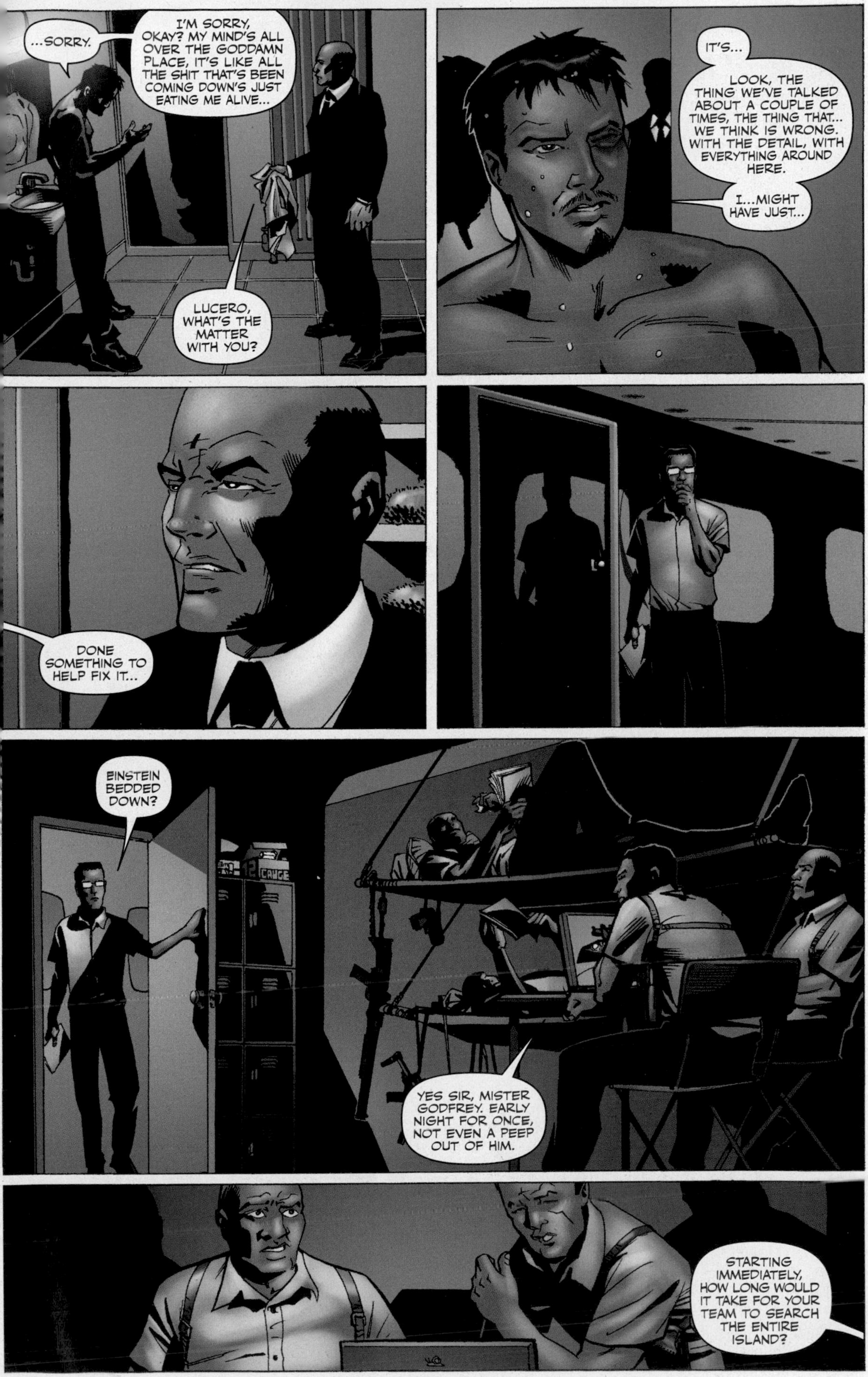
...SORRY.
I'M SORRY, OKAY? MY MIND'S ALL OVER THE GODDAMN PLACE, IT'S LIKE ALL THE SHIT THAT'S BEEN COMING DOWN'S JUST EATING ME ALIVE...
LUCERO, WHAT'S THE MATTER WITH YOU?
IT'S...
LOOK, THE THING WE'VE TALKED ABOUT A COUPLE OF TIMES, THE THING THAT... WE THINK IS WRONG. WITH THE DETAIL, WITH EVERYTHING AROUND HERE.
I...MIGHT HAVE JUST...
DONE SOMETHING TO HELP FIX IT...
EINSTEIN BEDDED DOWN?
YES SIR, MISTER GODFREY. EARLY NIGHT FOR ONCE, NOT EVEN A PEEP OUT OF HIM.
STARTING IMMEDIATELY, HOW LONG WOULD IT TAKE FOR YOUR TEAM TO SEARCH THE ENTIRE ISLAND?

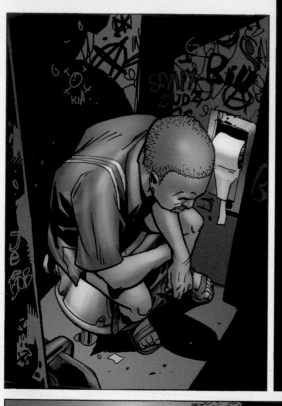

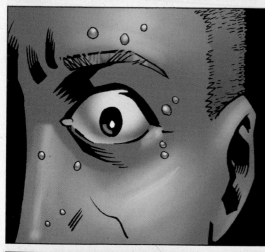

WHY'S HE NO' TOLD THEM ABOUT US?

AN' WHY--

WHY...

AND THE AWARD FOR *BEST NEW TEAM* GOES TO...*ELEMENT FORCE.*

ELEMENT FORCE HAIL FROM *DENVER, COLORADO,* AND CONSIST OF *FLAMEBURNER, THE DIVOT, FREEFLOW* AND TEAM LEADER *AIRHORN.*

HONNNNNK

TOLD YOU.

THERE'S A *FEELS MORE LIKE A BEGINNING* WAITING TO HAPPEN, IF EVER I SAW ONE.

HUH?

THING FROM THE COMIC BOOKS.

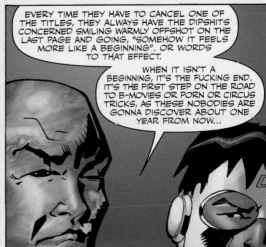

EVERY TIME THEY HAVE TO CANCEL ONE OF THE TITLES, THEY ALWAYS HAVE THE DIPSHITS CONCERNED SMILING WARMLY OFFSHOT ON THE LAST PAGE AND GOING, "SOMEHOW IT FEELS MORE LIKE A BEGINNING". OR WORDS TO THAT EFFECT.

WHEN IT ISN'T A BEGINNING, IT'S THE FUCKING END. IT'S THE FIRST STEP ON THE ROAD TO B-MOVIES OR PORN OR CIRCUS TRICKS, AS THESE NOBODIES ARE GONNA DISCOVER ABOUT ONE YEAR FROM NOW...

AND NOW, TO PRESENT THE AWARD IN THE VERY SPECIAL CATEGORY OF LIFETIME ACHIEVEMENT, PLEASE WELCOME... STARLIGHT.
AND WHOSE IDEA WAS IT TO MAKE THE DEEP M.C.? I MEAN FUCKING LOOK AT HIM UP THERE...!
UM... THANK YOU, DEEP.
YES.
THIS YEAR, THE, THE AWARD FOR LIFETIME ACHIEVEMENT GOES TO, UM...
UNCLE DREAMS.
WHY'S SHE...
LAST MINUTE REPLACEMENT FOR INVISI-LASS. SILLY BITCH FORGOT THE TAMPONS.
OH, WOULD YOU LOOK AT THIS, FOR CHRIST'S SAKE?
HHHHH
HHHHH
AHH-HHHHH

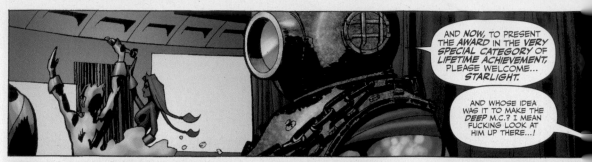

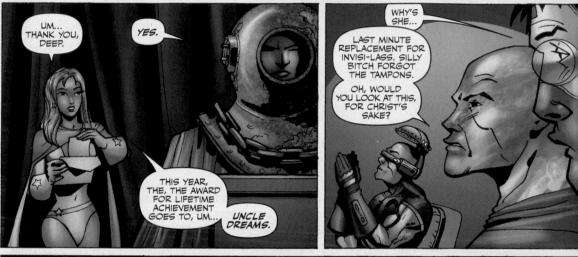

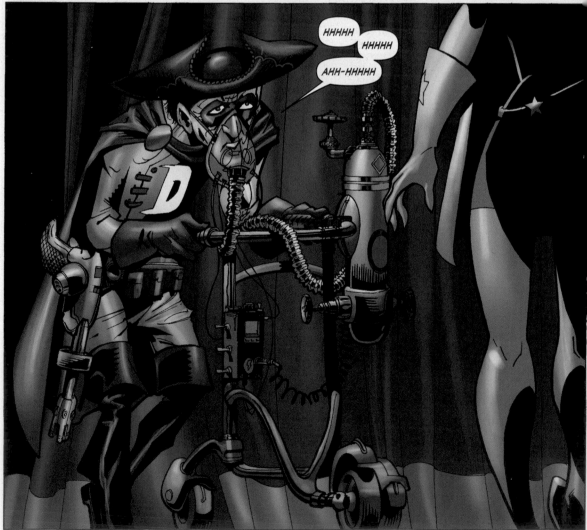

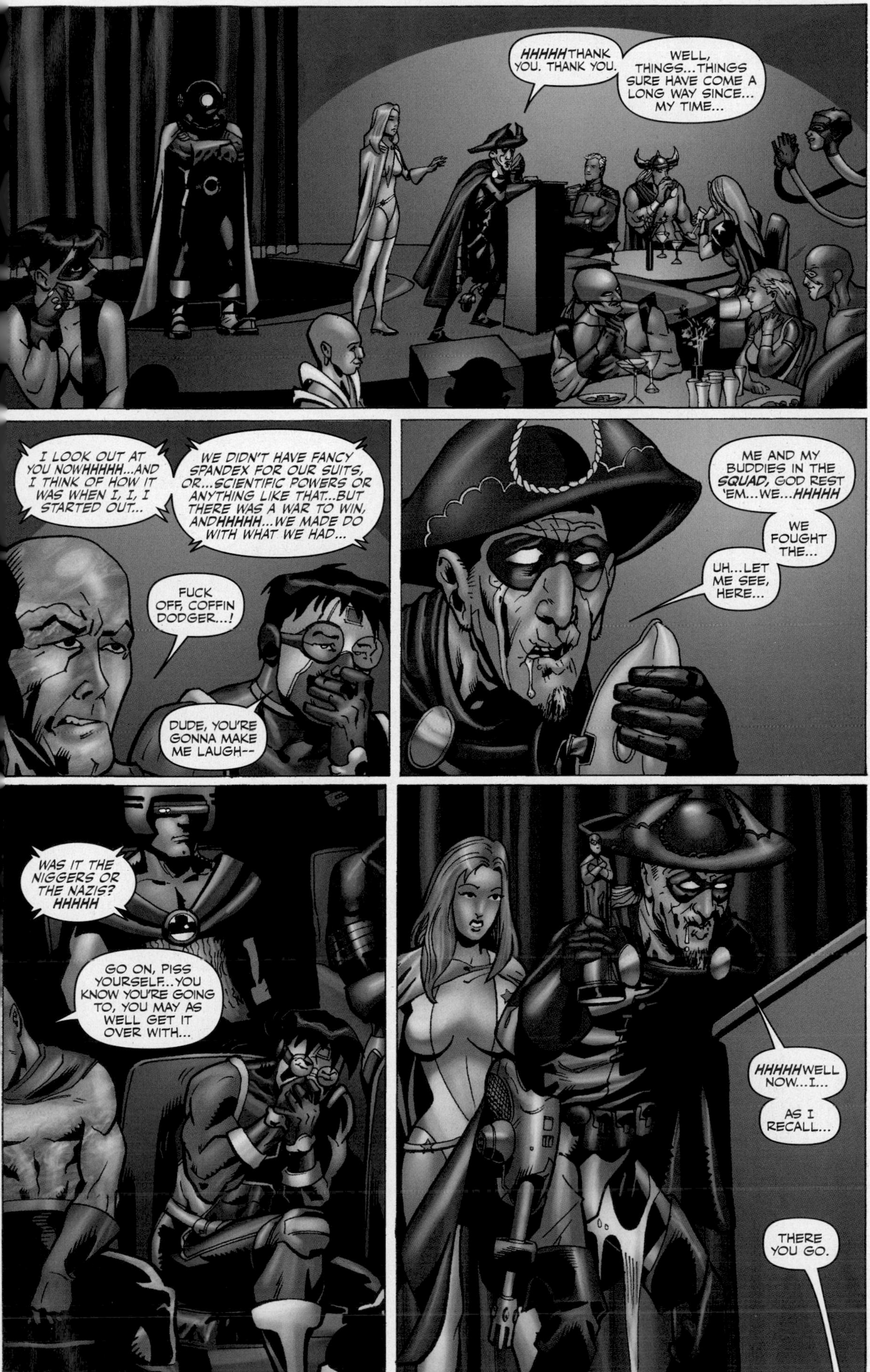
HHHHH THANK YOU. THANK YOU.
WELL, THINGS...THINGS SURE HAVE COME A LONG WAY SINCE... MY TIME...
I LOOK OUT AT YOU NOWHHHHH...AND I THINK OF HOW IT WAS WHEN I, I, I STARTED OUT...
WE DIDN'T HAVE FANCY SPANDEX FOR OUR SUITS, OR...SCIENTIFIC POWERS OR ANYTHING LIKE THAT...BUT THERE WAS A WAR TO WIN, ANDHHHHH...WE MADE DO WITH WHAT WE HAD...
FUCK OFF, COFFIN DODGER...!
DUDE, YOU'RE GONNA MAKE ME LAUGH--
ME AND MY BUDDIES IN THE SQUAD, GOD REST 'EM...WE...HHHHH
WE FOUGHT THE...
UH...LET ME SEE, HERE...
WAS IT THE NIGGERS OR THE NAZIS? HHHHH
GO ON, PISS YOURSELF...YOU KNOW YOU'RE GOING TO, YOU MAY AS WELL GET IT OVER WITH...
HHHHH WELL NOW...I...
AS I RECALL...
THERE YOU GO.

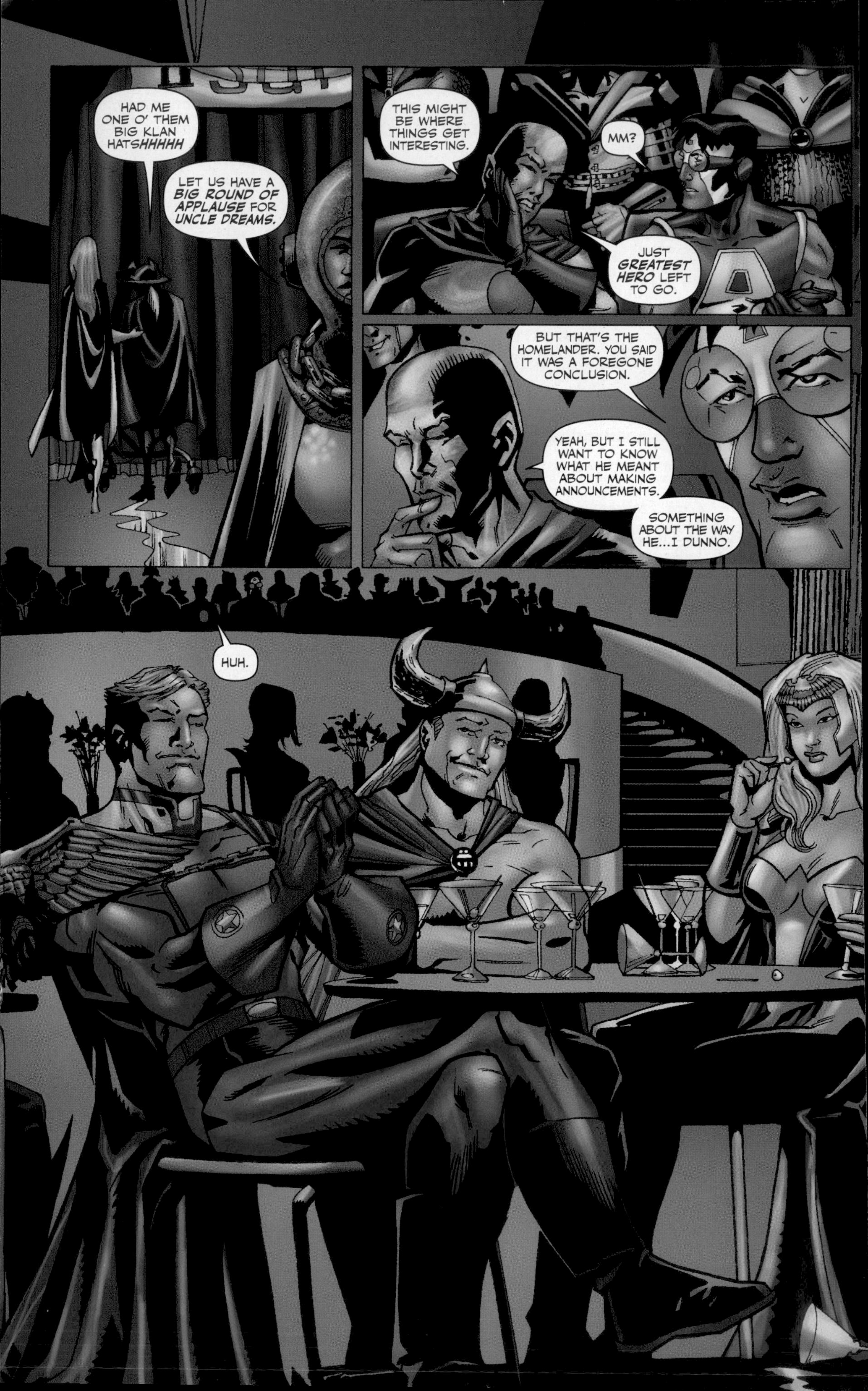
HAD ME ONE O' THEM BIG KLAN HATSHHHHH
LET US HAVE A BIG ROUND OF APPLAUSE FOR UNCLE DREAMS.
THIS MIGHT BE WHERE THINGS GET INTERESTING.
MM?
JUST GREATEST HERO LEFT TO GO.
BUT THAT'S THE HOMELANDER. YOU SAID IT WAS A FOREGONE CONCLUSION.
YEAH, BUT I STILL WANT TO KNOW WHAT HE MEANT ABOUT MAKING ANNOUNCEMENTS.
SOMETHING ABOUT THE WAY HE...I DUNNO.
HUH.

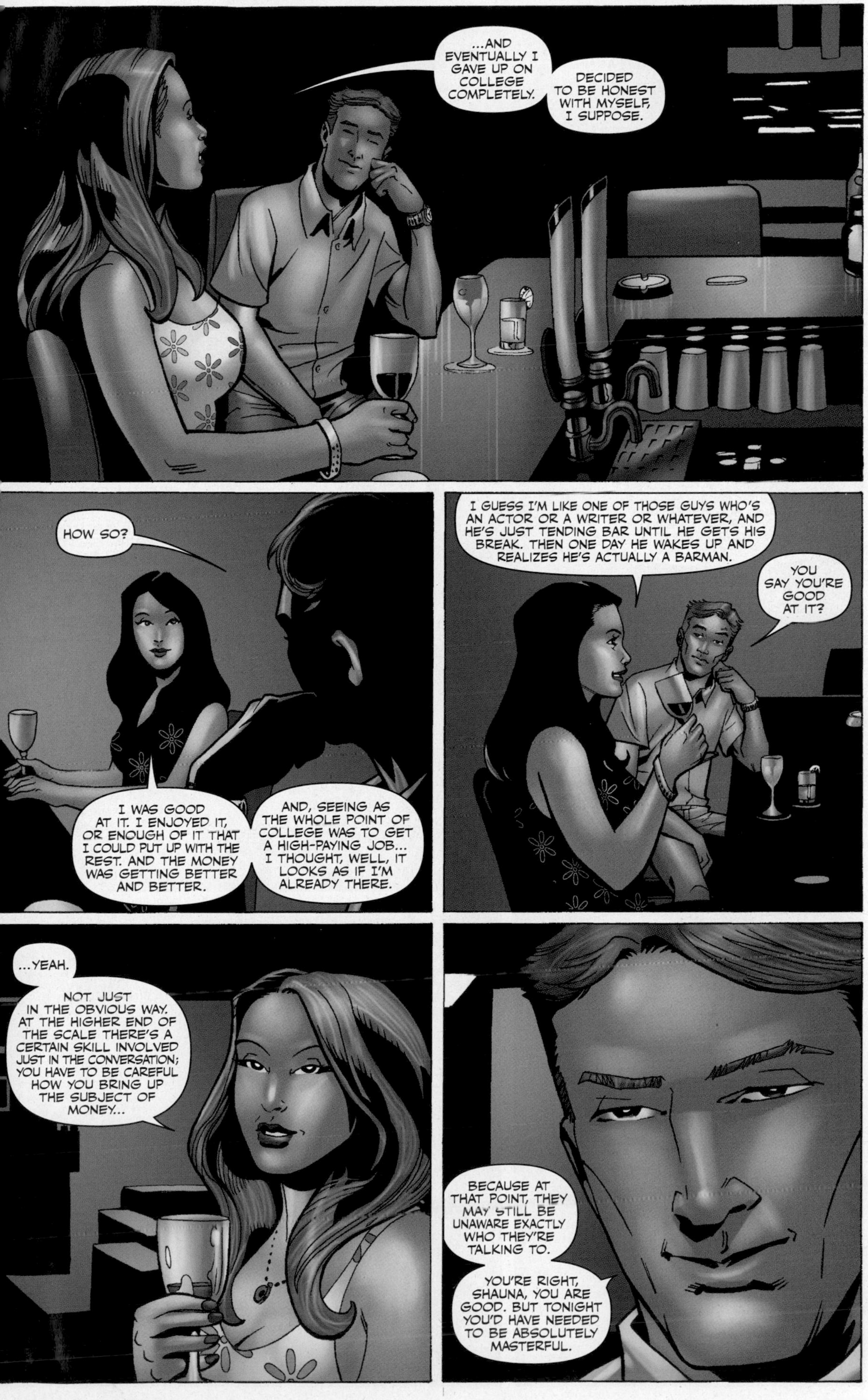
...AND EVENTUALLY I GAVE UP ON COLLEGE COMPLETELY.
DECIDED TO BE HONEST WITH MYSELF, I SUPPOSE.
HOW SO?
I WAS GOOD AT IT. I ENJOYED IT, OR ENOUGH OF IT THAT I COULD PUT UP WITH THE REST. AND THE MONEY WAS GETTING BETTER AND BETTER.
AND, SEEING AS THE WHOLE POINT OF COLLEGE WAS TO GET A HIGH-PAYING JOB... I THOUGHT, WELL, IT LOOKS AS IF I'M ALREADY THERE.
I GUESS I'M LIKE ONE OF THOSE GUYS WHO'S AN ACTOR OR A WRITER OR WHATEVER, AND HE'S JUST TENDING BAR UNTIL HE GETS HIS BREAK. THEN ONE DAY HE WAKES UP AND REALIZES HE'S ACTUALLY A BARMAN.
YOU SAY YOU'RE GOOD AT IT?
...YEAH.
NOT JUST IN THE OBVIOUS WAY. AT THE HIGHER END OF THE SCALE THERE'S A CERTAIN SKILL INVOLVED JUST IN THE CONVERSATION; YOU HAVE TO BE CAREFUL HOW YOU BRING UP THE SUBJECT OF MONEY...
BECAUSE AT THAT POINT, THEY MAY STILL BE UNAWARE EXACTLY WHO THEY'RE TALKING TO.
YOU'RE RIGHT, SHAUNA, YOU ARE GOOD. BUT TONIGHT YOU'D HAVE NEEDED TO BE ABSOLUTELY MASTERFUL.

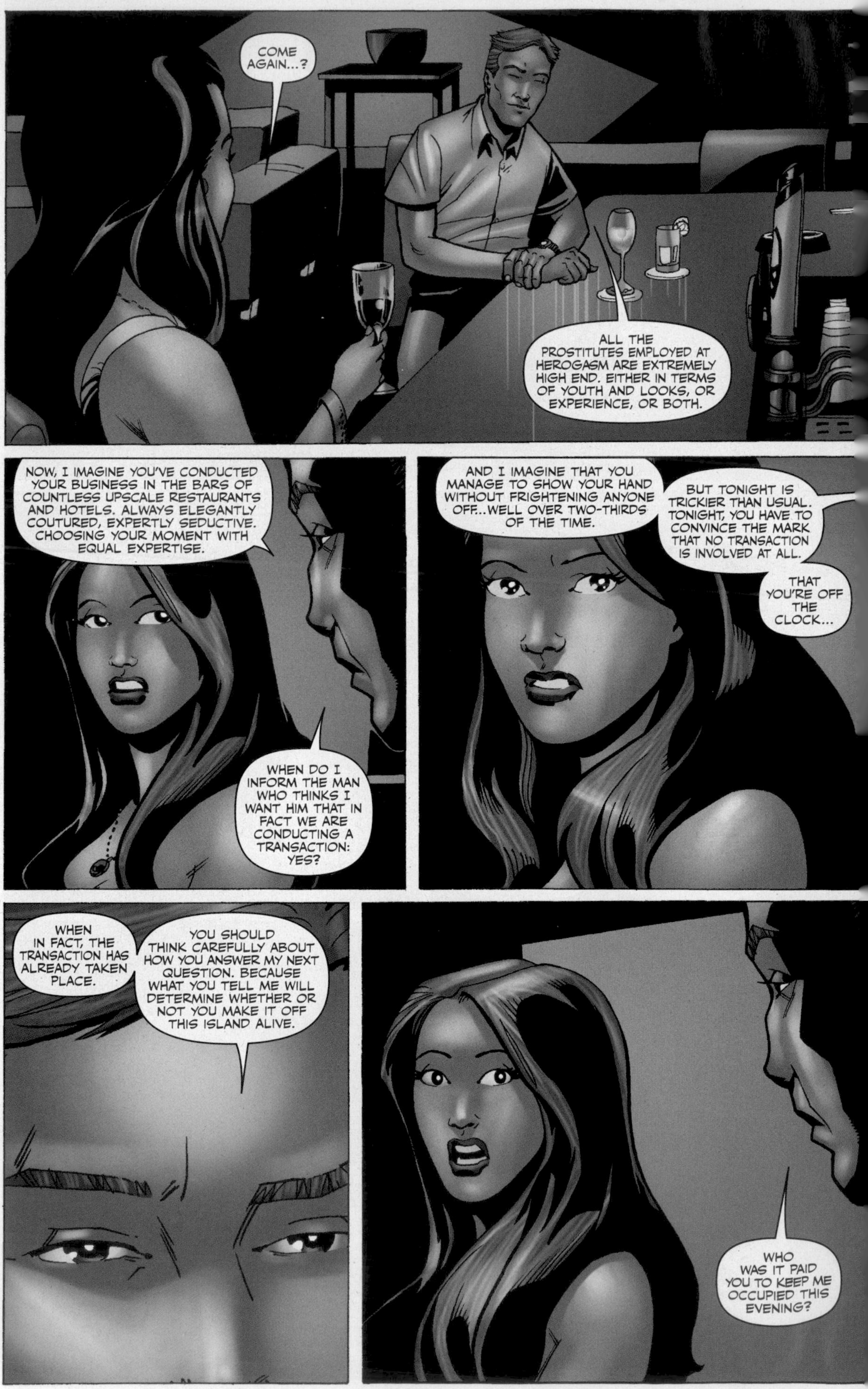
COME AGAIN...?
ALL THE PROSTITUTES EMPLOYED AT HEROGASM ARE EXTREMELY HIGH END. EITHER IN TERMS OF YOUTH AND LOOKS, OR EXPERIENCE, OR BOTH.
NOW, I IMAGINE YOU'VE CONDUCTED YOUR BUSINESS IN THE BARS OF COUNTLESS UPSCALE RESTAURANTS AND HOTELS. ALWAYS ELEGANTLY COUTURED, EXPERTLY SEDUCTIVE. CHOOSING YOUR MOMENT WITH EQUAL EXPERTISE.
WHEN DO I INFORM THE MAN WHO THINKS I WANT HIM THAT IN FACT WE ARE CONDUCTING A TRANSACTION: YES?
AND I IMAGINE THAT YOU MANAGE TO SHOW YOUR HAND WITHOUT FRIGHTENING ANYONE OFF...WELL OVER TWO-THIRDS OF THE TIME.
BUT TONIGHT IS TRICKIER THAN USUAL. TONIGHT, YOU HAVE TO CONVINCE THE MARK THAT NO TRANSACTION IS INVOLVED AT ALL.
THAT YOU'RE OFF THE CLOCK...
WHEN IN FACT, THE TRANSACTION HAS ALREADY TAKEN PLACE.
YOU SHOULD THINK CAREFULLY ABOUT HOW YOU ANSWER MY NEXT QUESTION. BECAUSE WHAT YOU TELL ME WILL DETERMINE WHETHER OR NOT YOU MAKE IT OFF THIS ISLAND ALIVE.
WHO WAS IT PAID YOU TO KEEP ME OCCUPIED THIS EVENING?

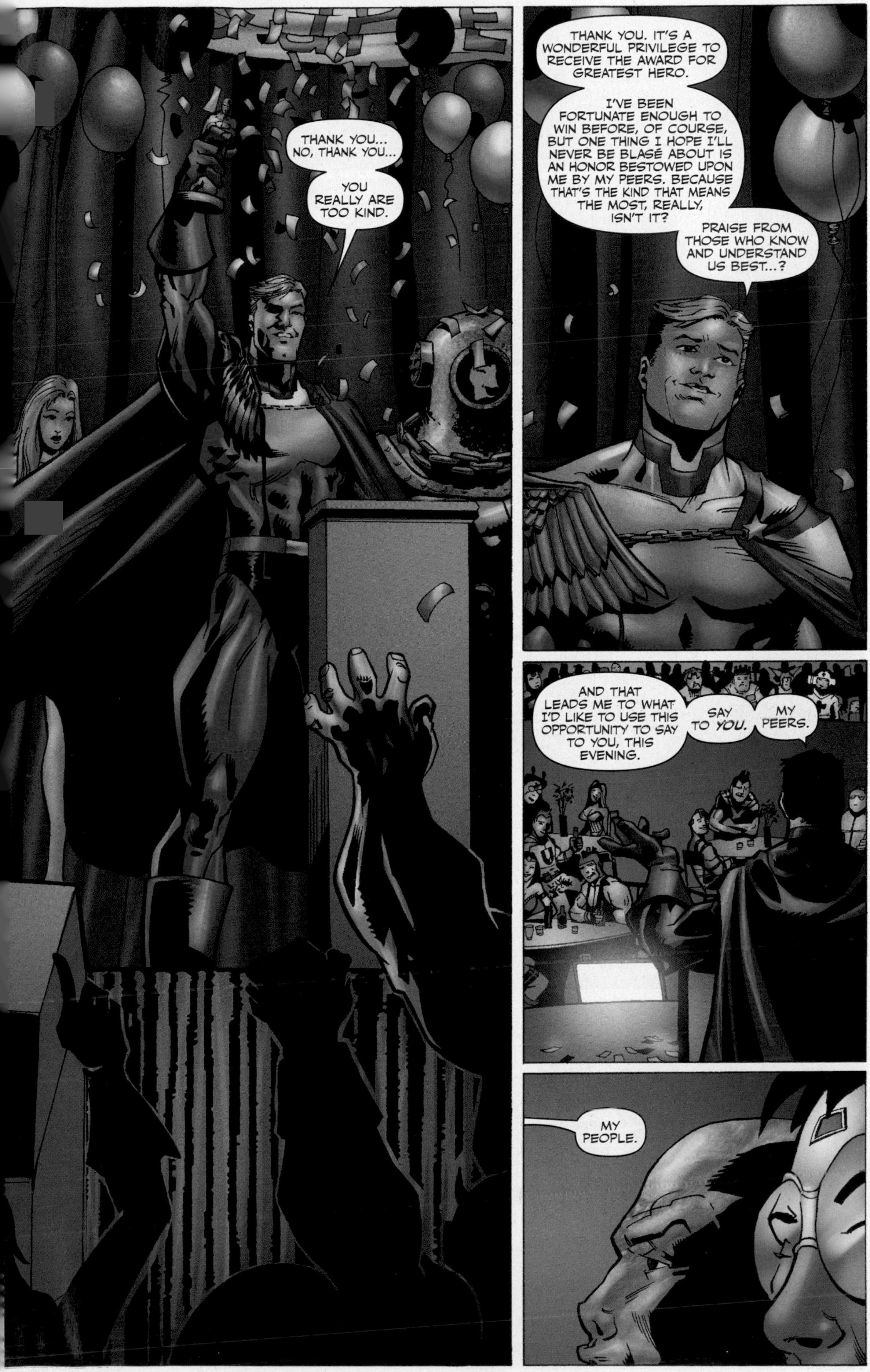
THANK YOU... NO, THANK YOU...
YOU REALLY ARE TOO KIND.
THANK YOU. IT'S A WONDERFUL PRIVILEGE TO RECEIVE THE AWARD FOR GREATEST HERO.
I'VE BEEN FORTUNATE ENOUGH TO WIN BEFORE, OF COURSE, BUT ONE THING I HOPE I'LL NEVER BE BLASÉ ABOUT IS AN HONOR BESTOWED UPON ME BY MY PEERS. BECAUSE THAT'S THE KIND THAT MEANS THE MOST, REALLY, ISN'T IT?
PRAISE FROM THOSE WHO KNOW AND UNDERSTAND US BEST...?
AND THAT LEADS ME TO WHAT I'D LIKE TO USE THIS OPPORTUNITY TO SAY TO YOU, THIS EVENING.
SAY TO *YOU.*
MY PEERS.
MY PEOPLE.

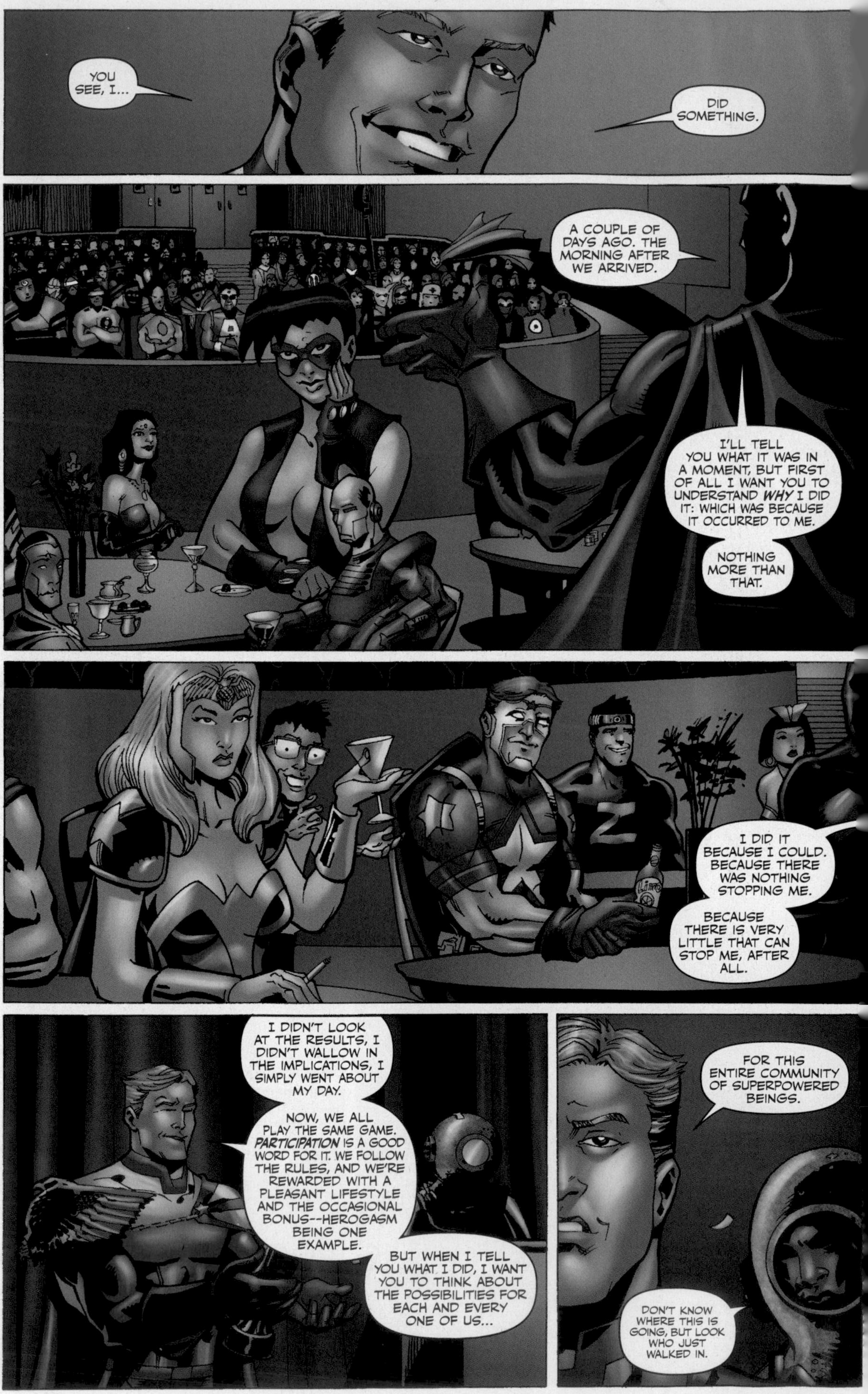
YOU SEE, I...
DID SOMETHING.
A COUPLE OF DAYS AGO. THE MORNING AFTER WE ARRIVED.
I'LL TELL YOU WHAT IT WAS IN A MOMENT, BUT FIRST OF ALL I WANT YOU TO UNDERSTAND *WHY* I DID IT: WHICH WAS BECAUSE IT OCCURRED TO ME.
NOTHING MORE THAN THAT.
I DID IT BECAUSE I COULD. BECAUSE THERE WAS NOTHING STOPPING ME.
BECAUSE THERE IS VERY LITTLE THAT CAN STOP ME, AFTER ALL.
I DIDN'T LOOK AT THE RESULTS, I DIDN'T WALLOW IN THE IMPLICATIONS, I SIMPLY WENT ABOUT MY DAY.
NOW, WE ALL PLAY THE SAME GAME. *PARTICIPATION* IS A GOOD WORD FOR IT. WE FOLLOW THE RULES, AND WE'RE REWARDED WITH A PLEASANT LIFESTYLE AND THE OCCASIONAL BONUS--HEROGASM BEING ONE EXAMPLE.
BUT WHEN I TELL YOU WHAT I DID, I WANT YOU TO THINK ABOUT THE POSSIBILITIES FOR EACH AND EVERY ONE OF US...
FOR THIS ENTIRE COMMUNITY OF SUPERPOWERED BEINGS.
DON'T KNOW WHERE THIS IS GOING, BUT LOOK WHO JUST WALKED IN.

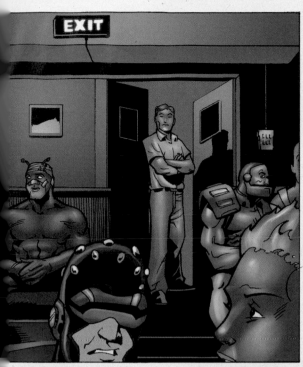

RIGHT AFTER "POSSIBILITIES".

I... HRRRMM

I'D LIKE TO THANK YOU ONCE AGAIN FOR THIS WONDERFUL AWARD AND I HOPE YOU ENJOY THE REST OF THE EVENING! GOODNIGHT!

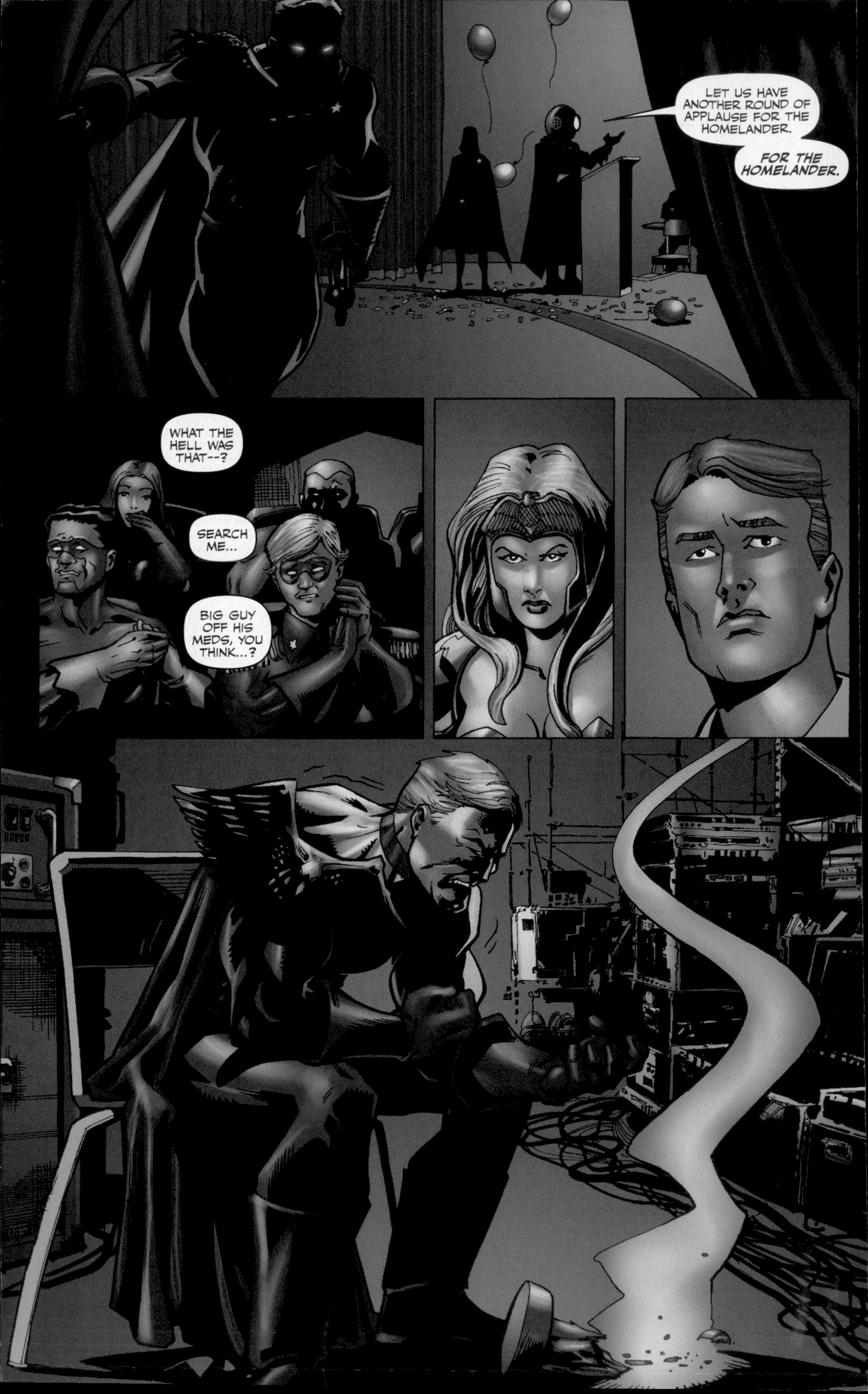
LET US HAVE ANOTHER ROUND OF APPLAUSE FOR THE HOMELANDER.
FOR THE HOMELANDER.
WHAT THE HELL WAS THAT--?
SEARCH ME...
BIG GUY OFF HIS MEDS, YOU THINK...?

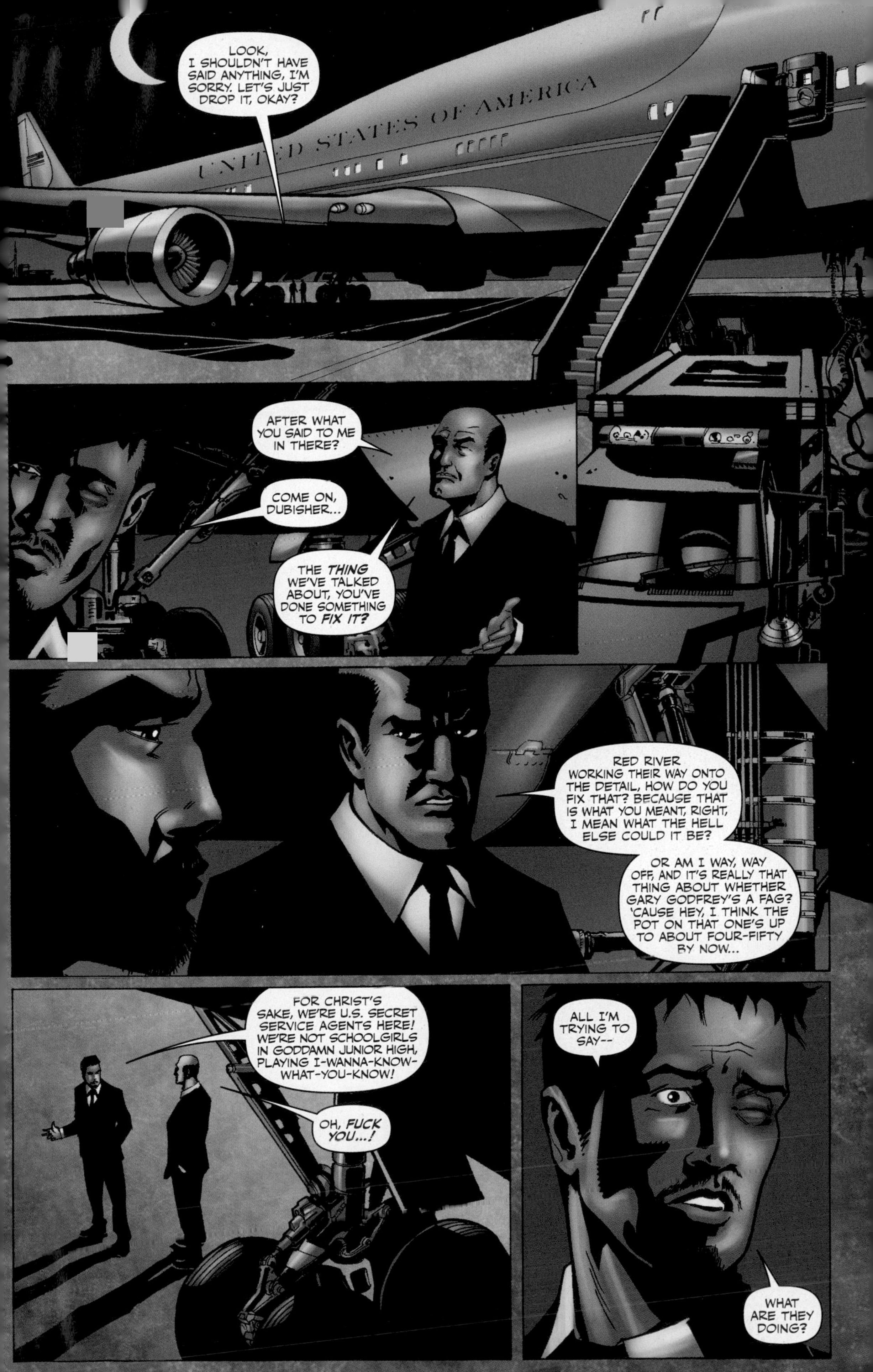
UNITED STATES OF AMERICA
LOOK, I SHOULDN'T HAVE SAID ANYTHING, I'M SORRY. LET'S JUST DROP IT, OKAY?
AFTER WHAT YOU SAID TO ME IN THERE?
COME ON, DUBISHER...
THE *THING* WE'VE TALKED ABOUT, YOU'VE DONE SOMETHING TO ***FIX IT?***
RED RIVER WORKING THEIR WAY ONTO THE DETAIL, HOW DO YOU FIX THAT? BECAUSE THAT IS WHAT YOU MEANT, RIGHT, I MEAN WHAT THE HELL ELSE COULD IT BE?
OR AM I WAY, WAY OFF, AND IT'S REALLY THAT THING ABOUT WHETHER GARY GODFREY'S A FAG? 'CAUSE HEY, I THINK THE POT ON THAT ONE'S UP TO ABOUT FOUR-FIFTY BY NOW...
FOR CHRIST'S SAKE, WE'RE U.S. SECRET SERVICE AGENTS HERE! WE'RE NOT SCHOOLGIRLS IN GODDAMN JUNIOR HIGH, PLAYING I-WANNA-KNOW-WHAT-YOU-KNOW!
OH, ***FUCK YOU...!***
ALL I'M TRYING TO SAY--
WHAT ARE THEY DOING?

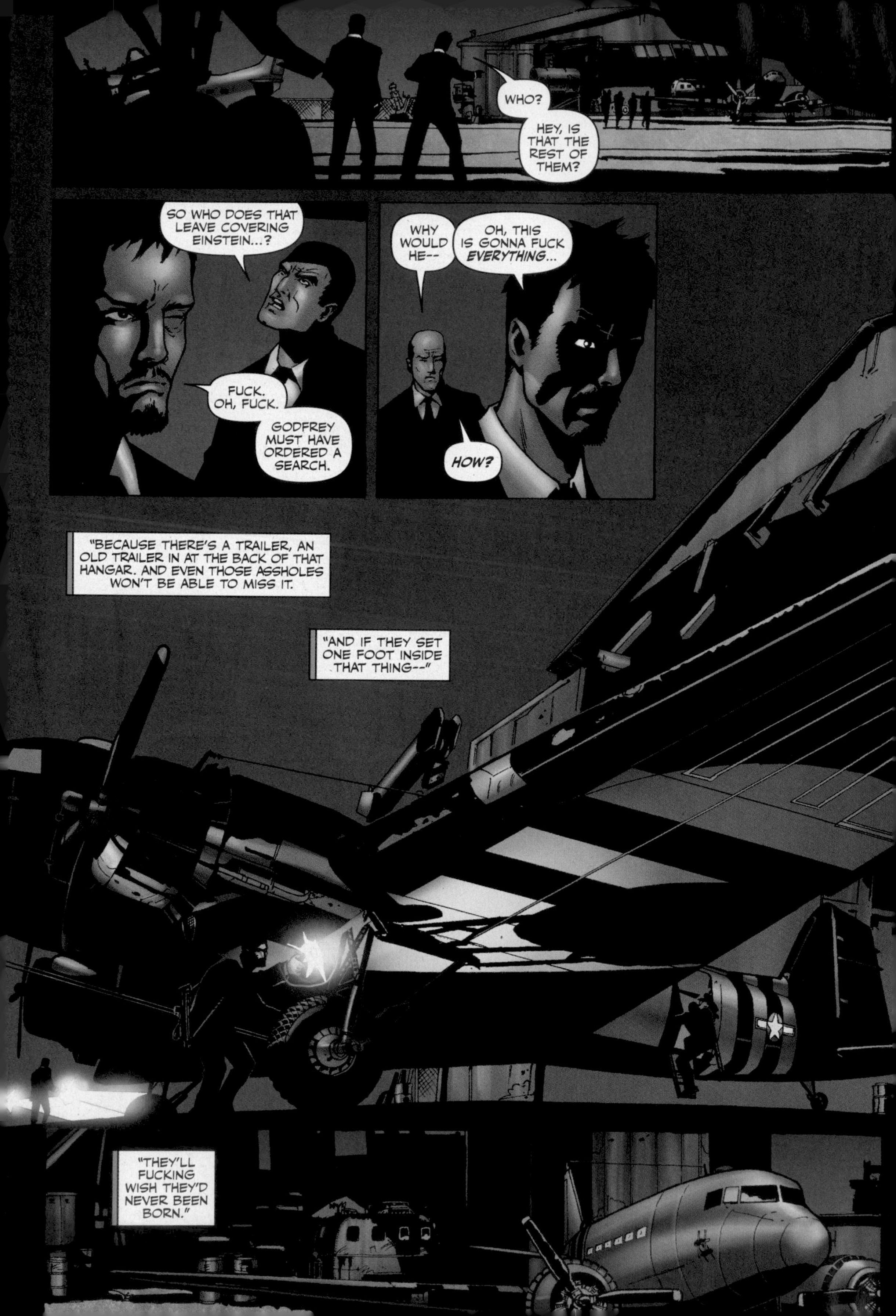
WHO?
HEY, IS THAT THE REST OF THEM?
SO WHO DOES THAT LEAVE COVERING EINSTEIN...?
FUCK. OH, FUCK.
GODFREY MUST HAVE ORDERED A SEARCH.
WHY WOULD HE--
OH, THIS IS GONNA FUCK *EVERYTHING*...
HOW?
"BECAUSE THERE'S A TRAILER, AN OLD TRAILER IN AT THE BACK OF THAT HANGAR. AND EVEN THOSE ASSHOLES WON'T BE ABLE TO MISS IT.
"AND IF THEY SET ONE FOOT INSIDE THAT THING--"
"THEY'LL FUCKING WISH THEY'D NEVER BEEN BORN."

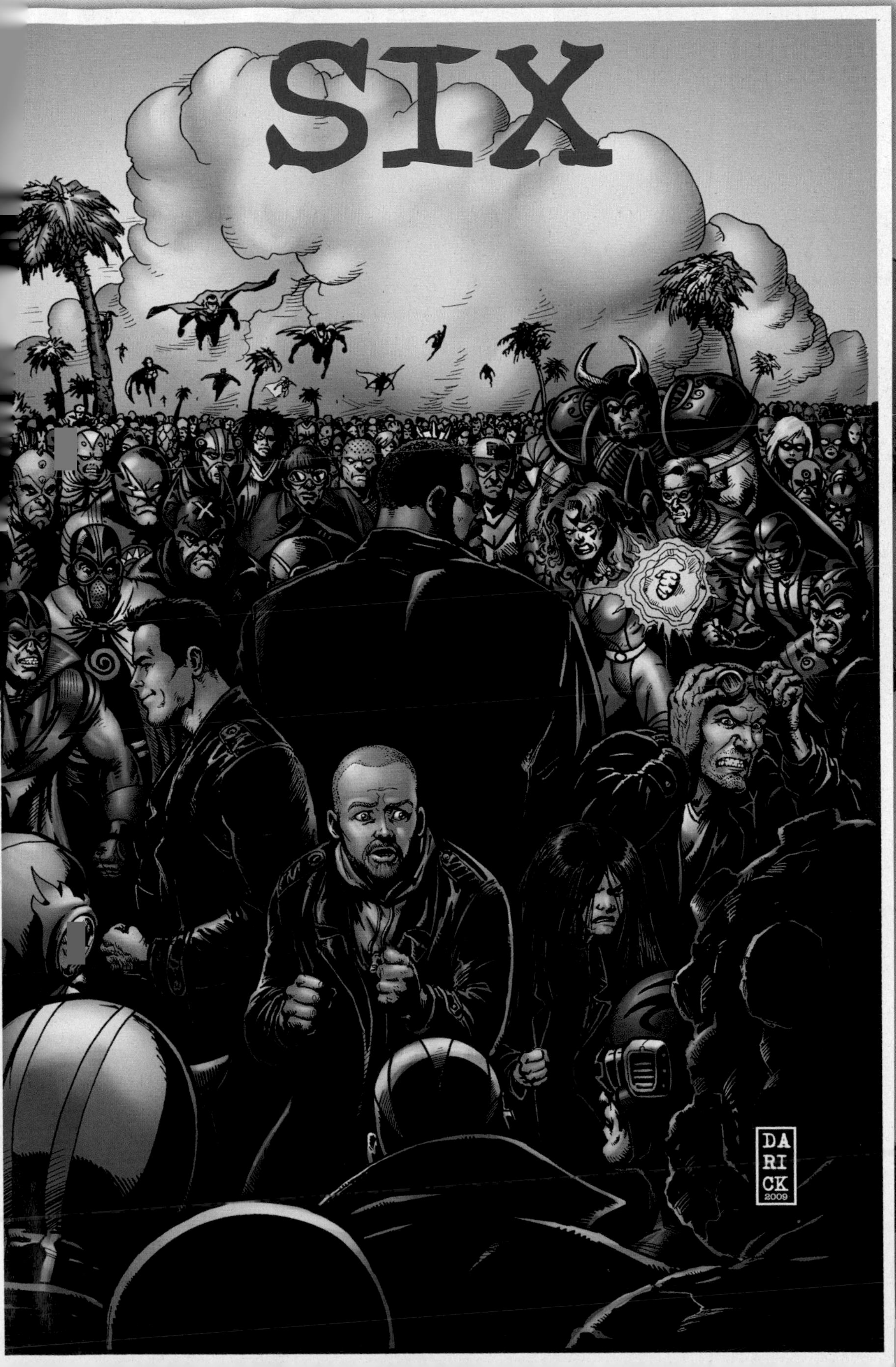
SIX
DA
RI
CK
2009

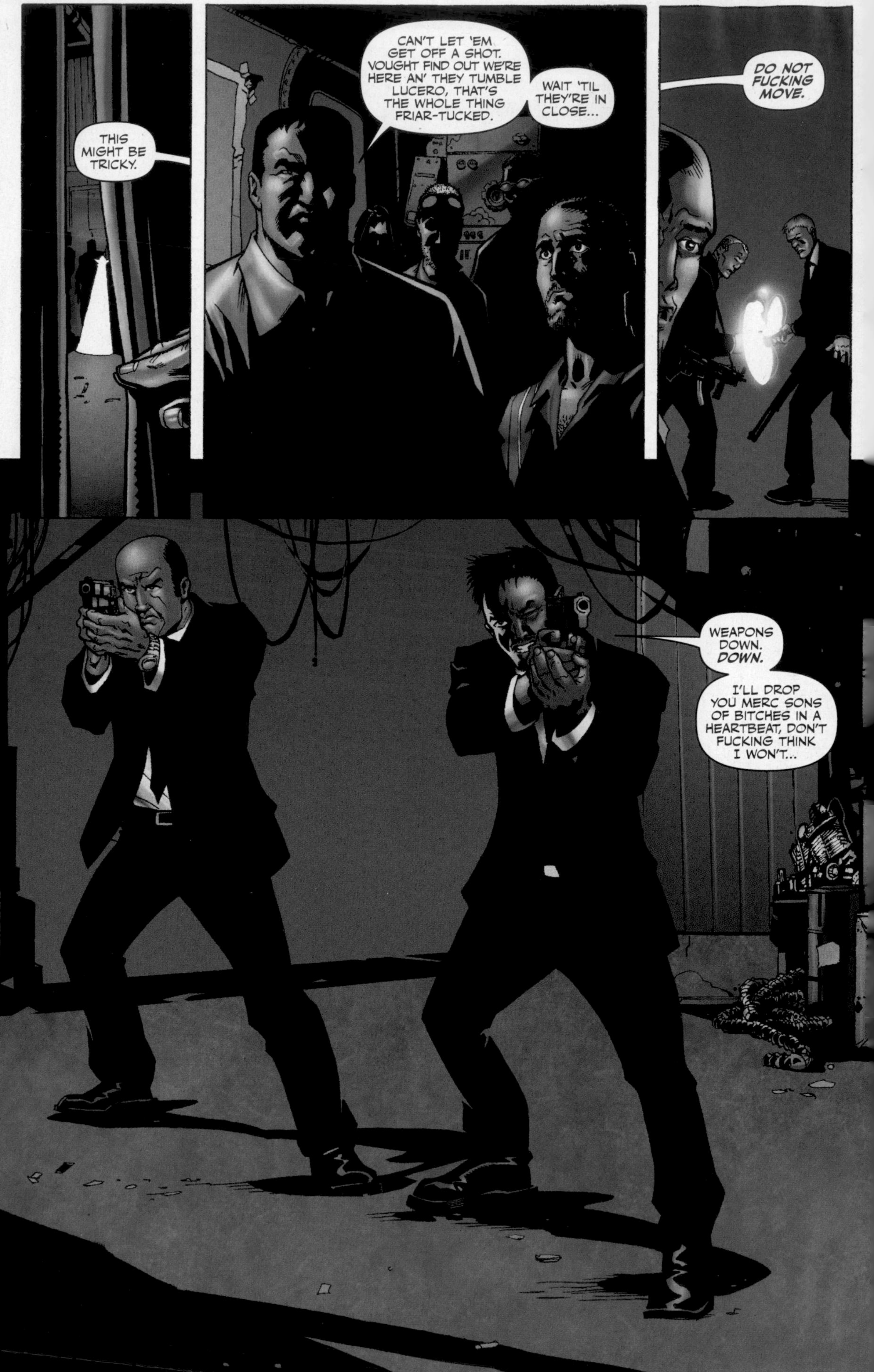
THIS MIGHT BE TRICKY.
CAN'T LET 'EM GET OFF A SHOT. VOUGHT FIND OUT WE'RE HERE AN' THEY TUMBLE LUCERO, THAT'S THE WHOLE THING FRIAR-TUCKED.
WAIT 'TIL THEY'RE IN CLOSE...
DO NOT FUCKING MOVE.
WEAPONS DOWN. DOWN.
I'LL DROP YOU MERC SONS OF BITCHES IN A HEARTBEAT, DON'T FUCKING THINK I WON'T...

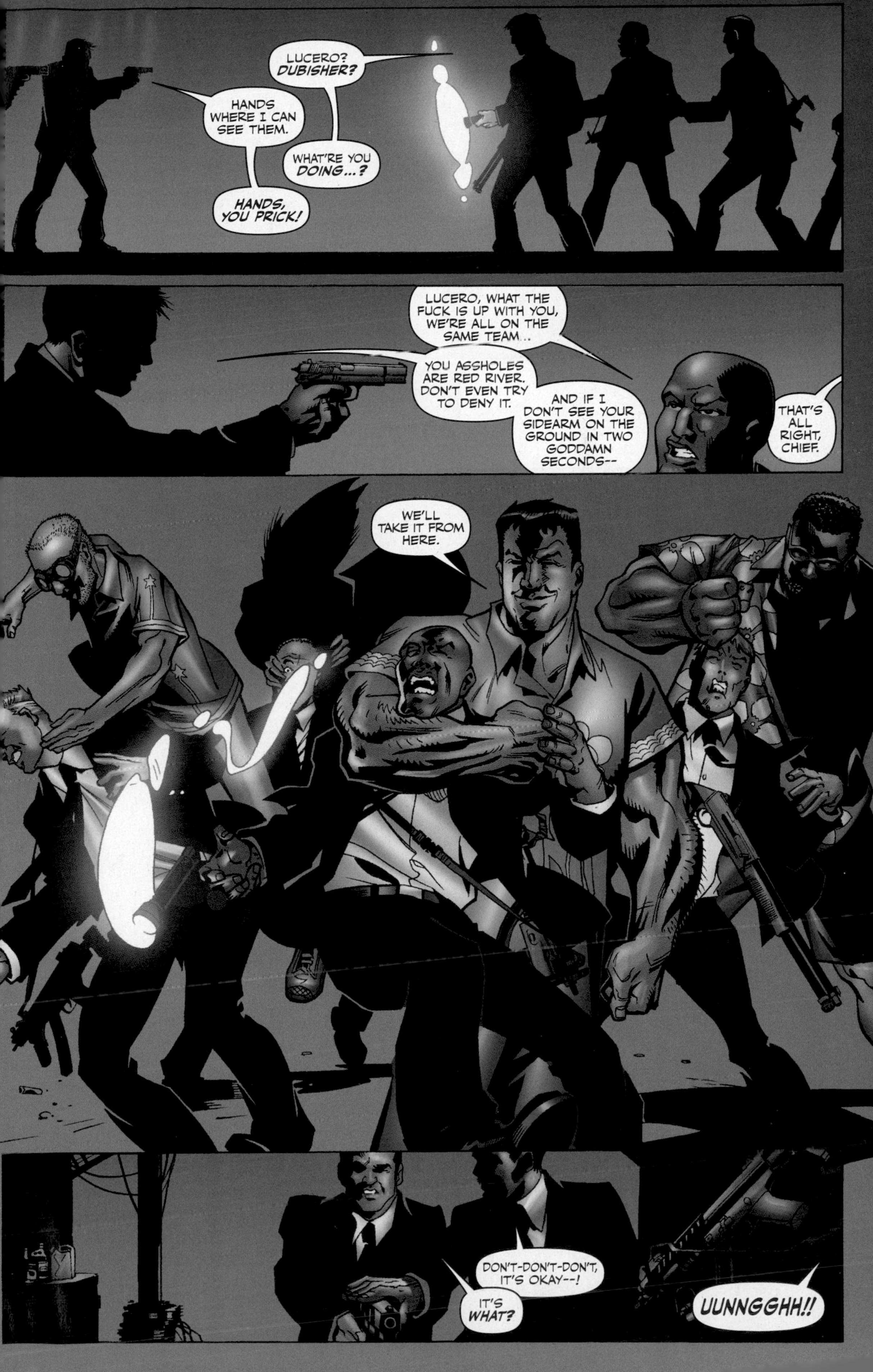
LUCERO? DUBISHER?
HANDS WHERE I CAN SEE THEM.
WHAT'RE YOU DOING...?
HANDS, YOU PRICK!
LUCERO, WHAT THE FUCK IS UP WITH YOU, WE'RE ALL ON THE SAME TEAM...
YOU ASSHOLES ARE RED RIVER. DON'T EVEN TRY TO DENY IT.
AND IF I DON'T SEE YOUR SIDEARM ON THE GROUND IN TWO GODDAMN SECONDS--
THAT'S ALL RIGHT, CHIEF.
WE'LL TAKE IT FROM HERE.
DON'T-DON'T-DON'T, IT'S OKAY--!
IT'S WHAT?
UUNNGGHH!!

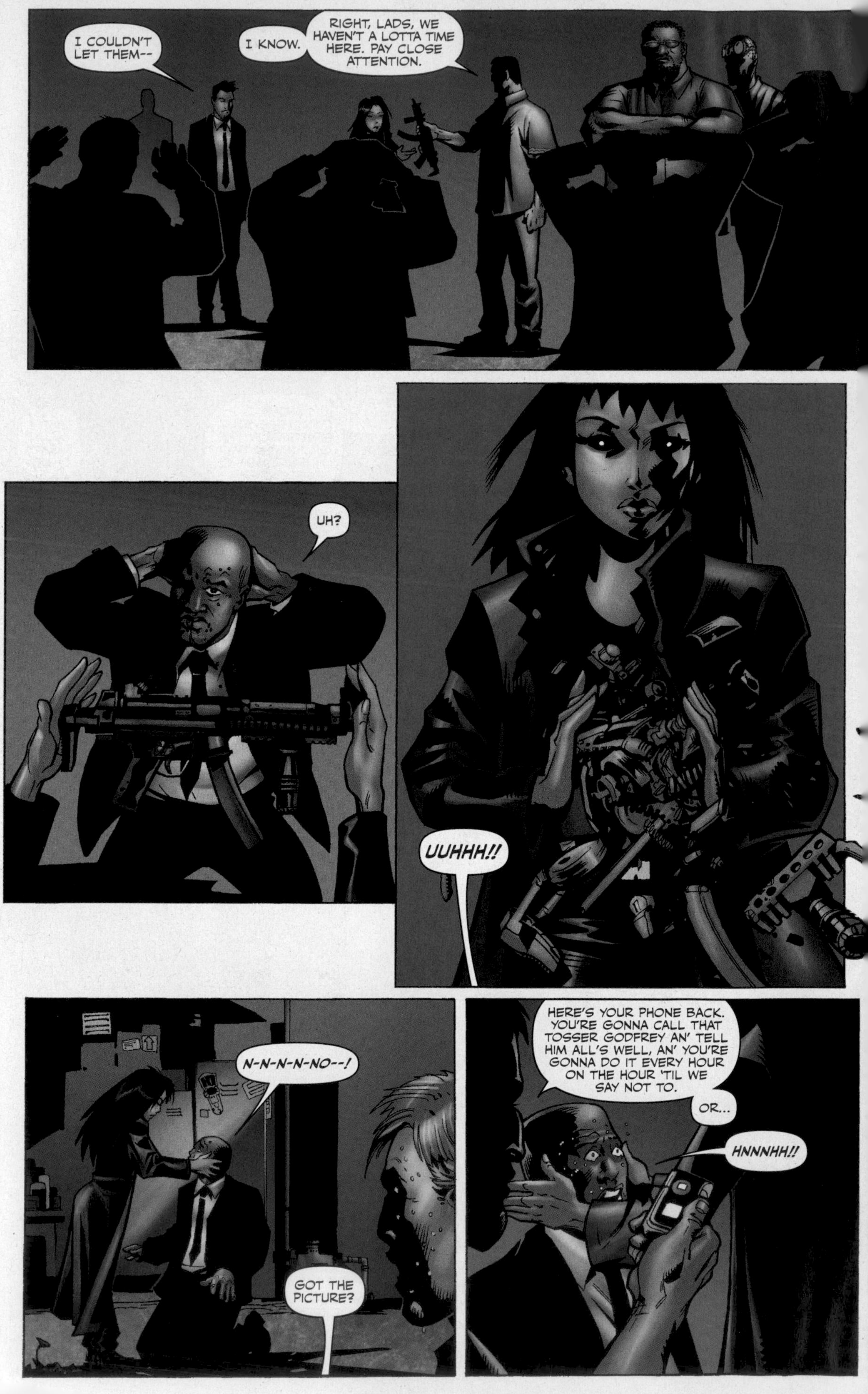
I COULDN'T LET THEM--
I KNOW.
RIGHT, LADS, WE HAVEN'T A LOTTA TIME HERE. PAY CLOSE ATTENTION.
UH?
UUHHH!!
N-N-N-N-NO--!
GOT THE PICTURE?
HERE'S YOUR PHONE BACK. YOU'RE GONNA CALL THAT TOSSER GODFREY AN' TELL HIM ALL'S WELL, AN' YOU'RE GONNA DO IT EVERY HOUR ON THE HOUR 'TIL WE SAY NOT TO.
OR...
HNNNHH!!

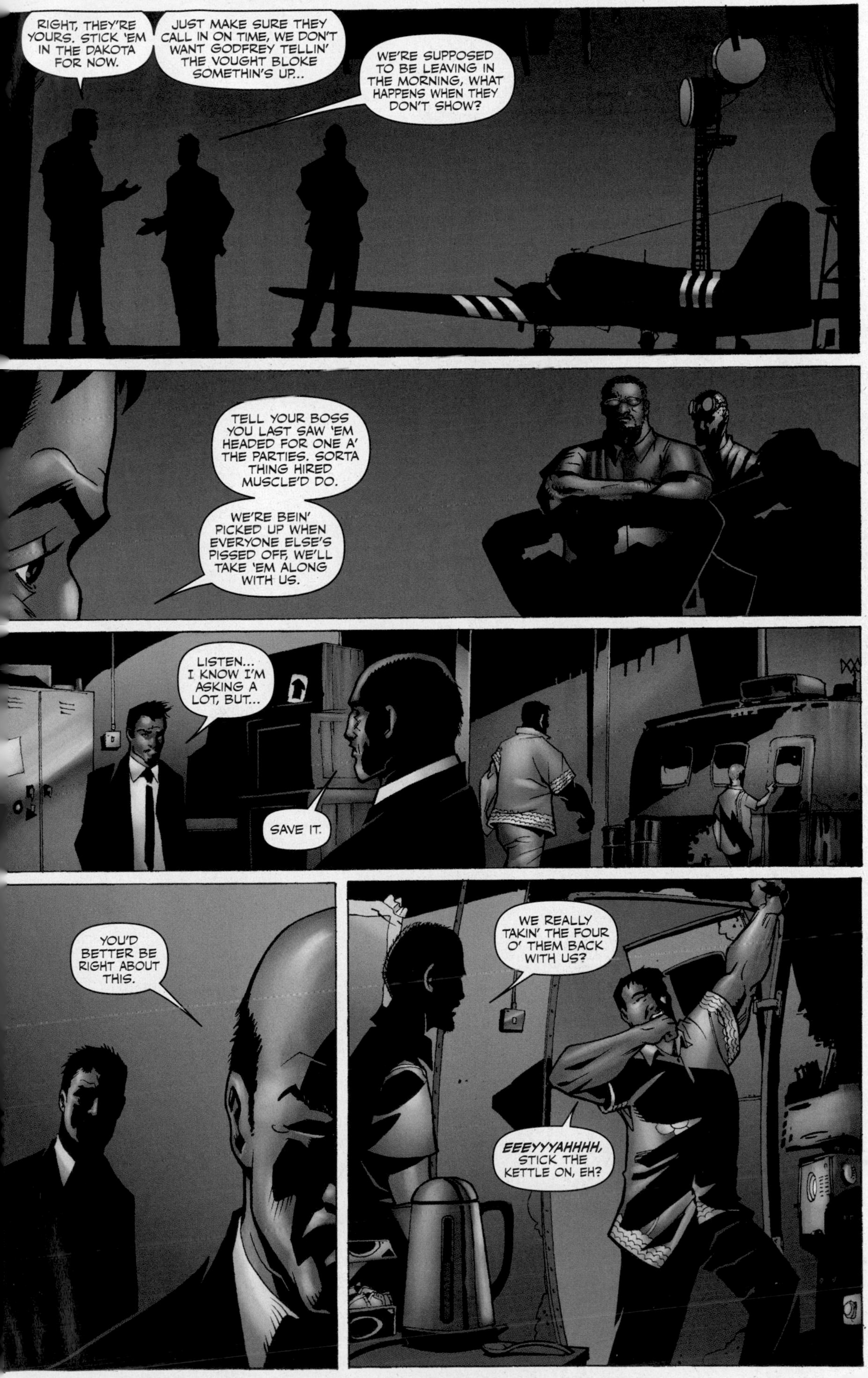
RIGHT, THEY'RE YOURS. STICK 'EM IN THE DAKOTA FOR NOW.
JUST MAKE SURE THEY CALL IN ON TIME, WE DON'T WANT GODFREY TELLIN' THE VOUGHT BLOKE SOMETHIN'S UP...
WE'RE SUPPOSED TO BE LEAVING IN THE MORNING, WHAT HAPPENS WHEN THEY DON'T SHOW?
TELL YOUR BOSS YOU LAST SAW 'EM HEADED FOR ONE A' THE PARTIES. SORTA THING HIRED MUSCLE'D DO.
WE'RE BEIN' PICKED UP WHEN EVERYONE ELSE'S PISSED OFF, WE'LL TAKE 'EM ALONG WITH US.
LISTEN... I KNOW I'M ASKING A LOT, BUT...
SAVE IT.
YOU'D BETTER BE RIGHT ABOUT THIS.
WE REALLY TAKIN' THE FOUR O' THEM BACK WITH US?
EEEYYYAHHHH, STICK THE KETTLE ON, EH?

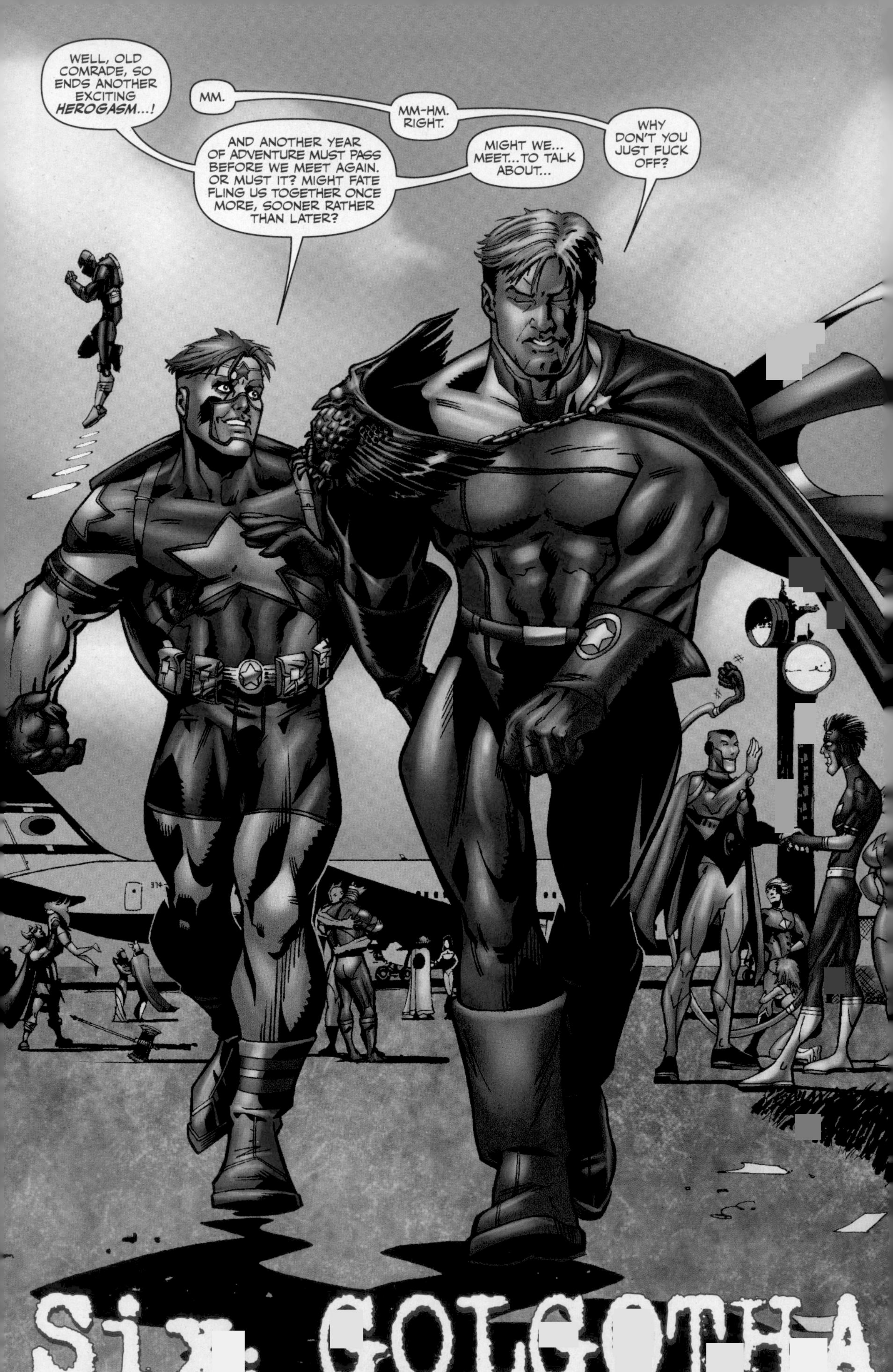
WELL, OLD COMRADE, SO ENDS ANOTHER EXCITING HEROGASM...!
MM.
AND ANOTHER YEAR OF ADVENTURE MUST PASS BEFORE WE MEET AGAIN. OR MUST IT? MIGHT FATE FLING US TOGETHER ONCE MORE, SOONER RATHER THAN LATER?
MM-HM. RIGHT.
MIGHT WE... MEET...TO TALK ABOUT...
WHY DON'T YOU JUST FUCK OFF?

Six: GOLGOTHA

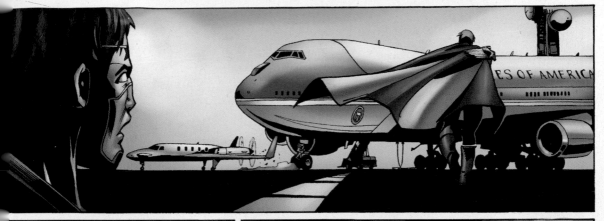

...I BEG YOUR PARDON, COULD YOU REPEAT THAT?

YES, CORRECT. SHAUNA MATTHESON. SHE'S ON THE HEROGASM MANIFEST.

NO, NOT ON THE FLIGHT. HAVE HER MET AT L.A.X.

GOOD.

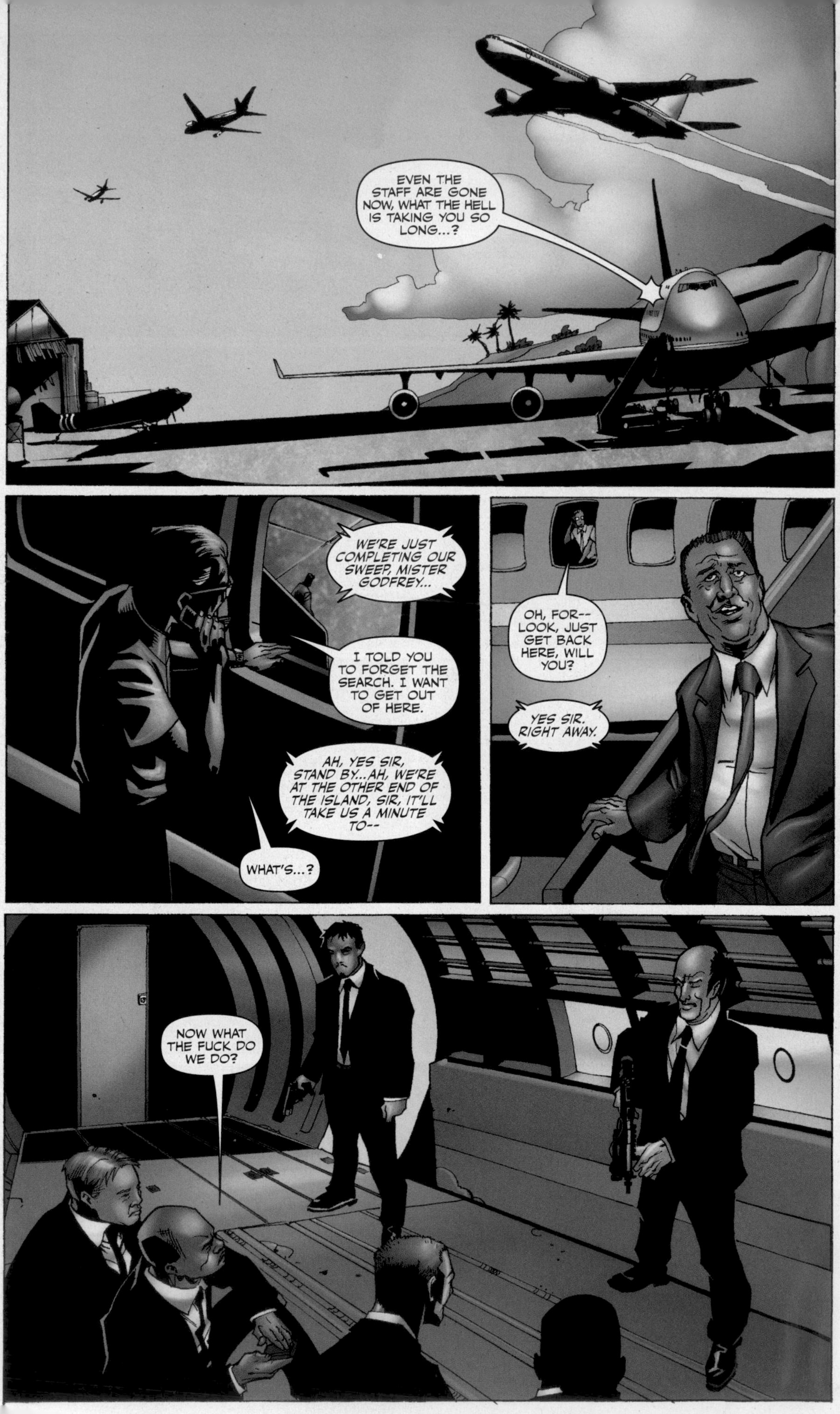
EVEN THE STAFF ARE GONE NOW, WHAT THE HELL IS TAKING YOU SO LONG...?
WE'RE JUST COMPLETING OUR SWEEP, MISTER GODFREY...
I TOLD YOU TO FORGET THE SEARCH. I WANT TO GET OUT OF HERE.
AH, YES SIR, STAND BY...AH, WE'RE AT THE OTHER END OF THE ISLAND, SIR, IT'LL TAKE US A MINUTE TO--
WHAT'S...?
OH, FOR-- LOOK, JUST GET BACK HERE, WILL YOU?
YES SIR. RIGHT AWAY.
NOW WHAT THE FUCK DO WE DO?

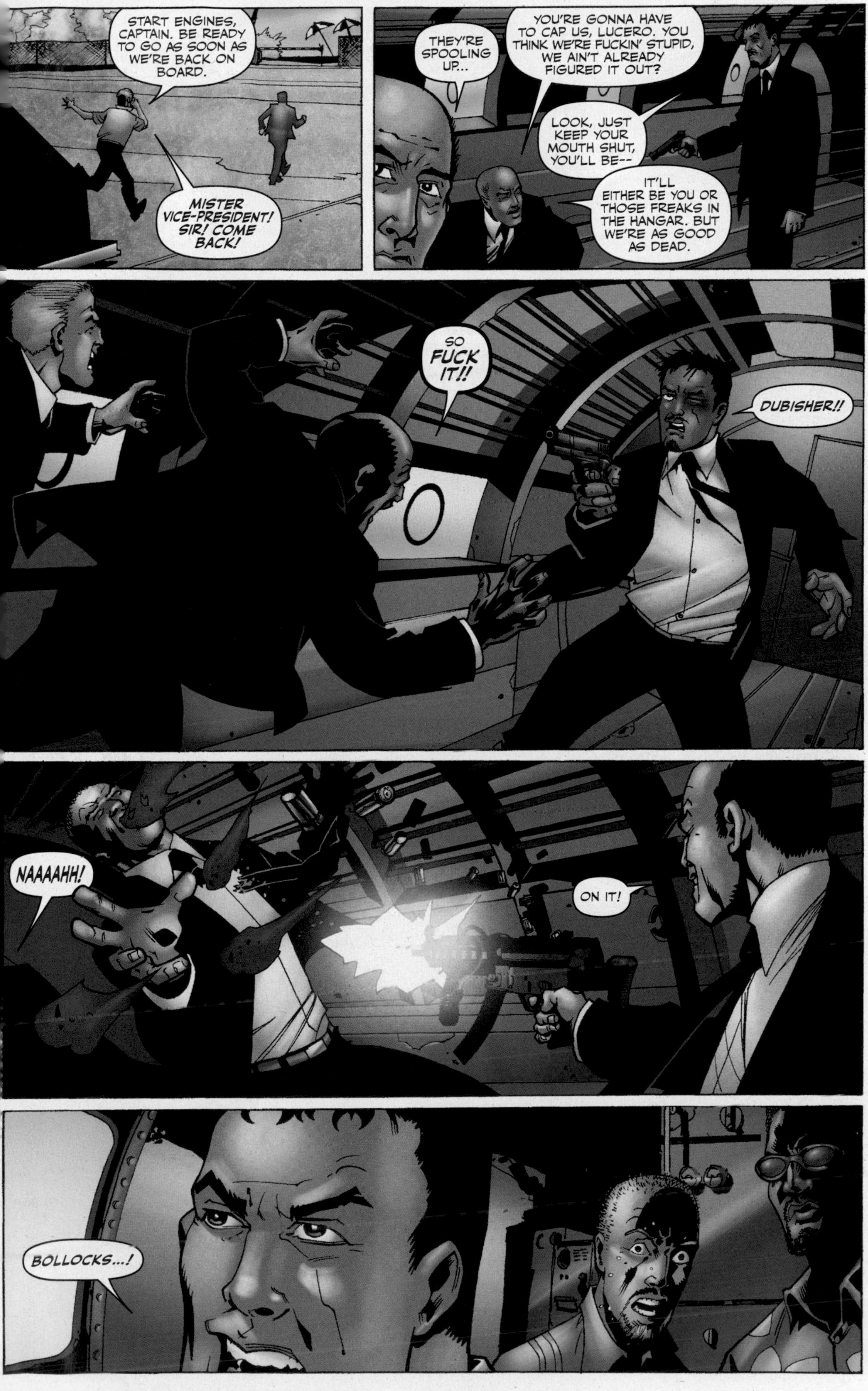
START ENGINES, CAPTAIN. BE READY TO GO AS SOON AS WE'RE BACK ON BOARD.
MISTER VICE-PRESIDENT! SIR! COME BACK!
THEY'RE SPOOLING UP...
YOU'RE GONNA HAVE TO CAP US, LUCERO. YOU THINK WE'RE FUCKIN' STUPID, WE AIN'T ALREADY FIGURED IT OUT?
LOOK, JUST KEEP YOUR MOUTH SHUT, YOU'LL BE--
IT'LL EITHER BE YOU OR THOSE FREAKS IN THE HANGAR. BUT WE'RE AS GOOD AS DEAD.
SO FUCK IT!!
DUBISHER!!
NAAAAHH!
ON IT!
BOLLOCKS...!

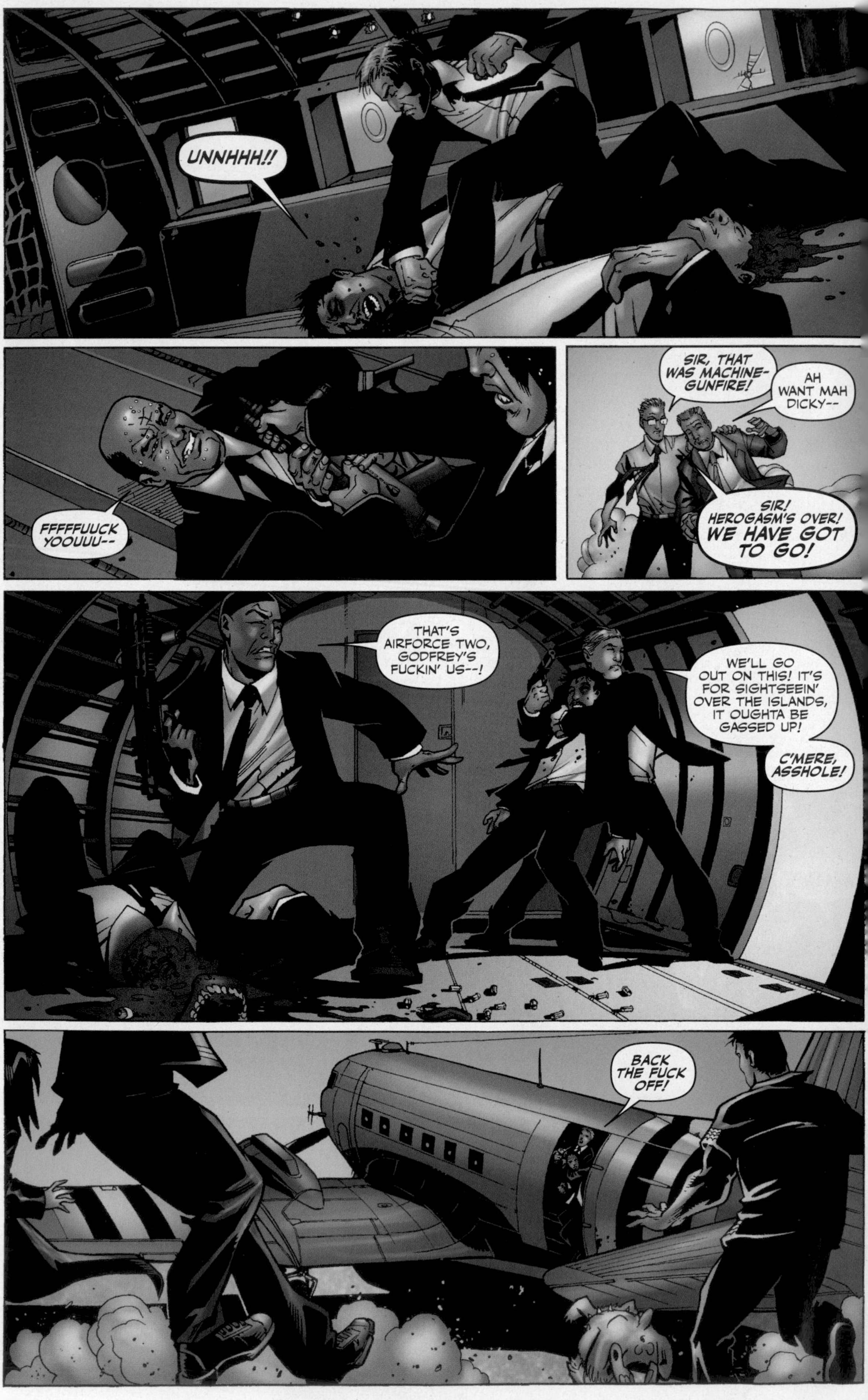
UNNHHH!!
FFFFFUUCK YOOUUU--
SIR, THAT WAS MACHINE-GUNFIRE!
AH WANT MAH DICKY--
SIR! HEROGASM'S OVER! WE HAVE GOT TO GO!
THAT'S AIRFORCE TWO, GODFREY'S FUCKIN' US--!
WE'LL GO OUT ON THIS! IT'S FOR SIGHTSEEIN' OVER THE ISLANDS, IT OUGHTA BE GASSED UP!
C'MERE, ASSHOLE!
BACK THE FUCK OFF!

EASY DOES IT, SUNSHINE. YOU AIN'T GOIN' ANYWHERE WITHOUT A PILOT.

FUCK YOU! YOU KNOW HOW MANY THIRD WORLD SHITHOLES WE BLASTED OUT OF IN WRECKS LIKE THIS?

YOU GOT NO IDEA WHO YOU'RE DEALIN' WITH, ASSHOLE!!

NEITHER DOES THIS SPIC FUCK RIGHT HERE! BUT WE GET HIM HOME, WE'RE ALL GONNA FIND OUT WHERE WE STAND!

NAHHH--

SHIT!

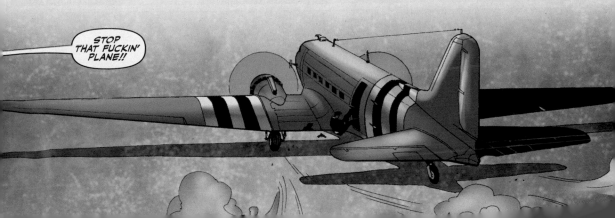

STOP THAT FUCKIN' PLANE!!

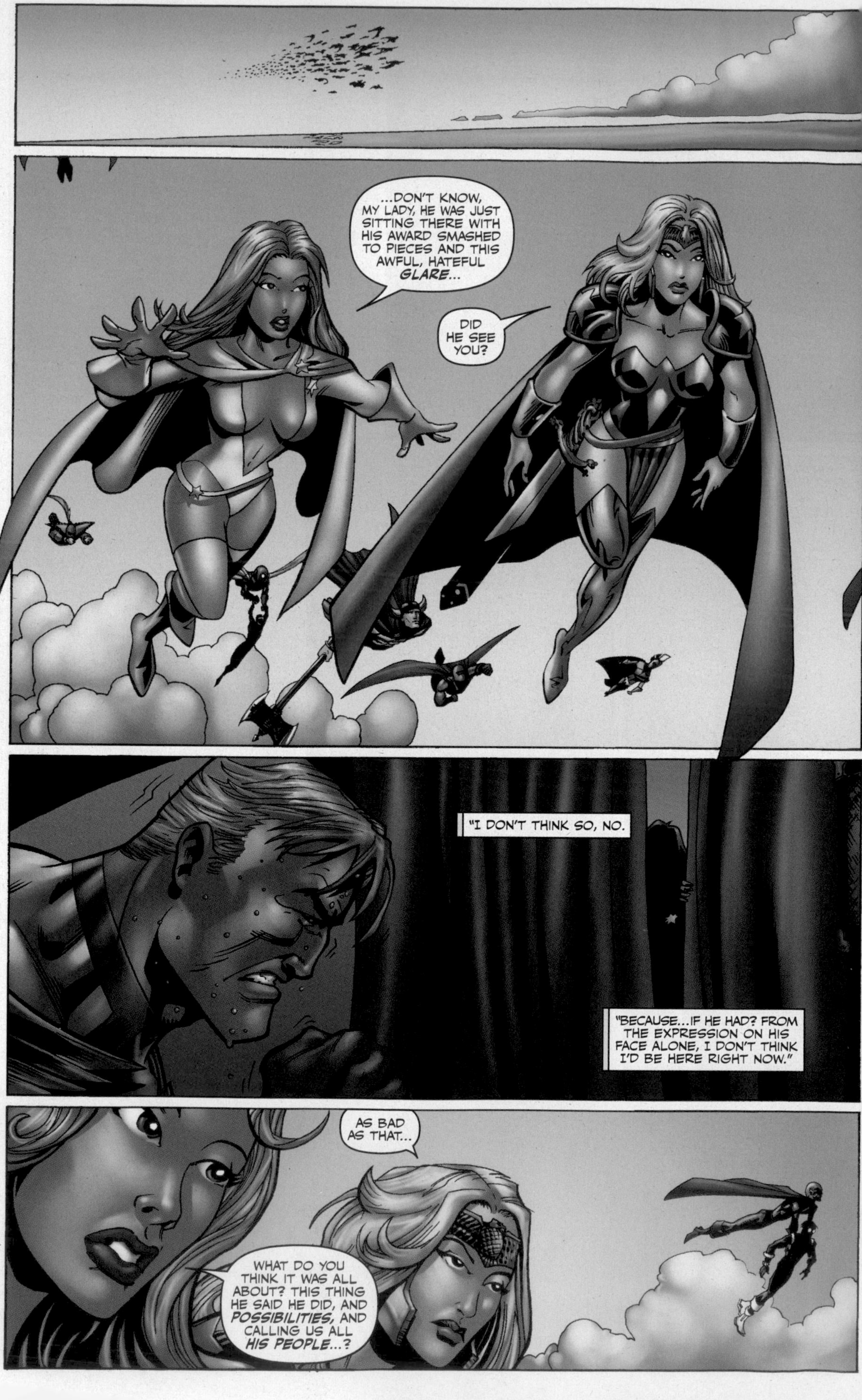
...DON'T KNOW, MY LADY, HE WAS JUST SITTING THERE WITH HIS AWARD SMASHED TO PIECES AND THIS AWFUL, HATEFUL *GLARE*...
DID HE SEE YOU?
"I DON'T THINK SO, NO.
"BECAUSE...IF HE HAD? FROM THE EXPRESSION ON HIS FACE ALONE, I DON'T THINK I'D BE HERE RIGHT NOW."
AS BAD AS THAT...
WHAT DO YOU THINK IT WAS ALL ABOUT? THIS THING HE SAID HE DID, AND *POSSIBILITIES,* AND CALLING US ALL *HIS PEOPLE*...?

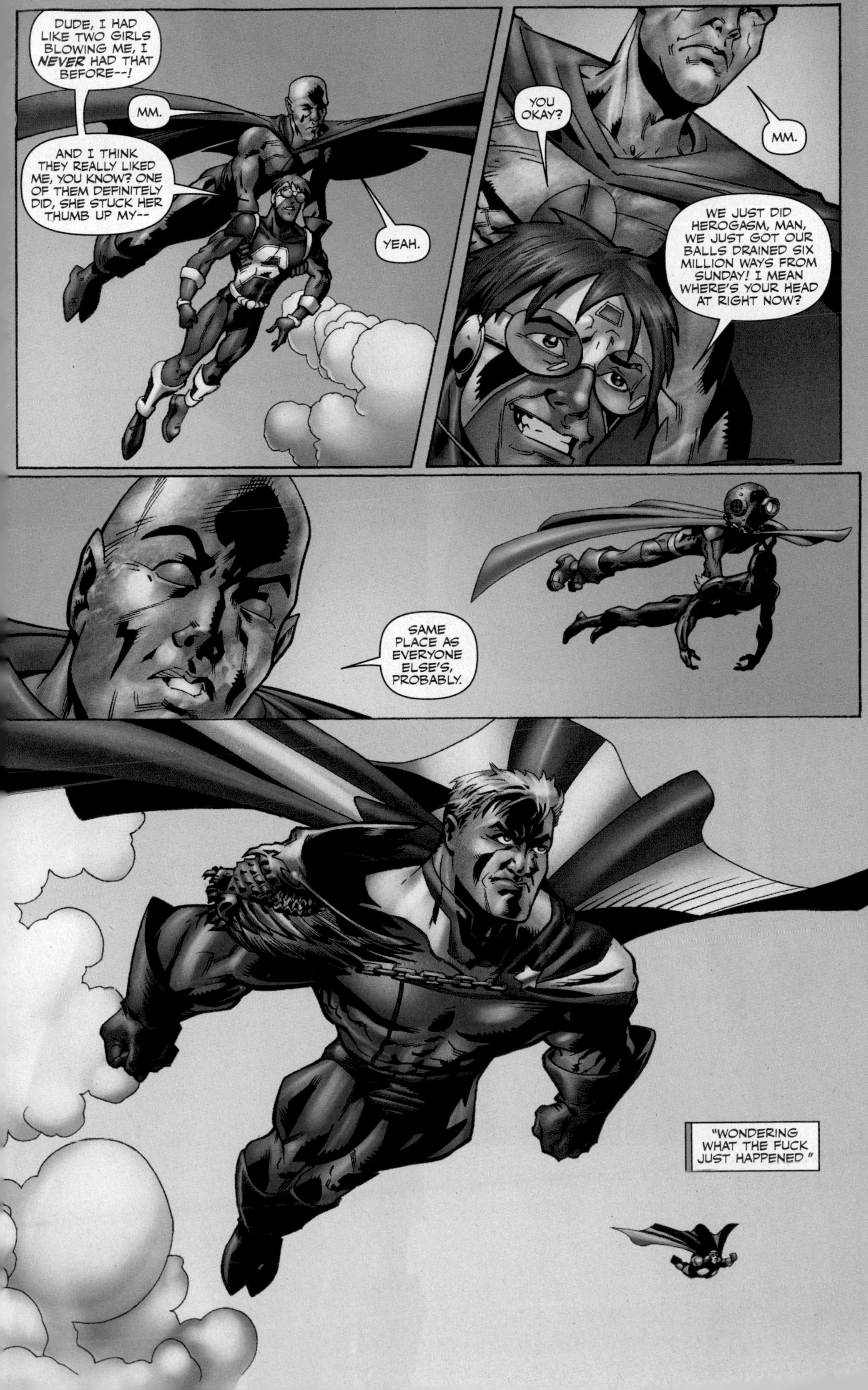
DUDE, I HAD LIKE TWO GIRLS BLOWING ME, I NEVER HAD THAT BEFORE--!
MM.
AND I THINK THEY REALLY LIKED ME, YOU KNOW? ONE OF THEM DEFINITELY DID, SHE STUCK HER THUMB UP MY--
YEAH.
YOU OKAY?
MM.
WE JUST DID HEROGASM, MAN, WE JUST GOT OUR BALLS DRAINED SIX MILLION WAYS FROM SUNDAY! I MEAN WHERE'S YOUR HEAD AT RIGHT NOW?
SAME PLACE AS EVERYONE ELSE'S, PROBABLY.
"WONDERING WHAT THE FUCK JUST HAPPENED"

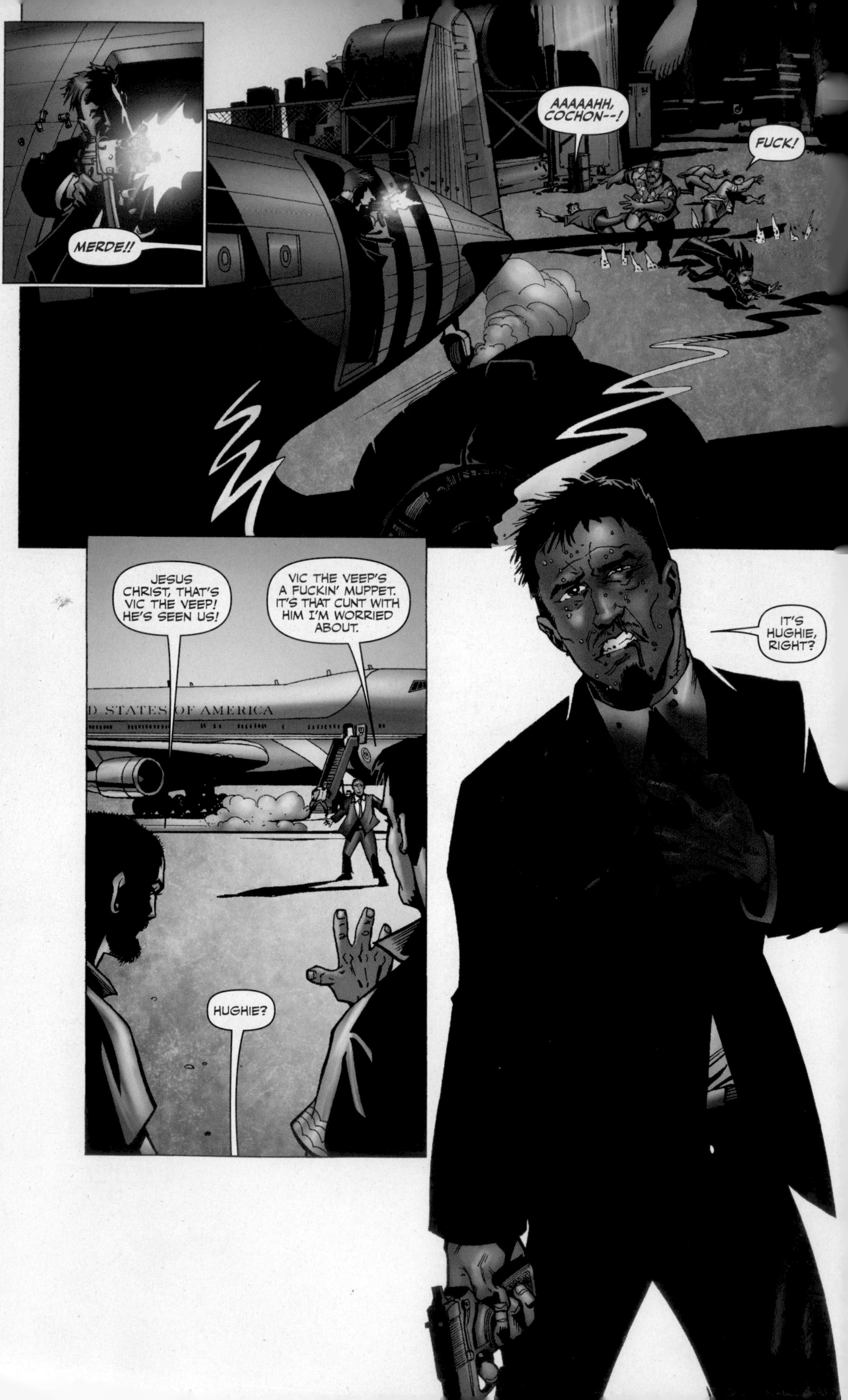
MERDE!!
AAAAAHH, COCHON--!
FUCK!
JESUS CHRIST, THAT'S VIC THE VEEP! HE'S SEEN US!
VIC THE VEEP'S A FUCKIN' MUPPET. IT'S THAT CUNT WITH HIM I'M WORRIED ABOUT.
D STATES OF AMERICA
HUGHIE?
IT'S HUGHIE, RIGHT?

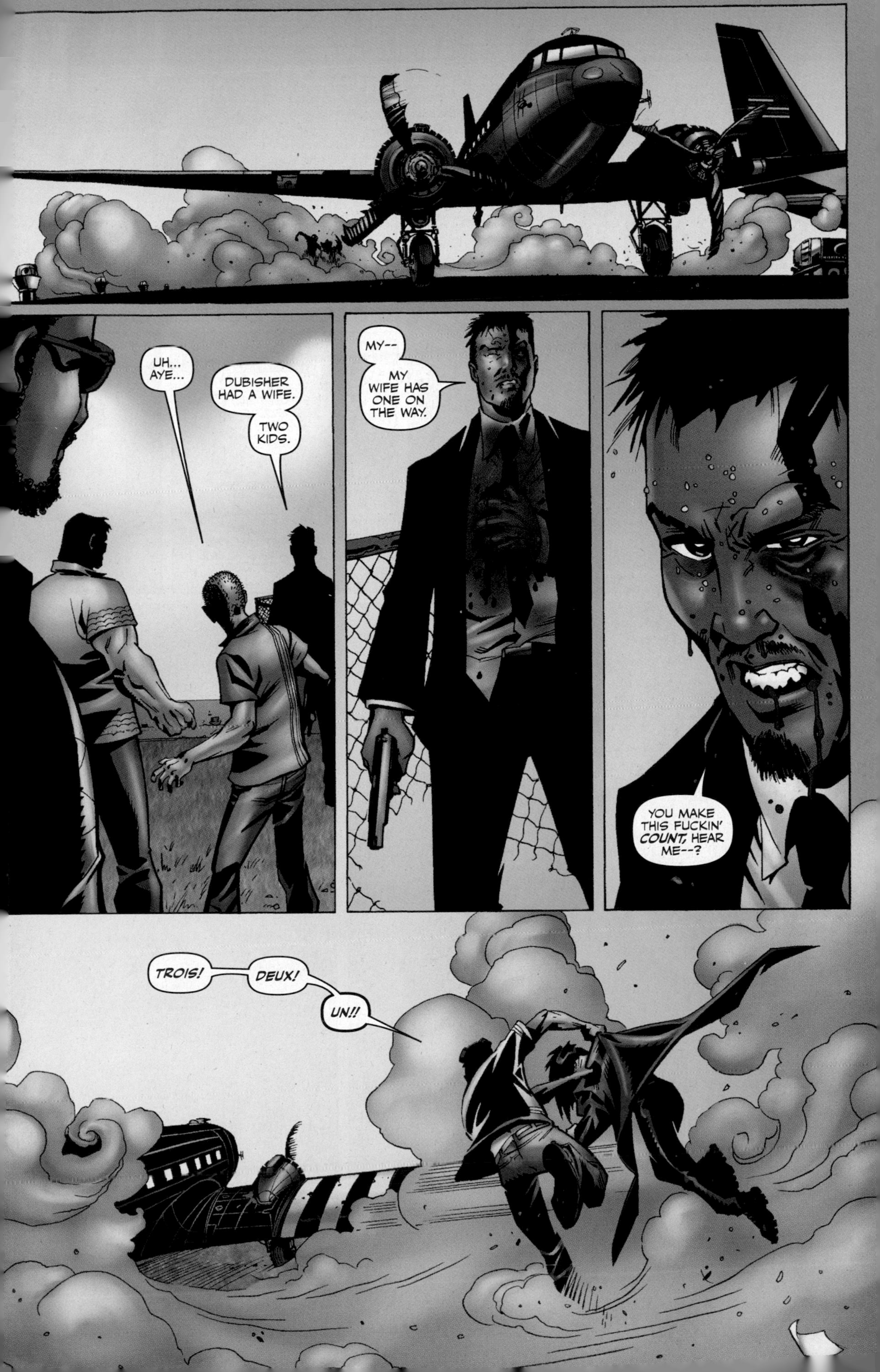
UH... AYE...
DUBISHER HAD A WIFE.
TWO KIDS.
MY--
MY WIFE HAS ONE ON THE WAY.
YOU MAKE THIS FUCKIN' COUNT, HEAR ME--?
TROIS!
DEUX!
UN!!

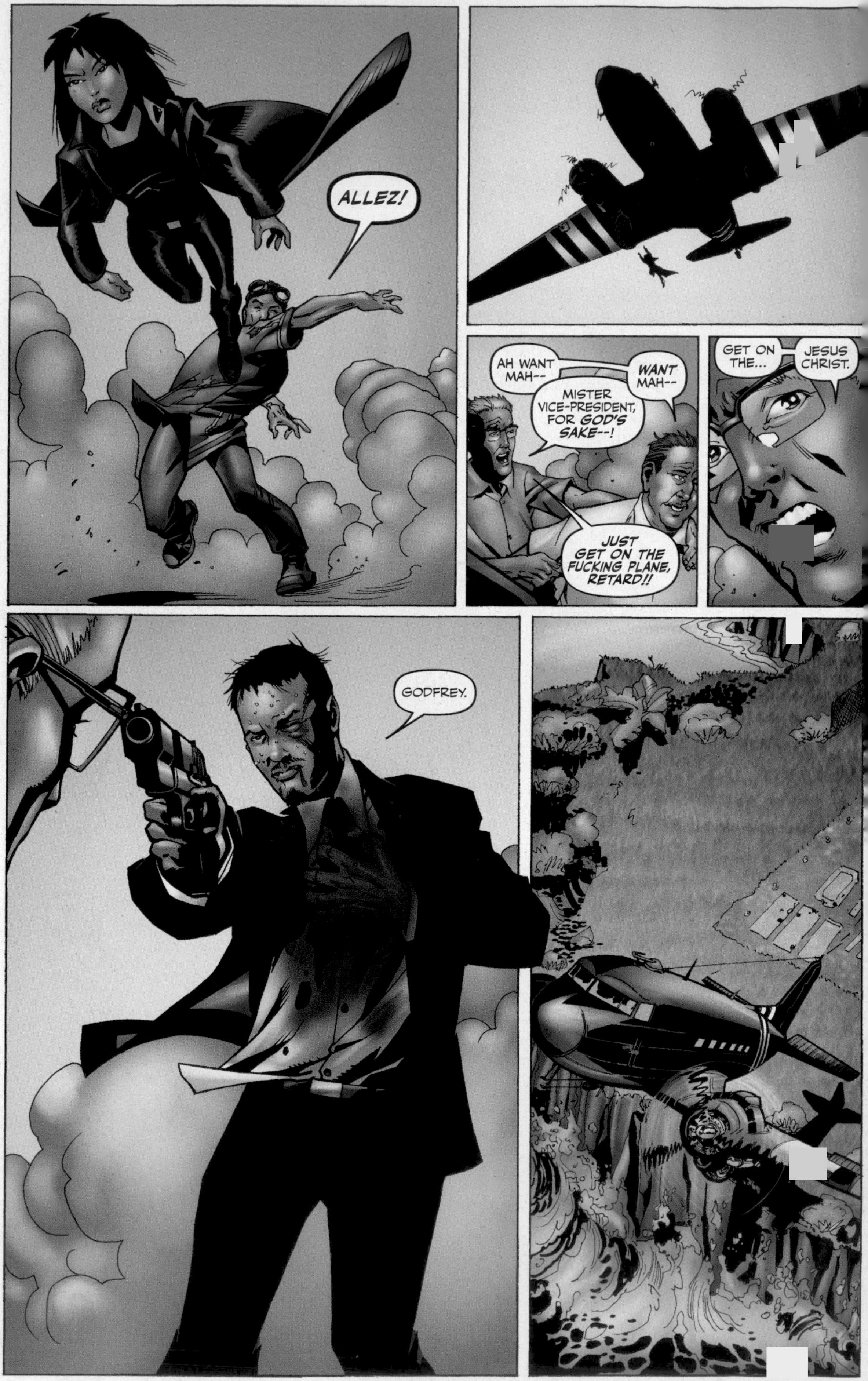
ALLEZ!
AH WANT MAH--
WANT MAH--
MISTER VICE-PRESIDENT, FOR GOD'S SAKE--!
JUST GET ON THE FUCKING PLANE, RETARD!!
GET ON THE...
JESUS CHRIST.
GODFREY.

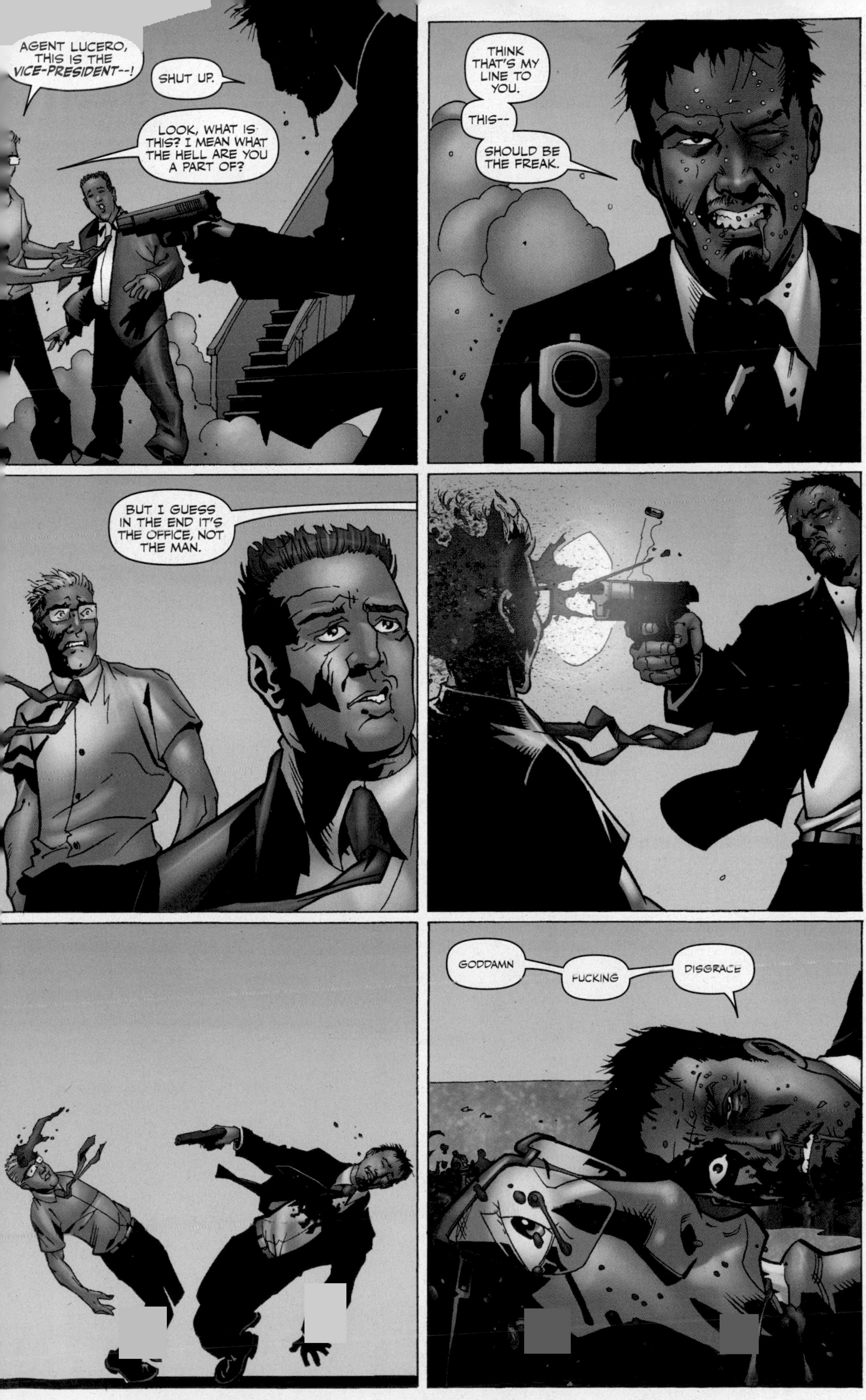
AGENT LUCERO, THIS IS THE VICE-PRESIDENT--!
SHUT UP.
LOOK, WHAT IS THIS? I MEAN WHAT THE HELL ARE YOU A PART OF?
THINK THAT'S MY LINE TO YOU.
THIS--
SHOULD BE THE FREAK.
BUT I GUESS IN THE END IT'S THE OFFICE, NOT THE MAN.
GODDAMN
FUCKING
DISGRACE

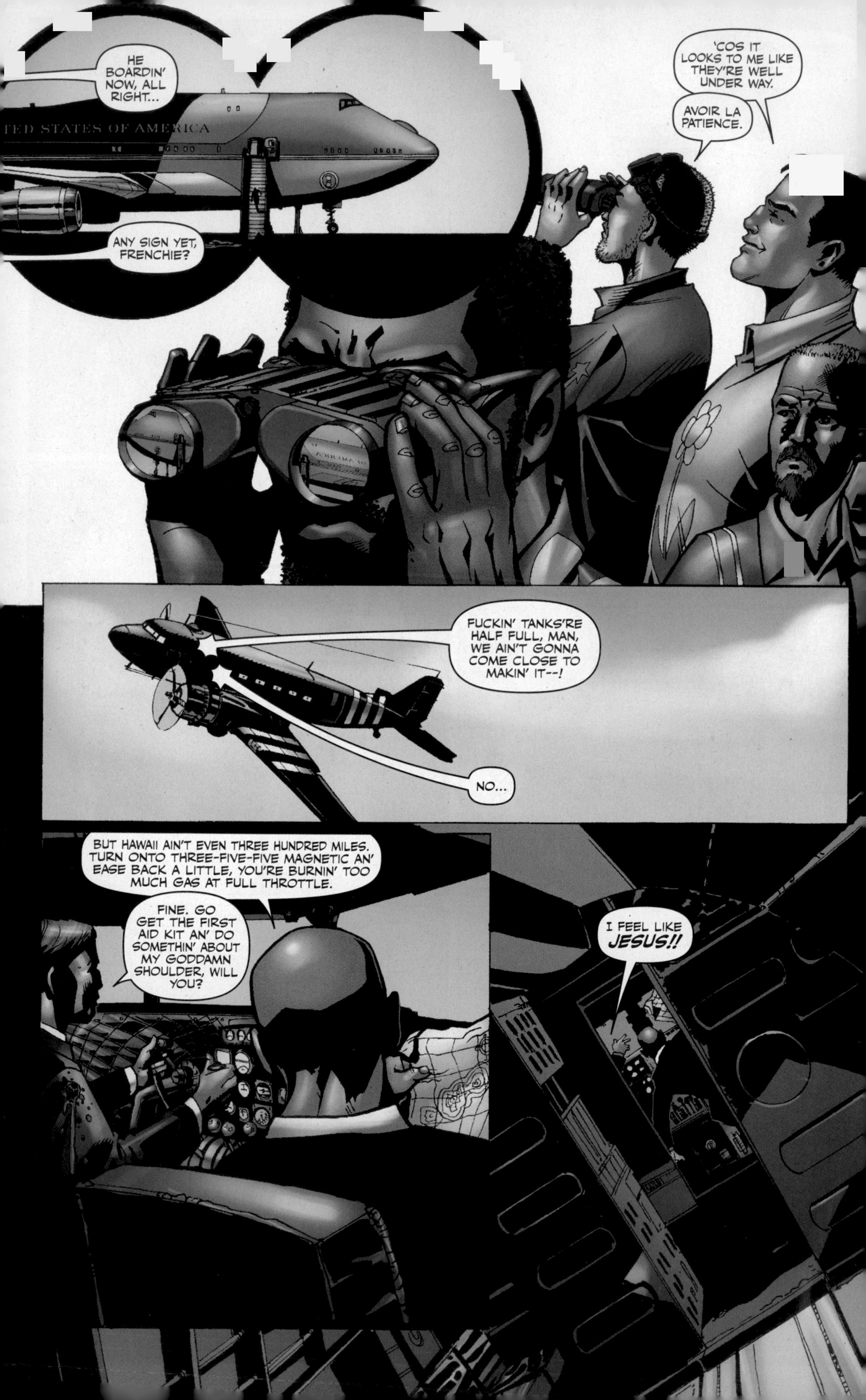
HE BOARDIN' NOW, ALL RIGHT...
ANY SIGN YET, FRENCHIE?
AVOIR LA PATIENCE.
'COS IT LOOKS TO ME LIKE THEY'RE WELL UNDER WAY.
FUCKIN' TANKS'RE HALF FULL, MAN, WE AIN'T GONNA COME CLOSE TO MAKIN' IT--!
NO...
BUT HAWAII AIN'T EVEN THREE HUNDRED MILES. TURN ONTO THREE-FIVE-FIVE MAGNETIC AN' EASE BACK A LITTLE, YOU'RE BURNIN' TOO MUCH GAS AT FULL THROTTLE.
FINE. GO GET THE FIRST AID KIT AN' DO SOMETHIN' ABOUT MY GODDAMN SHOULDER, WILL YOU?
I FEEL LIKE *JESUS!!*

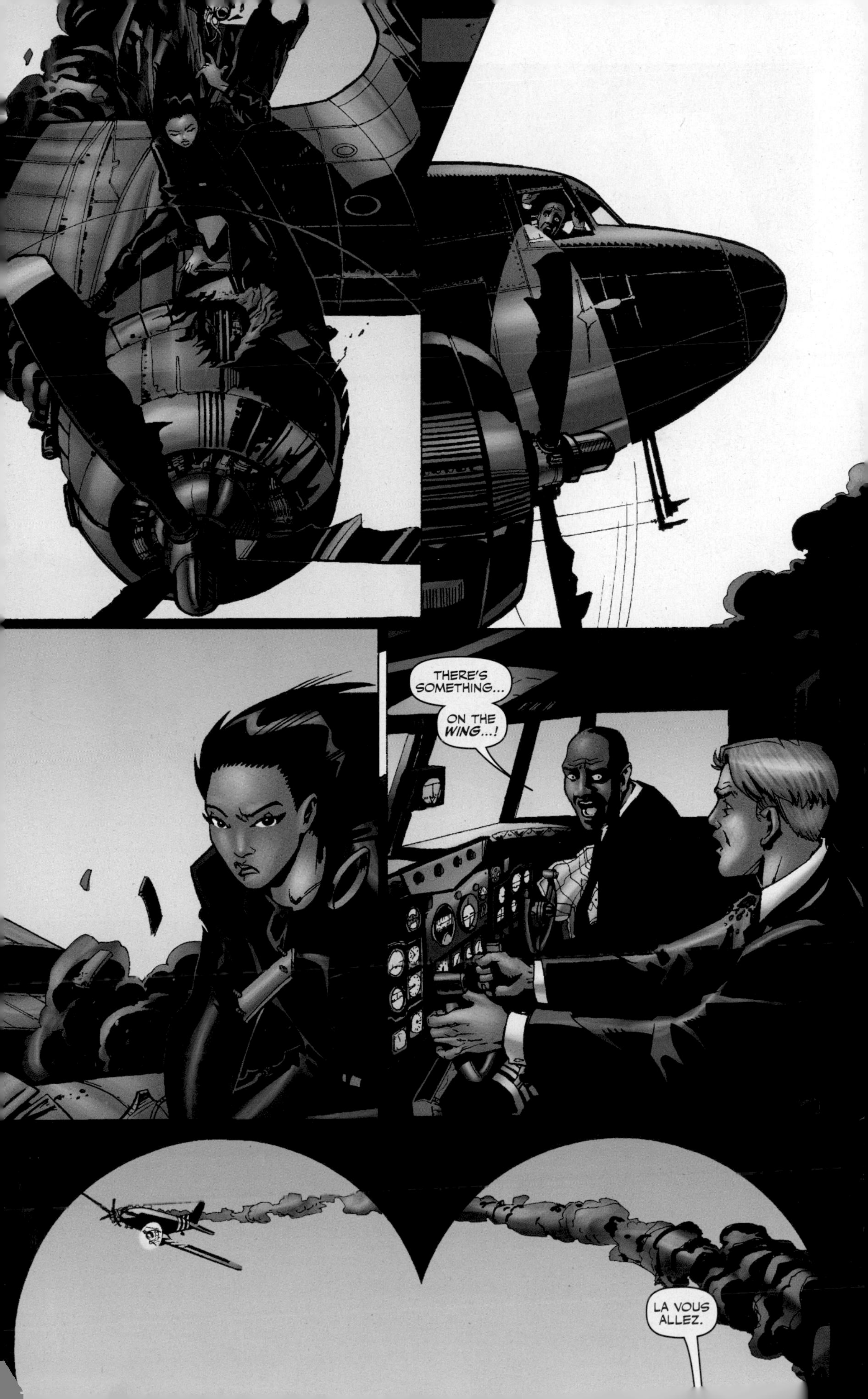
THERE'S SOMETHING...
ON THE *WING*...!
LA VOUS ALLEZ.

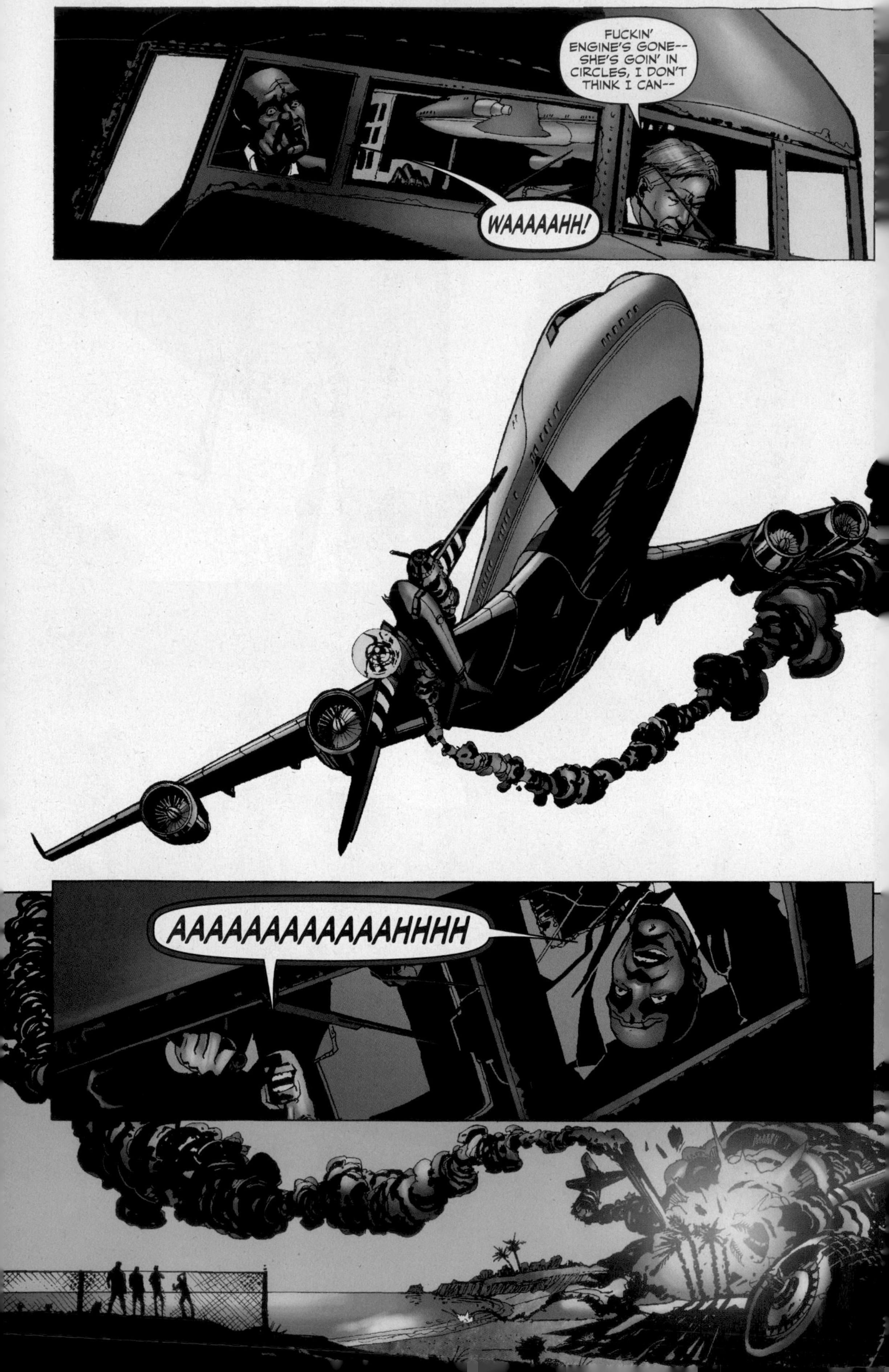
FUCKIN' ENGINE'S GONE-- SHE'S GOIN' IN CIRCLES, I DON'T THINK I CAN--
WAAAAAHH!
AAAAAAAAAAAAHHHH

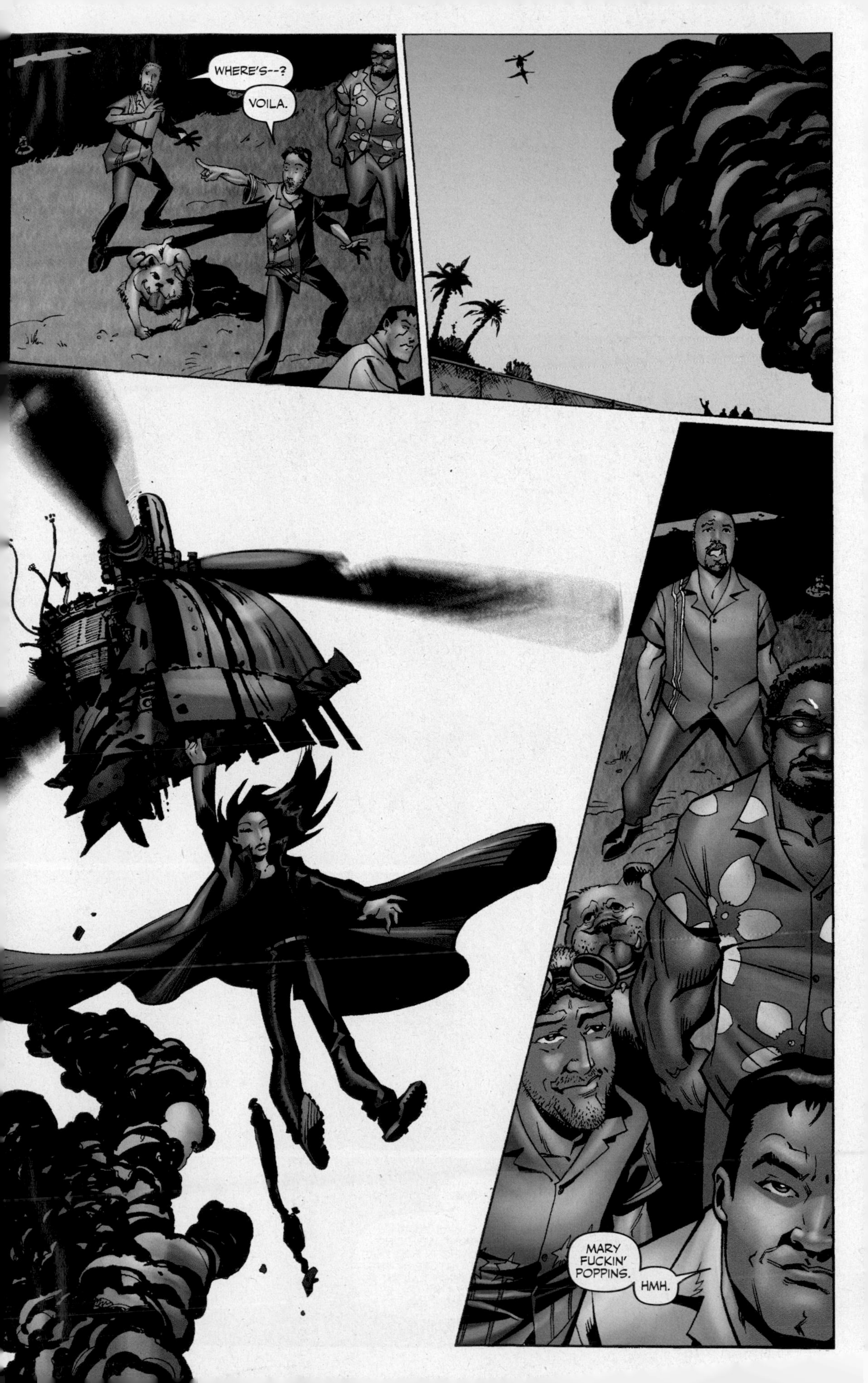
WHERE'S--?
VOILA.
MARY FUCKIN' POPPINS.
HMH.

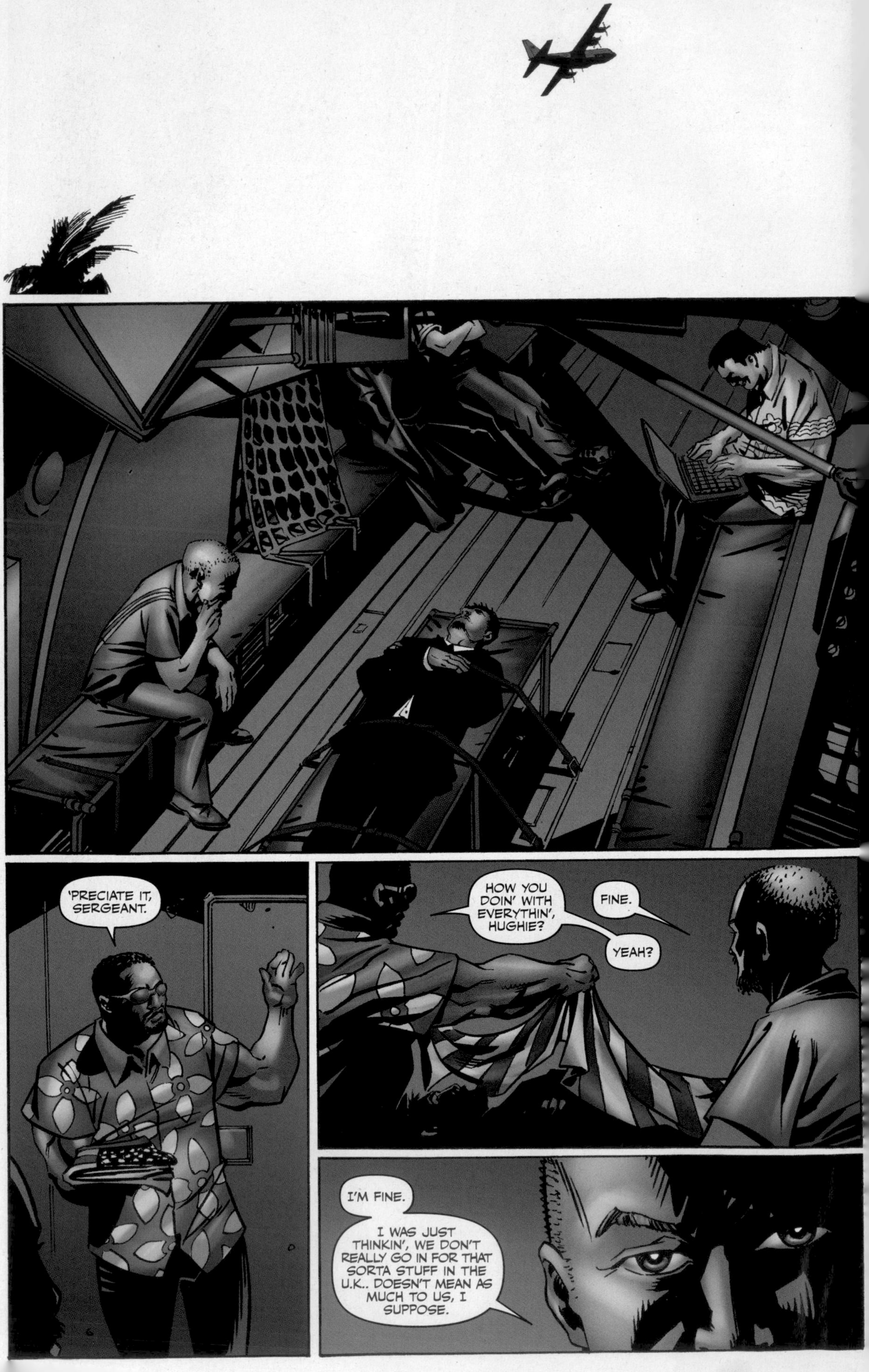
'PRECIATE IT, SERGEANT.
HOW YOU DOIN' WITH EVERYTHIN', HUGHIE?
FINE.
YEAH?
I'M FINE.
I WAS JUST THINKIN', WE DON'T REALLY GO IN FOR THAT SORTA STUFF IN THE U.K.. DOESN'T MEAN AS MUCH TO US, I SUPPOSE.

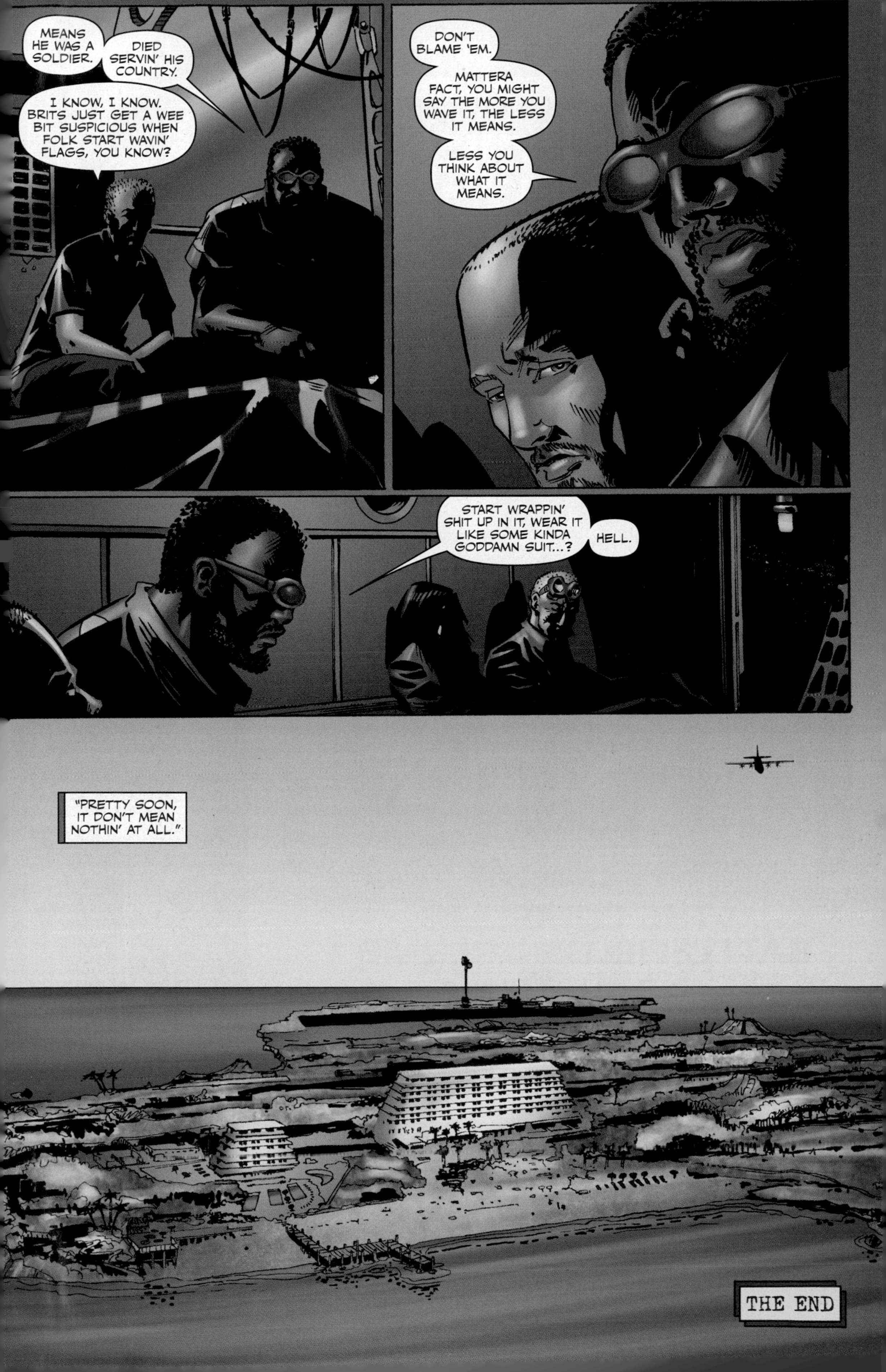
MEANS HE WAS A SOLDIER.
DIED SERVIN' HIS COUNTRY.
I KNOW, I KNOW. BRITS JUST GET A WEE BIT SUSPICIOUS WHEN FOLK START WAVIN' FLAGS, YOU KNOW?
DON'T BLAME 'EM.
MATTERA FACT, YOU MIGHT SAY THE MORE YOU WAVE IT, THE LESS IT MEANS.
LESS YOU THINK ABOUT WHAT IT MEANS.
START WRAPPIN' SHIT UP IN IT, WEAR IT LIKE SOME KINDA GODDAMN SUIT...?
HELL.
"PRETTY SOON, IT DON'T MEAN NOTHIN' AT ALL."
THE END

From *New York Times* Best-Selling Writer

GARTH ENNIS (Preacher, The Boys)

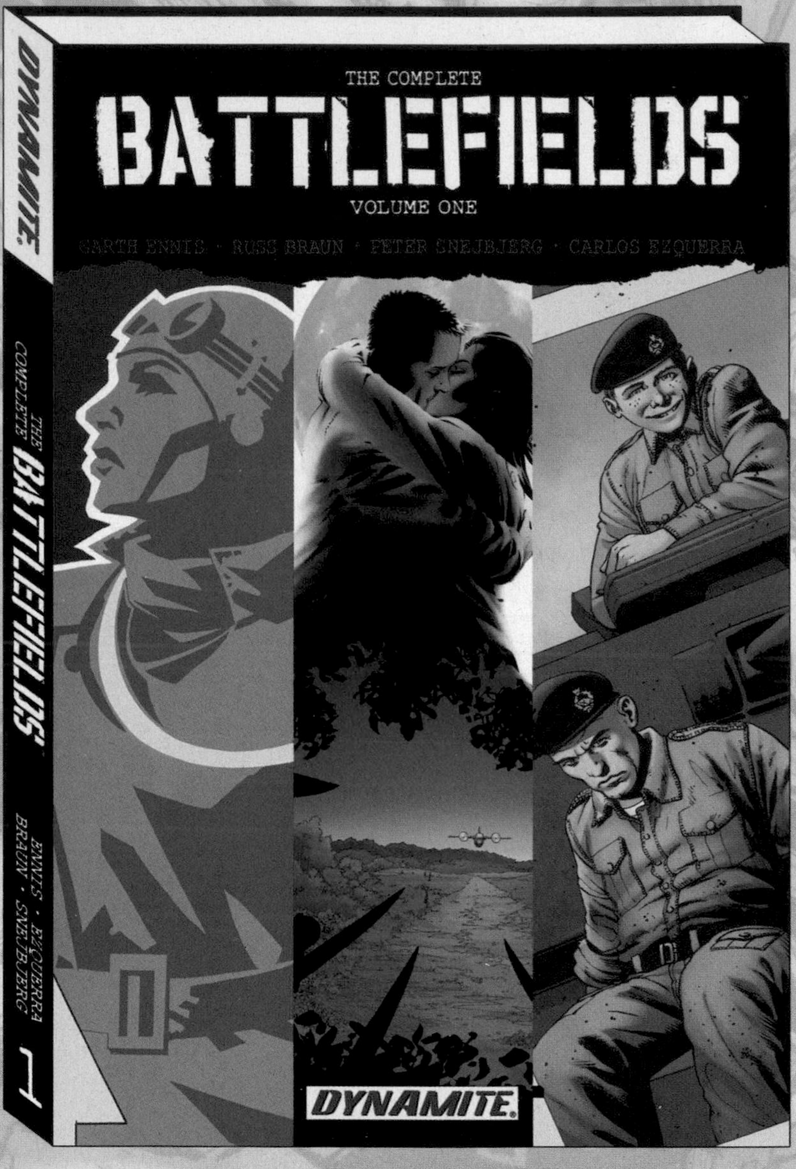
THE COMPLETE
BATTLEFIELDS
VOLUME ONE
GARTH ENNIS · RUSS BRAUN · PETER SNEJBJERG · CARLOS EZQUERRA
DYNAMITE
DYNAMITE
THE COMPLETE BATTLEFIELDS
ENNIS · EZQUERRA
BRAUN · SNEJBJERG
1

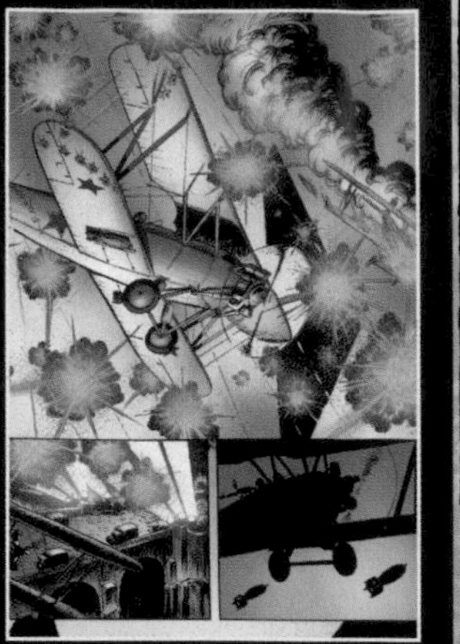

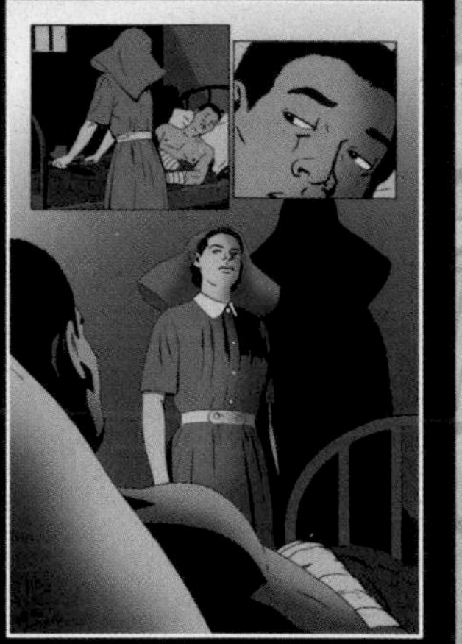

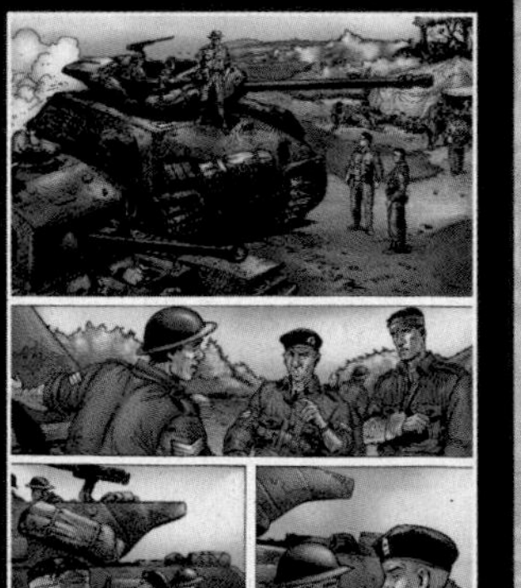

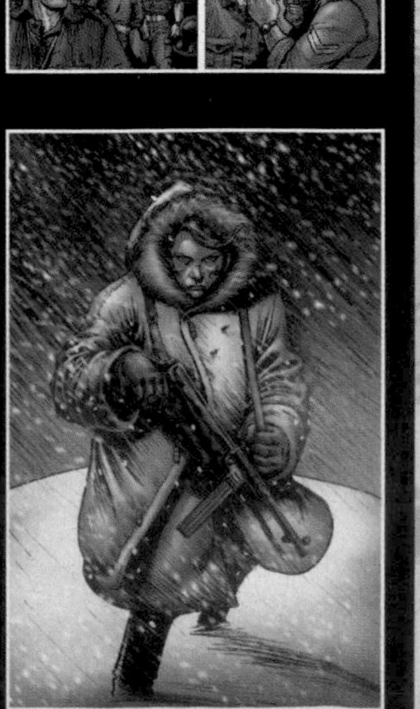

THE COMPLETE BATTLEFIELDS VOLUME 1 HARDCOVER

THE WAR THAT TORE THE WORLD APART.

Three tales of lost innocence, tragedy and suspense set during the Second World War, by writer Garth Ennis and artists Russ Braun, Peter Snejbjerg and Carlos Ezquerra.

Collects the first three Battlefields mini-series: THE NIGHT WITCHES, DEAR BILLY and THE TANKIES, features 25 pages of bonus materials and all of the covers by John Cassaday and Garry Leach!

IN STORES NOW FROM DYNAMITE!

WWW.DYNAMITEENTERTAINMENT.COM

DON'T MISS THESE GREAT COLLECTIONS FROM *NEW YORK TIMES* BEST-SELLING AUTHOR

GARTH ENNIS & DYNAMITE

Garth Ennis Darick Robertson
The BOYS
VOLUME ONE: THE NAME OF THE GAME

THE COMPLETE
BATTLEFIELDS
VOLUME ONE
DYNAMITE

JUST A
PILGRIM
GARTH ENNIS • CARLOS EZQUERRA

GARTH ENNIS GARY ERSKINE
DAN DARE
DYNAMITE

HARDCOVERS

THE BOYS DEFINITIVE EDITION VOL. 1 HARDCOVER........1933305800
- Collecting issues 1-14 of the hit series by Ennis and Robertson

THE BOYS DEFINITIVE EDITION VOL. 2 HARDCOVER........1606900730
- Collecting issues 15-30 of the hit series by Ennis and Robertson

THE COMPLETE BATTLEFIELDS VOL. 1 HARDCOVER........160690079X
- Collecting the first 3 Battlefields mini-series by Ennis, Braun, Snejbjerg and Ezquerra

THE COMPLETE JUST A PILGRIM HARDCOVER........160690003X
- Both mini-series by Ennis and Ezquerra collected together for the first time

DAN DARE OMNIBUS HARDCOVER........1606900277
- Collecting issues 1-7 by Ennis and Erskine

TRADE PAPERBACKS

THE BOYS VOL. 1: THE NAME OF THE GAME........1933305738
- Collects issues 1-6 by Ennis & Robertson

THE BOYS VOL. 2: GET SOME........1933305681
- Collects issues 7-14 by Ennis, Robertson and Snejbjerg

THE BOYS VOL. 3: GOOD FOR THE SOUL........1933305924
- Collects issues 15-22 by Ennis & Robertson

THE BOYS VOL. 4: WE GOTTA GO NOW........160690035
- Collects issues 23-30 by Ennis, Robertson and Higgins

THE BOYS VOL. 5: HEROGASM........160690082X
- Collects issues 1-6 of the hit mini-series by Ennis and McCrea

BATTLEFIELDS VOL. 1: THE NIGHT WITCHES........1606900285
- Collects issues 1-3 by Ennis and Braun

BATTLEFIELDS VOL. 2: DEAR BILLY........1606900579
- Collects issues 1-3 by Ennis and Snejbjerg

BATTLEFIELDS VOL. 3: THE TANKIES........1606900757
- Collects issues 1-3 by Ennis and Ezquerra

THE COMPLETE JUST A PILGRIM........1606900072
- Both mini-series by Ennis and Ezquerra collected together for the first time

DAN DARE OMNIBUS........1606900404
- Collecting issues 1-7 by Ennis and Erskine

DYNAMITE ENTERTAINMENT

For more information on these titles and more, visit us at:
WWW.DYNAMITEENTERTAINMENT.COM

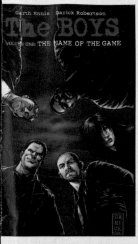

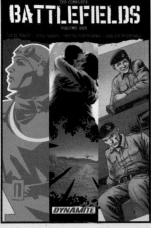

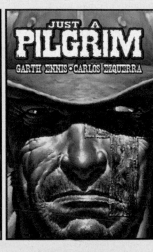

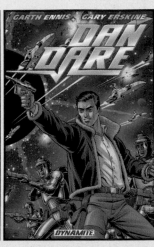

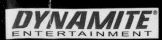

CURRENTLY AVAILABLE AND UPCOMING COLLECTIONS FROM DYNAMITE ENTERTAINMENT

Adventures of Red Sonja Vol. 1
Thomas, Thorne, More
SC ISBN: 1-933305-07-X

Adventures of Red Sonja Vol. 2
Thomas, Thorne, More
SC ISBN: 1-933305-12-6

Adventures of Red Sonja Vol. 3
Thomas, Thorne, More
SC ISBN: 1-933305-98-3

American Flagg! Definitive Collection Vol. 1
Chaykin
HC ISBN: 978-1-58240-983-2
SC part 1 ISBN: 978-1-5824-418-9
SC part 2 ISBN: 978-1--5824-419-6

Army of Darkness: Movie Adaptation
Raimi, Raimi, Bolton
SC ISBN: 1-933305-17-7

Army of Darkness: Ashes to Ashes
Hartnell, Bradshaw
SC ISBN: 0-9749638-9-5

Army of Darkness: Shop 'Till You Drop Dead
Kuhoric, Bradshaw, Greene
SC ISBN: 1-933305-26-6

Army of Darkness vs. Re-Animator
Kuhoric, Bradshaw, Greene
SC ISBN: 1-933305-13-4

Army of Darkness: Old School & More
Kuhoric, Sharpe
SC ISBN: 1-933305-18-5

Army of Darkness: Ash vs. The Classic Monsters
Kuhoric, Sharpe, Blanco
SC ISBN: 1-933305-41-X

Army of Darkness: From The Ashes
Kuhoric, Blanco
SC ISBN: 1-933305-77-0

Army of Darkness: The Long Road Home
Kuhoric, Raicht, Blanco
SC ISBN: 1-933305-86-X

Army of Darkness: Home Sweet Hell
Kuhoric, Raicht, Perez
SC ISBN: 1-60690-016-1

Army of Darkness: Hellbillies & Deadnecks
Kuhoric, Raicht, Cohn
SC ISBN: 1-60690-076-5

Army of Darkness vs. Xena Vol. 1: Why Not?
Layman, Jerwa, Montenegro
SC ISBN: 1-60690-008-0

Xena vs. Army of Darkness Vol. 2: What...Again?!
Jerwa, Serrano, Montenegro
SC ISBN: 1-60690-032-3

Bad Boy 10th Anniv. Edition
Miller, Bisley
HC ISBN: 1-933305-54-1

Borderline Vol. 1
Risso, Trillo
SC ISBN: 1-933305-05-3

Borderline Vol. 2
Risso, Trillo
SC ISBN: 1-933305-99-1

Borderline Vol. 3
Risso, Trillo
SC ISBN: 1-933305-22-3

The Boys Vol. 1: The Name of the Game
Ennis, Robertson
SC ISBN: 1-933305-73-8

The Boys Vol. 2: Get Some
Ennis, Robertson, Snejbjerg
SC ISBN: 1-933305-68-1

The Boys Vol. 3: Good For The Soul
Ennis, Robertson,
SC ISBN: 1-933305-92-4

The Boys Vol. 4: We Gotta Go Now
Ennis, Robertson,
SC ISBN: 1-606900-35-8

The Boys Vol. 5: Herogasm
Ennis, McCrea,
SC ISBN: 1-60690-082-X

The Boys Definitive Edition Vol. 1
Ennis, Robertson,
HC ISBN: 1-933305-80-0

The Boys Definitive Edition Vol. 2
Ennis, Robertson,
HC ISBN: 1-606900-73-0

Classic Battlestar Galactica Vol. 1
Remender, Rafael
SC ISBN: 1-933305-45-2

Classic Battlestar Galactica Vol. 2: Cylon Apocalypse
Grillo-Marxuach, Rafael
SC ISBN: 1-933305-55-X

The Complete Dracula
Stoker, Moore, Reppion, Worley
HC ISBN: 1-60690-060-9

Dan Dare Omnibus
Ennis, Erskine
HC ISBN: 1-60690-027-7

Darkman vs. Army of Darkness
Busiek, Stern, Fry
SC ISBN: 1-933305-48-7

Darkness vs. Eva Vol. 1
Moore, Reppion, Salazar
SC ISBN: 1-933305-85-1

Dead Irons
Kuhoric, Alexander, Lee
HC ISBN: 1-606900-69-2

Dreadstar The Definitive Collection
Starlin
HC ISBN: 0-9749638-0-1
SC part 1 ISBN: 0-9749638-1-X
SC part 2 ISBN: 0-9749638-2-8

Dreadstar: The Beginning
Starlin
HC ISBN: 1-933305-10-X

Eduardo Risso's Tales of Terror
Risso, Trillo
SC ISBN: 1-933305-23-1

Garth Ennis' Battlefields Vol. 1: The Night Witches
Ennis, Braun
SC ISBN: 1-60690-028-5

Garth Ennis' Battlefields Vol. 2: Dear Billy
Ennis, Snejbjerg
SC ISBN: 1-60690-057-9

Garth Ennis' Battlefields Vol. 3: The Tankies
Ennis, Ezquerra
SC ISBN: 1-60690-075-7

Garth Ennis' The Complete Battlefields Vol. 1
Ennis, Braun, Snejbjerg, Ezquerra
HC ISBN: 1-60690-075-7

Hellshock
Lee, Chung
HC ISBN: 1-58240-505-0
SC ISBN: 1-58240-504-2

Highlander Vol. 1: The Coldest War
Oeming, Jerwa, Moder, Sharpe
HC ISBN: 1-933305-31-2
SC ISBN: 1-933305-34-7

Highlander Vol. 2: Dark Quickening
Jerwa, Laguna
SC ISBN: 1-933305-59-2

Highlander Vol. 3: Armageddon
Jerwa, Rafael
SC ISBN: 1-933305-67-3

Highlander Way Of The Sword
Krul, Rafael
SC ISBN: 1-933305-87-8

Jungle Girl Vol. 1
Cho, Murray, Batista
HC ISBN: 1-933305-78-9

Jungle Girl Vol. 2
Cho, Murray, Batista
HC ISBN: 1-60690-036-6

Just A Pilgrim
Ennis, Ezquerra
HC ISBN: 1-60690-003-X

Kid Kosmos: Cosmic Guard
Starlin
SC ISBN: 1-933305-02-9

Kid Kosmos: Kidnapped
Starlin
SC ISBN: 1-933305-29-0

The Lone Ranger Vol. 1: Now & Forever
Matthews, Cariello, Cassaday
HC ISBN: 1-933305-39-8
SC ISBN: 1-933305-40-1

The Lone Ranger Vol. 2: Lines Not Crossed
Matthews, Cariello, Cassaday, Pope
HC ISBN: 1-933305-66-5
SC ISBN: 1-933305-70-3

The Lone Ranger Vol. 3: Scorched Earth
Matthews, Cariello, Cassaday
HC ISBN: 1-60690-031-5
SC ISBN: 1-60690-041-2

The Man With No Name Vol. 1: Saints and Sinners
Gage, Dias
SC ISBN: 1-60690-012-9

Masquerade Vol. 1
Ross, Hester, Paul
SC ISBN: 1-60690-065-X

Mercenaries Vol. 1
Reed, Salazar
SC ISBN: 1-933305-71-1

Monster War
Golden, Chin, more
SC ISBN: 1-933305-30-4

New Battlestar Galactica Vol. 1
Pak, Raynor
HC ISBN: 1-933305-33-9
SC ISBN: 1-933305-34-7

New Battlestar Galactica Vol. 2
Pak, Raynor
HC ISBN: 1-933305-53-3
SC ISBN: 1-933305-49-5

New Battlestar Galactica Vol. 3
Pak, Raynor, Lau
HC ISBN: 1-933305-58-4
SC ISBN: 1-933305-57-6

New Battlestar Galactica Complete Omnibus V1
Pak, Raynor, Jerwa, Lau
SC ISBN: 1-606900-90-0

New Battlestar Galactica: Zarek
Jerwa, Batista
SC ISBN: 1-933305-50-9

New Battlestar Galactica: Season Zero Vol. 1
Jerwa, Herbert
SC ISBN: 1-933305-81-9

New Battlestar Galactica: Season Zero Vol. 2
Jerwa, Herbert
Mass SC ISBN: 1-606900-17-X
Direct SC ISBN: 1-606900-18-8

New Battlestar Galactica Origins: Baltar
Fahey, Lau
SC ISBN: 1-933305-88-6

New Battlestar Galactica Origins: Adama
Napton, Lau
SC ISBN: 1-606900-15-3

New Battlestar Galactica Origins: Starbuck & Helo
Fahey, Lau
SC ISBN: 1-606900-38-2

New Battlestar Galactica: Ghosts
Jerwa, Lau
SC ISBN: 1-606900-29-3

Essential Painkiller Jane Vol. 1
Quesada, Palmiotti, Leonardi, more
SC ISBN: 1-933305-97-5

Painkiller Jane Vol. 1: The Return
Quesada, Palmiotti, Moder
SC ISBN: 1-933305-42-8

Painkiller Jane Vol. 2: Everything Explodes
Quesada, Palmiotti, Moder
SC ISBN: 1-933305-65-7

Painkiller Jane vs. Terminator
Palmiotti, Raynor
SC ISBN: 1-933305-84-3

Power & Glory
Chaykin
SC ISBN: 1-933305-06-1

Project Superpowers Chapter 1
Ross, Krueger, Paul, Sadowski
HC ISBN: 1-933305-91-6
TPB ISBN: 1-60690-014-5

Raise The Dead
Moore, Reppion, Petrus
HC ISBN: 1-933305-56-8

Red Sonja She-Devil With a Sword Vol. 1
Oeming, Carey, Rubi
HC ISBN: 1-933305-36-3
SC ISBN: 1-933305-11-8

Red Sonja She-Devil With a Sword Vol. 2: Arrowsmiths
Oeming, Rubi, more
HC ISBN: 1-933305-44-4
SC ISBN: 1-933305-43-6

Red Sonja She-Devil With a Sword Vol. 3: The Rise of Kulan Gath
Oeming, Rubi, more
HC ISBN: 1-933305-51-7
SC ISBN: 1-933305-52-5

Red Sonja She-Devil With a Sword Vol. 4: Animals & More
Oeming, Homs, more
HC ISBN: 1-933305-64-9
SC ISBN: 1-933305-63-0

Red Sonja She-Devil With a Sword Vol. 5: World On Fire
Oeming, Reed, Homs
HC ISBN: 1-933305-89-4
SC ISBN: 1-933305-90-8

Red Sonja She-Devil With a Sword Vol. 6: Death
Marz, Ortega, Reed, more
HC ISBN: 1-933305-89-4
SC ISBN: 1-933305-90-8

Red Sonja She-Devil With a Sword Vol. 7: Born Again
Marz, Ortega, Reed, more
HC ISBN: 1-60690-010-2
SC ISBN: 1-60690-011-0

Red Sonja vs. Thulsa Doom Vol. 1
David, Lieberman, Conrad
SC ISBN: 1-933305-96-7

Savage Red Sonja: Queen of the Frozen Wastes
Cho, Murray, Homs
HC ISBN: 1-933305-37-1
SC ISBN: 1-933305-38-X

Red Sonja: Travels
Marz, Ortega, Thomas, more
SC ISBN: 1-933305-20-7

Sword of Red Sonja: Doom of the Gods (Red Sonja vs. Thulsa Doom 2)
Lieberman, Antonio
SC ISBN: 1-933305-76-2

Savage Tales of Red Sonja
Marz, Gage, Ortega, more
SC ISBN: 1-60690-081-1

Scout Vol. 1
Truman
SC ISBN: 1-933305-95-9

Scout Vol. 2
Truman
SC ISBN: 1-933305-60-6

Sherlock Holmes Vol. 1: The Trial of Sherlock Holmes
Moore, Reppion, Campbell
HC ISBN: 1-606900-58-7

Six From Sirius
Moench, Gulacy
SC ISBN: 1-933305-03-7

Street Magik
Lieberman, McCarthy, Buchemi
SC ISBN: 1-933305-47-9

Super Zombies
Guggenheim, Gonzales, Rubi
HC ISBN: 1-60690-067-6

Terminator: Infinity
Furman, Raynor
SC ISBN: 1-933305-74-6

Terminator: Revolution
Furman, Antonio
SC ISBN: 1-606900-30-7

Witchblade: Shades of Gray
Moore, Reppion, Segovia, Geovani
SC ISBN: 1-933305-72-X

Xena Vol. 1: Contest of Pantheons
Layman, Neves
SC ISBN: 1-933305-35-5

Xena Vol. 2: Dark Xena
Layman, Champagne, Salonga
SC ISBN: 1-933305-61-4

Zorro Vol. 1: Year One Trail of the Fox
Wagner, Francavilla
HC ISBN: 1-60690-019-6
TPB ISBN: 1-606900-13-7